BREEDER

Real-Life Stories
from the New Generation of Mothers

Edited by Ariel Gore and Bee Lavender
Foreword by Dan Savage
Illustrated by Jonny Thief

Seal Press

Cover design by Kathleen Kincaid
Cover photograph by Nealy Blau
Text design by Alison Rogalsky
Illustrations by Jonny Thief

A version of "Edging" by Joy Castro originally appeared in the *Mid-American
Review,* Autumn 1991, Volume XII, Number 1. Used by permission of the author.

Library of Congress Cataloging-in-Publication Data
Breeder : real-life stories from the new generation of mothers / edited by
Ariel Gore and Bee Lavender.
     p. cm.
   ISBN 1-58005-051-4
     1. Mothers—United States. 2. Motherhood—United States. 3.
Parenting—United States. I. Gore, Ariel, 1970– II. Lavender, Bee.

HQ759 . B753 2001
306.874'3—dc21   00-054914

Printed in Canada

First printing, May 2001
Text font: Adobe Garamond

10   9   8   7   6   5   4   3   2   1

Distributed to the trade by Publishers Group West
In Canada: Publishers Group West Canada, Toronto, Ontario
In Australia: Banyan Tree Book Distributors, Kent Town, South Australia
In the United Kingdom, Europe and South Africa: Hi Marketing, London
In Asia and the Middle East: Michelle Morrow Curreri, Beverly, MA

PRAISE FOR *HIP MAMA*

"A search for sites related to mothers—or to Mother's Day—can be depressing: it turns up Hallmark images, twee Victoriana, and links to merchandise. How refreshing, then, is this Web counterpart to *Hip Mama,* the California parenting zine 'for parents who didn't check their personalities at the door when their kids were born.' . . . The site ultimately provides succor to moms who cannot relate to our culture's mawkish notions of motherhood."   —*New Yorker*

"Fun and irreverent."   —*USA Today*

"No sanctified endorsement of the usual myths about motherhood here. No neat checklists of all-too-easy parenting solutions or slick write-ups of professional experts telling how it's supposed to be. . . . *Hip Mama* explores the real stuff of parenting with a proper recognition of the ambiguity of it all—and plenty of love and humanity."
                                        —*Utne Reader*

"*Hip Mama* is considered one of the best zines out there."
                              —*San Francisco Chronicle*

"Proof that being a mother doesn't have to be boring or apolitical."
                          —Heather Irwin, *Fast Company*

"Child-rearing gets cutting edge treatment."   —*Chicago Tribune*

"Gore's strong attitudes are making her a hot commodity."
—*Working Woman*

"It's about real-life mothering, where the kids are smeared with spaghetti sauce and money is tight, where new mamas may find themselves in college, in culture shock or in family court."   —*Parents' Press*

"Traditional or not, the topics are handled with serious insight."
—*San Jose Mercury News*

"Is there a revolution of mamas going on? If so, Ariel Gore has written the manifesto."   —*Common Ground*

CONTENTS

FLESH AND BLOOD

HONEY FROM THE ROCK

F OREWORD

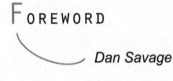

Dan Savage

My Irish-Catholic mother stayed home, made eight peanut butter sandwiches every day for four kids and smoked at the kitchen sink in our small, crowded apartment. My Irish-Catholic dad was a cop and, like all the dads at the time, he wasn't home much. Stay-at-home moms terrorized our Northside Chicago neighborhood, a few square blocks of two-flat apartments a half-mile from the lake. Moms were stationed like sentries up and down every block, and there was no escape from their prying eyes. Knock over a garbage can two blocks from home, and half a dozen moms would get on the phone. Your mom would announce you were grounded as you walked in the door for lunch.

In the afternoons the neighborhood moms—Mrs. Lamont, Mrs. Kasher, Mrs. Brady, Mrs. McDonald—would gather in my mother's kitchen while their husbands were at work. They came to sit, talk, drink coffee and—most important—have human contact with other adults. Looking up at these women from under the kitchen table—I was a mama's boy, always underfoot—these women all seemed the same to me. They were moms, their lives defined and limited by the expectations of their husbands, their children, their church and their own mothers. My mother's own mother lived right downstairs, in the very apartment my mother had grown up in, and she was always quick to criticize the way my mother raised her children. Because there was one right way to be a mom: the way your mom was a mom.

All of the women who sat at my mother's kitchen table were, as I would later learn, not nearly as content as they pretended to be over coffee. They had been brought up to believe they had two things to do: breed (lots of children) and feed (their children and their husbands). They were making the best of it.

Then it was 1970 and people started getting divorced. Mrs. Kasher, I think, was first. Then Mrs. Brady. Then someone else's mother. Pretty soon, everyone was getting divorced, including my own parents, and the mothers who still gathered in our kitchen were suddenly having to improvise, to re-create their roles. They had to shrug off the expectations that came with motherhood in the same way they had been shrugged off by their first husbands. They were the last generation to blindly take on the role of mother, allowing other people's opinions about what a mother is or does or thinks or wears to limit them.

The first time I heard someone use the word "breeder," I was sixteen years old and nearly naked. The guy who used the word was quite a bit older than I was, completely naked and only the second guy I'd ever slept with. I was in love, clumsily slogging through an awkward coming out—as if there's any other kind of coming out—and it took me a moment to realize what my crush meant by "breeders." He meant my parents. Straight people. Breeders make babies, he explained, they breed. We don't. Gay people don't have to worry about birth control or children or expectations. It was 1980, and soon gay people would have a lot to worry about—death control, for instance—but I bought into the gay-people-don't-have-children stuff for more than a decade.

Then I went and bred. Sort of.

When my boyfriend and I adopted a baby, a boy, from a young woman who, while pregnant, wasn't ready to be a full-time mom, I didn't immediately make the connection between my son's mother and my own. But my son's mother wasn't much older than my mother was when she had her first child. Holding my son, talking on the phone with my son's mother, I can't help but wonder at the changes that have taken place in my short life. There are now so many different ways to be or become a mother, and each individual woman gets to determine for herself which route she will take—if, of course, she decides to become a mother at all. It's not up to her husband—if she has a husband—or her church, or her own mother. The women who gathered in my mother's kitchen when I was a child weren't free. The women whose voices are gathered in this remarkable collection are—and that's a difference worth celebrating and a development that must be documented.

I still think of myself as a mama's boy, and I'm often on the phone, asking my mother for her advice about kid stuff: potty training, discipline, daycare. My Irish-Catholic mother isn't shy about telling me exactly what she thinks my boyfriend and I should do; she takes a healthy, almost proprietary, interest in her grandson's well-being. But my mother always wraps up her advice with this: "That's what I would do if I were you. But I'm not you. You have to parent your own way." I don't believe my grandmother ever said anything like that to my mother when I was a child. It's kind of a miracle, isn't it?

INTRODUCTION

Ariel Gore

When I was in high school, all the coolest punk rockers hung out in the shopping mall parking lot across the street from campus. I sat with them, smoking Drum tobacco, even though I was neither cool nor terribly punk rock. Whenever an unsuspecting pregnant woman would walk by our group, one of the high schoolers—probably a white girl with dyed black dreadlocks, crosses carved into her skin and thick kohl eyeliner—would narrow her eyes in disgust and shout, "Breeder!"

As the pregnant woman hurried away, pretending not to see or hear, the punk would mutter something to the effect of: "Bringing children into *this* world? How deluded is *that?*"

The incident would be forgotten soon enough. The conversation would drift to more pressing issues: black clothing dye, United States involvement in Central America or who was playing at the Vortex on Friday night.

Of course, most of those cool punk rockers have kids of their own now. They've reconciled the pure cynicism of our youth with the most poignant act of hope I know—bringing children into *this* world. How did it happen?

Women of my generation grew up in a blur of ERA demonstrations and disco dancing. We were commune babies, latchkey kids, the daughters of women who changed what it meant to be female in America. If our own parents were married, most of our friends' parents were divorced. We don't remember when the first man walked on the moon (but we do remember when the *Challenger* blew up). We became riot grrls, sometime-slackers, student-loan queens. We published zines, pioneered the new high-tech economy, revitalized the American tradition of political protest. We have plenty in common, but growing up in the 1970s and '80s meant different things to each of us. To one contributor, it meant being the only black girl at an elite private school, the daughter of a music industry executive who was funding the Black Panthers as well as the family's Hollywood Hills lifestyle; to another, it meant being homeschooled by hippie parents on a Northern California homestead; and to another, it meant learning from her immigrant parents that children meant sacrifice.

My own childhood was as typical as anyone else's—I was raised by activists, an artist and a Roman Catholic priest, in the pre–Silicon Valley Bay Area. Before she married the reverend, my twice-divorced welfare mom would lie to potential landlords, claiming she was a widow. She tried to give me an androgynous name so I could pass for a man on paper. The world was changing, but it wasn't safe to bet on how fast. Thirty years later, "Ariel" is a girl's name and I can afford to roll my eyes at potential landlords who care about my marital status.

◯

Bee Lavender and I started this project in part to understand our own experiences. We both became mothers in our teens—Bee as a married, working-class youth activist; I as a single, international bag lady who grew up to the soundtrack of *Free to Be . . . You and Me*. In a culture where women often delay childbearing as long as nature and science will allow, we chose to have our kids *while,* not *instead of,* following our other dreams. We were anomalies in our college classes, but a decade later, more than half the women of our generation have kids. With more choices than our grandmas ever dreamed of, and less support, many of us have struggled with the judgment of our peers and elders who told us we couldn't do it as students, as travelers, as dykes, as bread-winners, as single girls or as alterna-freaks. We excuse their ignorance. As the daughters of the 1970s feminist movement, we cherish our re-productive freedom. And as willing breeders, we refuse to be oppressed by the institution of motherhood.

We make mistakes, build communities, fight the good fight. Cyni-cism was the natural response when youthful naiveté was slapped out of us, but through love and hard work we're finding our way back—not to naiveté, but to a kind of optimism based in real-life experiences, an optimism that allows us to find joy in resistance, and hope in real, shit-kicking progress.

In the pages you're about to read, real women who came up during the hippie and punk eras chronicle what it means to be "mama" here and now. We aren't the neo–June Cleaver corporate beauties you see in the mainstream parenting magazines, and we aren't the purer-than-thou organic earth mamas you see in the alternative glossies. We are imperfect, and we are impure.

We are also brave—rejecting medical advice and giving birth at home, waiting to be inseminated in a stark doctor's office, dealing with an unexpected pregnancy in a chaotic foreign country. We face struggles that hearken back to our moms' time: the difficulty of adopting as a lesbian, the fight to be allowed to parent as a teenager.

We know that all moms are working moms, but that doesn't make the dance between desire and necessity in our work-lives any simpler. We are pilots, teaching our daughters to fly; we are strippers, forced back onto the stage with the "success" of welfare reform; we are poets, and we have something to say.

We are sick of silences, so we are telling the truth about our family histories—the eating disorders, the suicidal depressions. We are intent on offering our children a different legacy.

We believe in true love—not in marketed romantic bullshit, but in love of children, partners, communities, friends. Sometimes the sexiest thing somebody can do is the laundry.

It's a good thing we don't take ourselves too seriously or we might just lose it in motherhood's chaos when the vibrator stops working; as the youngsters go about their daily business of eating, sleeping, crying, drooling and peeing all over the place; when we find ourselves shining a flashlight into our sleeping kid's butt crack on pinworm patrol.

Our lives are intense, chaotic, excellent. We don't know too much about "settling down," but we are finding, after a long ramble, ways to mother soulfully in *this* world—the one we swore we would never bring children into, the one that spawned our cynicism and the one that, ultimately, nurtures our hope.

Rock on, breeder chicks!

Breeder Rites of Passage
Kimberly Bright

1. Birth
2. Expulsion from preschool
3. First Judy Blume book
4. Menarche
5. First shoplifted pack of cigarettes
6. First zine, guitar, band, mosh pit
7. First date: a) with a boy; b) with a girl
8. First political demonstration
9. Spiritual crisis (choose your own religion)
10. Deflected rape attempt
11. Trip to Planned Parenthood
12. Tattoos
13. Trip to Europe (Montmartre, Soho, Prague)
14. College: obscure liberal arts school on scholarship
15. First hangover: "Where am I and where are my panties?"
16. First stalker
17. HIV test
18. Death of a peer or sibling: a) suicide; b) auto accident; c) drug overdose; d) murder
19. Exploration of non-Western medicine
20. Psychotherapy; detox center or first Prozac prescription
21. Graduation
22. Piercings
23. Motherhood
24. Own business
25. Marriage/long-term commitment to one or more individuals
26. Volvo purchase
27. Mortgage (funky cottage, townhouse or bungalow in artsy neighborhood)
28. First trip to Nepal
29. Continuous search for joy
30. Enlightenment

◯

When my boy was about a week old, I was on the phone with the doctor's office, making an appointment for his checkup, and I started say something about "needing an appointment for my son." Hearing myself saying "my son" totally freaked me out. It was then that I realized I was this child's mother. I couldn't believe it. I still can't believe it, and he is five years old now. —Priscilla

Motherhood and the Indian Post Office

Liesl Schwabe

I promised myself I would take a pregnancy test in the morning, but that night I was still free—unpregnant for all intents and purposes. I decided to buy a bottle of Honey Bee Brandy.

Women in rural India don't buy alcohol openly. I figured that if I was actually going to buy alcohol, buying brandy instead of the local Guru beer or Royal Stag whiskey would somehow help me to keep my respectable reputation intact. It was also, I suppose, a small act of denial as it was the last time I was to drink anything alcoholic for a long, long time.

I got the brandy from the liquor shop, which wasn't really a liquor shop. It was more like a shack, Mafia-run, on a back road, which wasn't really a road. It was more like a dirt path. I was living in Bodh Gaya, Bihar, the site in India of the Buddha's enlightenment twenty-five hundred years ago.

I first came to Bodh Gaya as an eighteen-year-old college student exploring Buddhism. At twenty-three, I was back. I had just attended a two-week Buddhist seminar with a former boyfriend named Justin, and was planning to see the Dalai Lama. I had also begun practice of prostrations, the Buddhist pushups through which one aspires to attain the mind, speech and body of the Buddha. This practice is considered fundamental to gaining realization of the preciousness of human birth and existence.

I didn't buy the pregnancy test myself. I wasn't even sure if tests were available in Bihar, the poorest, most rural state in India. It is the only state where, despite India's recent years of economic growth, per capita income has declined. I was known by and friendly with most of the local shopkeepers and restaurant owners. I was also known, at least by face, by most of the men who worked in the pharmacies where I imagined a pregnancy test would be sold. During my visit five years earlier I had learned from a fellow American woman about the risks associated with appearing promiscuous: Deborah was confided in by a close Indian friend who was pregnant with her third child, whom she could not afford. In order to help her friend, she asked about the abortion pill at a pharmacy. Deborah had been paying a man from town to tutor her in Hindi. It was a business friendship, and they were often seen together, going through conjugations and prepositions over chai. But when she inquired about the abortion pill, word got around. Her Hindi tutor was beaten up, and Deborah eventually left town because of public disapproval—*What was a married man doing with this young American woman?*

I, too, had sipped tea with young men in Bodh Gaya. These men were just friends, but I was still hesitant to buy my own pregnancy test for fear someone else would be beaten up due to a misunderstood friendship with an American girl. I asked a friend, an inconspicuous Greek guy, to buy the test for me. He bought it the day I purchased the brandy, though apparently not without everyone in the pharmacy stopping mid-conversation to stare.

I was in denial over having to take a pregnancy test in the first place, let alone grapple with the results.

In India, where uncertainties are guaranteed, there were no immediate little plus or minus signs, no blue or white X's or O's, no obvious opposites to offer certainty. The pregnancy test I took would stay light pink (no) or turn dark pink (yes) after half an hour or so. *Pink or pink,* I thought. *Great.* In a country where the word for yesterday is the same as the word for tomorrow, it wasn't much of a surprise. Though I had decided not to worry Justin until I was certain, I couldn't have reached him even if I had wanted to. Justin was living in Mirik, a small village in the foothills of the Himalayas, about three hours outside of Darjeeling, where the intra-India phone lines had been down for months. All my calls were futile. A tape-recorded operator's voice instructed me to "Please call back after some time."

Luckily, the day I took the test was Valentine's Day, and Justin called me from Darjeeling to tell me the phone lines were down in Mirik—as if I didn't already know. His call came during the half-hour I was waiting for my test tube to turn a distinct shade of pink, supposedly as light as a petal or as fervent as alizarin. When he called, it looked somewhere in between—plain old bubblegum pink, where it would remain.

The call came to the office of the Burmese Vihar, where I had been living. The Vihar is a small monastery, home to a few monks, accommodations for yearly rounds of Burmese pilgrims and, during the fall and winter, a place for western travelers and Buddhist practitioners to stay. The office had, just that week, gotten a television with cable, so there were a dozen people crowded around it, watching a Backstreet Boys video. They were all Indian men, and I knew them all individually. As in most small, rural towns the world over, premarital sex—especially when it results in pregnancy—is seen as a disgrace. Bodh Gaya is no different. I had often struggled with the gap between how I carry myself as an independent, western woman, and how Indian men view western women. I am critical of the travelers-scene girls who wander around in dirty tank tops and wear sari petticoats as skirts. I know that western women's disrespectful reputation is a direct product of western media and is reinforced by travelers ignorant of basic cleanliness standards that are a cornerstone of Hinduism. I never pretended I could *be* Indian, but I dressed as appropriately as possible in traditional *salwar kamiz,* and my Hindi, though far from effortless, was becoming increasingly fluid. I knew that my occasional cigarettes and cups of chai with male friends were luxuries not enjoyed by the women of Bodh Gaya, but I was not a Bodh Gaya woman and never would be. I fit somewhere in between, and everyone had become comfortable with my place. I felt that I had established friendships built on mutual respect with the men in that room, and I did not want it all to go to hell because of an overheard phone conversation about something even I could barely comprehend. I did not want to lose the respect I had earned and to prove again that western ladies are only good for the "sexy free" I was often asked for on the train.

It is extremely difficult to whisper on an Indian phone. There is usually a delay and a lot of static. In rural India, and in a monastery where "no sexual misconduct" is one of five precepts one agrees to while staying there, the prospect of yelling that I might be pregnant and I was just waiting for the pink to pinken was overwhelming. I told Justin about the Honey Bee brandy instead. Then I realized the blessing of the Backstreet Boys. The lure *(Everybody, yeah)* of bad special effects *(Rock your body, yeah)* meant that no one was listening to me *(Backstreet's back, all right!).* I am still grateful to those boys and their gimmicks. Over the next few days of emotional, dreamlike phone conversations, they would provide a surreal soundtrack and at least a mirage of privacy. I told Justin I was sure it was negative, and that I would have a blood test from the doctor in town the next day.

I knew the clinic was another arena for possible gossip. Though I asked the doctor for confidentiality, I wasn't surprised by his team of five young assistants who came to take my blood. Nor was I fazed when one of them proceeded to throw the used syringe like a dart into the side of a cardboard box in the corner. Preoccupied with the idea that my life was about to change more drastically than I would've ever imagined, I hardly noticed the other used syringes that had also missed the bull's-eye and were piled up around it. The test was confirmed. I was pregnant and feeling very alone in a country of one billion people.

I went to the main temple to cry. Lighting candles, the traditional Buddhist offering to dispel the darkness of ignorance, I aspired to dispel my own and prayed I could be open enough to receive this teacher who would be my child. I realized my practice had become intensely literal. I thought I had been gaining insight into the profundity of human life, and suddenly I understood how little I knew. I was petrified, but felt somehow blessed. Everything I thought I knew about myself and the world at large felt different, and I didn't know how I felt about anything at all. Maybe I would understand later, after I let go of what I thought was supposed to be and accepted what was. A woman who had become like a surrogate mother to me in Bodh Gaya told me that other women she knew spoke of how grounding pregnancy is during meditation. I felt anything but grounded.

Despite losing myself in my worries, India was still all around me. The heat was coming fast, and the unnerving chaos did not belong to me alone. Life's everyday trials remained. Most of my letters, both outgoing and incoming, had a very low arrival rate. I felt isolated in every way. I was getting giardia. The onset of Holi, a spring festival of color where everyone winds up covered from head to toe in staining pink powder, added to the craziness. Suddenly everywhere I looked was the positive pink my pregnancy test never turned, as if every person and inanimate object was now screaming, "Yes, you're pregnant!"

Politically, things were no less dramatic. As my own world was being overturned, so was the Bihari government. That week, for the first time ever, the national Indian government forcefully took over Bihar's state government, which was rampant with corruption. Patna, Bihar's capital, was in turmoil, and Justin's thirty-hour bus ride to Bodh Gaya required a five-hour stop there. The previous evening several people had been killed in the mayhem, including one family who had been burned alive. But he arrived safely on the day of Losar, the Tibetan New Year. It was a new moon, an unarguably auspicious time for new beginnings.

We went to visit the one and only woman doctor in a nearby city. My sore breasts bounced and ached during the bumpy rickshaw ride. This doctor, too, had her team of young assistants, although fortunately this time they were women. The office felt more professional than the pile of rubble and bricks that constituted the open-air clinic in Bodh Gaya, but it bore a frightening resemblance to those asylums in turn-of-the-century photographs of women with hysteria. Everything was cold stainless steel, and the operating tables I passed on my way to the bathroom had scary leather straps and belts hanging from them. All the medicine cabinets were empty. I think the electricity was out that day as well—the electric company was supposedly being bribed by the candle company. They took more blood and had the same cardboard-box-in-the-corner method of disposal. Eventually, while her assistants giggled at the skimpiness and the pattern of my underwear, the lady doctor examined me and told us everything was fine. She pointed to a fetal development chart on the wall, and we stared dizzily at Week Six and the funny little prehistoric-looking shrimp. She started to calculate the due date and smiled brightly as she told us this would be a New Year Baby. It was February, mind you, so my first thought was, *How can I be pregnant for a year?* Justin later told me he was excitedly thinking, *Maybe it will be an Aquarius!* Then we looked at each other with recognition. Diwali. The Indian New Year begins in October. She interrupted my persistent interrogation, exasperated, and told me to stop asking so many questions. Pregnancy and birth, she assured me, happen all the time.

As we packed our bags and made arrangements to leave India, we began to tell people the news. We made calls home and started to whisper and stammer to some folks around town. The excitement and faith were unbelievable. With the exception of my father (and he soon came around), everyone seemed pretty unfazed, as if it were obvious to them that Justin and I would make good parents. The support was reassuring, and there was joy enough to counter my doubts. Countless people offered their blessings, from the silent Austrian who tipped his hat to us, to Justin's teacher, a Tibetan lama, who prayed and touched our heads with a fourteenth-century statue. We were gaining confidence and momentum.

Grateful for the lessons learned and the ones to come, I understood why it had been so important for me to return to India. It was here that I had struggled with notions of control and had found release. I was realizing, more than ever, the necessity to stay present, moment to moment.

I had always had an extremely difficult time with mail in Bodh Gaya. I would write letters as efficiently as I knew how, on airmail paper, and fold them into uninteresting envelopes, plainly addressed. I would bring exact change to the post office, knowing how much the old man at the counter resented having to make it for me. I would stand patiently, without hovering, and watch as he pounded with authority the official seal of the Indian post office onto the corners of my letters. I would smile. Still, very few of my letters made it to their destinations. I struggled constantly not to have a mental breakdown in the post office, and on particularly trying days, I avoided it altogether. It was the one aspect of living in Indian chaos that I could not come to terms with. I was angry that I couldn't control what would happen to my letters. And I always blamed the curmudgeon behind the counter. Just before leaving Bodh Gaya, seven weeks pregnant and with a stack of letters saying so, I went to the post office for the last time. I gave the old man my letters, exact change and a big box of Indian sweets—my offering to the unknown.

Getting Dick

Beth Kohl Feinerman

Below the bellybutton is the best place for it. If I pinch a thick enough flesh biscuit, I barely feel the prick. It's only after I press my thumb toward my index finger that I sense the invasion. It's not painful, really. It's more of a psychic shock, a rubber band snapped on my wrist. *I shouldn't have to do this,* I think. *Why should I have to go through this?* The vials look so decorative, teardrop-shaped and lovely. I pretend I'm a doctor, a junkie. Anything but what I am.

What I am is a patient, a statistic, number 20125 at the clinic I visit thrice weekly. What I am is one of a handful of women—ten or twelve of us at any one time—languishing in unplush waiting-room chairs, hoping against all hope to discover a new article in the same nineteen magazines that have been there, fanned on the Formica coffee table, at least since I started coming here over a year ago.

⬯

Each time the lab technician appears from behind the door to the back of the office—the place where things get done, hopes are realized—I hold my breath and pray to hear my name called. I watch somebody else, some other severely bloated woman who slides the April 1997 *Better Homes and Gardens* back into its position in the fan, rise from her chair and smile at the technician who holds the door open. Before returning to my article on forcing narcissus bulbs (I've memorized the first four lines and half of the fifth), I listen to the receptionist on the phone. I agree with her, her baby's father is a selfish motherfucker, and I, too, would just as soon not even know who the daddy was, for all he ever does for us. Selfish motherfucker.

Every night at exactly 9:45 P.M. I'm in the kitchen, mixing up and injecting a brew of insufficiently tested substances bearing stamps warning, "Awaiting FDA Approval." My husband, who, selfish motherfucker, tries to remember to ask how it went at the clinic, has a thing about needles and leaves the room when the vials start popping. When I've administered the shots, one for follicular growth and another for hormonal balance, I call for him, tell him the coast is clear, no more bleeding injection sites, it's safe to come back in and watch *ER*.

And as I go through all of these paces, a voice in the back of my head keeps at me. *This is your fault*, it says. *Shit like this doesn't just happen*. My mom blames it on my avoidance of full-fat salad dressing, real potato chips, Coca-Cola Classic. My grandmother swears it's because I run around too much, eat at restaurants too often, wear jeans that pinch me at the waist. And my sister-in-law says it's from taking birth control pills for too many years.

"Anything over five years is bad news," she says as she directs her nipple into a gaping one-month-old mouth and glances toward the den, the direction from which come the screams of her two- and five-year-olds.

"That's ridiculous," I say. "If they were bad for me, certainly my OB/GYN wouldn't have prescribed them for over ten years."

"I took a college course called 'Women and Their Bodies in Health and Disease.' We studied birth control, and I still remember the section on the Pill because I had already been on it for four and a half years. Thank God for that class or we'd both be up shit creek. No offense."

I, on the other hand, took the Pill without compunction, swallowing it nightly like candy, which it may as well have been since I barely even kissed anybody in high school. But then I went to college and made up for lost time, reassured nightly by the solid plastic snap of my pill case. Four years and many boyfriends later, I graduated, met my husband-to-be, and continued taking the Pill, certain that when I wanted to have a baby, I'd have a baby, boom.

As soon as we made that decision—a no-brainer for me, but a soul-searching, friend-interviewing, guidebook-reading rigmarole for my husband—I threw away my birth control pill stockpile. I'm not talking two or three packets, either. I'm talking supply, thanks to my generous pharmacist father-in-law who sported me whole cases of whatever brand I wanted, no prescription required. But figuring I'd purge the house of all counterproductive substances to create a fertile environment, I pitched my stash and filled the newly vacant spot in the medicine cabinet with ovulation kits and EPT tests, thanks again to the generosity, and grandfatherly ambition, of my father-in-law the pharmacist.

Then, I figured, it would only take a minute. It was a simple enough equation. Being on the pill prevented pregnancy. Ergo, ditch the pills, put your head between your knees and prepare to collide with the Progeny Express. After all, if the 3,780 pills I had faithfully jammed into the back of my throat hadn't kept me from having a baby, why had I spent all that money on those little pink bullets that caused me to bloat and kept me from smoking?

I was sixteen when I filled my first prescription. Ortho-Novum. It seemed so exciting, so ERA. It seemed so political, so adult, so Gloria Bunker. Granted, I wasn't doing it yet. But I was thinking about it, just like I was thinking about someday having tits and buying a white eyelet demi bra, even though it would be years before I'd even remove the tags.

So there it was, 1985, and there I was, sophisticated in my Country Day School black watch-plaid skirt and navy knee socks, trying to conjure the spirit of an independent woman in desperate need of something to foil my sex partner's semen. (I had seen the filmstrips in health class and knew how wily and persistent those bulbous-headed, thrashing-tailed spermatozoa could be.)

I loitered outside Fitzgerald's Pharmacy, one eye toward the parking lot, scanning for a familiar Wagoneer or Suburban, the other eye on McDonald's, where some of my friends occasionally hung. As I stood there, still but for my knocking knees, a folded slip of paper glowed neon from the innermost pocket of my JanSport backpack.

Baby, it blinked. Baby. Baby.

I was no baby. I'll show you who's a baby.

I unzipped the backpack, fished beneath my Trapper Keeper for the prescription, breathed deep, swung open the front door and raced down aisle three, past the greeting cards and wrapping paper, past the diapers and wipes, all the way back to where the pharmacy counter floated in a sea of fluorescence. I stood there, my heartbeat fluttering against my shirt, the tinkling of the front-door bell tolling my imminent rebirth.

Okay, Beth, get ahold of yourself. Listen to the music. That's nice. Sounds familiar. It was a piped-in Muzak rendition of "Papa Don't Preach"—proving that not only did God exist but he was a member of the Moral Majority.

"Can I help you?" A man wearing a light-blue smock had surfaced behind the pharmacy counter. What had I been so afraid of? He was wearing powder blue, for Chrissakes. The medical color, empathic and efficient. I grasped the accordioned paper and handed it over. The pharmacist—"Richard" was embroidered over his heart in navy cursive letters—held the paper between two fingers as if it were a soiled napkin. Clearing his throat, he unfolded it, read it and, after firing a quick glance at me over the top of his glasses, read it again.

"How old are you, young lady?"

"Sixteen."

"Sixteen? You don't look sixteen. Do you have any identification, Miss, um, Kohl?" I flinched, sure that every last person in the pharmacy had heard my name and figured out that not only was I there for birth control pills, but that I was wearing thong underwear and had shared a cigarette with Tracy MacNeil in an alley behind school during lunch hour.

"Identification? I walked here from home and forgot my wallet."

"Is your mother at home?" *Fuck.*

"No. My mom and dad are both out of town. Together. I'm not sure where."

"Well, give me your phone number so I can leave a message for your parents."

"Sir. I don't understand what the problem is. I'm allowed to get these. I went to the doctor and got a prescription and everything. If you don't believe it's my prescription, you can call Dr. Barwig and ask her yourself."

"I think I'll do just that. Be back in a minute."

I stood there, waiting for the return of Dick. I was in the most conspicuous spot in the place, the apse where all rows converged and all shoppers strolled, red plastic baskets hooked over their arms, wholesome, good-neighborly smiles for all.

I turned around to find a hideout and found myself face to face with a rack of granny-style reading glasses. I examined them and they stared back. I heard a chorus of grandmothers wondering what was wrong with kids today. One, horn-rimmed and oversized, called me easy while another, silver and cheap-looking, warned me that if anyone found out, my reputation would be ruined. I jerked the rack ninety degrees, giving the dusty old biddies a clear shot of the LifeStyles condom display. Finally, after a complete lunar phase had passed, communism had been implemented and deemed a failure, and my nails had grown an inch, Dick came back.

"Miss Kohl?" He was talking loud. Visiting-your-Uncle-Leon-at-Brookhaven-Rest-Home-and-having-to-get-his-attention-even-though-*Wheel of Fortune*-is-on loud. "Here are your birth control pills. Sorry for the wait."

My face burned. "That's okay," I lied. I had them. I couldn't believe I was holding them in my hands.

I turned and started for the nearest exit, trying to duck the line that had formed behind me, when Dick arrested my escape.

"Miss Kohl? How are you going to take care of this?"

"What?"

"Do you want me to put them on your family's house charge?"

I most certainly did not.

"Well?"

"I'll come back when I have my wallet." And I shoved the already damp and wrinkled bag toward the light-blue-wearing, buzz-killing sentinel to my womanhood.

"Okay, Miss. I'll be the fellow back here holding his breath."

That was a long time ago, at least 150 prescriptions ago, and I've become a real pro at buying the personal stuff. Tampax, Tucks and Metamucil plunked down at the checkout, screw them if they think anything of it. These days, while I wait for my pharmacist to hand over the drugs made from the urine of expectant women, I chat up the other patrons, as comfortable about my need for pregnant pee as I am about the Goody barrettes in my shopping basket.

"Are you sick, dear?" one regular asks. "I see you here an awful lot for such a young gal."

"No, I'm not sick. Not really. I can't get pregnant."

This information is usually followed by the older lady scoffing at whatever medication I'm on and recommending an alternate home remedy, which usually involves changing my diet to an almost exclusively vagina-resembling smorgasbord. Figs and dates, oranges and oysters. I've also been told to eat kreplachs, potstickers, tacos and anything snuggled deep within the warm folds of pita bread.

What a waste—all those years spent skulking around in pharmacies scattered around my hometown. The countless pastel-colored cases whisked into my pocket the moment the pharmacist laid them on the counter. The plastic-cased caches buried beneath woolen knee socks at the back of my sock drawer. And the most goddamned most hysterical part about all of it? I couldn't have gotten pregnant even if I had wanted to. Good one, God.

My husband and I tried to conceive for a couple of months, but it was impossible to figure out when I was ovulating since I hadn't seen a period since the Reagan Administration. So we went to a fertility specialist. He examined me, told my husband it was my problem, not his, and started writing us prescriptions for fertility drugs.

"Try the Clomid first," he said, looking up while his pen continued scratching out illegible marks. "They come in pill form. So much more pleasant than the others. But I'm also writing you prescriptions for Fertinex and Follistim and some syringes just in case the Clomid isn't working after a couple of tries."

My husband and I didn't know enough to think up any questions, so we thanked the doctor, filled the sundry prescriptions and started debating names.

The Clomid didn't work. I saw double and my ovaries swelled up to the size of cantaloupes, which made me appear five months pregnant. That was some good fun when well-meaning folks would congratulate me and ask when the little one was due. "November," I'd say, not wanting to make them feel bad for assuming I was just like everybody else.

With little choice, we dumped the Clomid and moved on to hardcore drugs. So now, twice a week, I pick up my supply of tinkling vials filled halfway with a liquid looking a bit too much like purified water. But that's no water. No, Ma'am. That's the stuff making women all over the world give birth not to one baby, but to legions of them. But willing to defy nature and possibly God's will, I sail into the drugstore and shimmy through the metal turnstile. The assistant pharmacist, young and variously pierced, welcomes me.

"If it isn't Beth Kohl, would-be mother and customer of the century!"

I'm on a mission and don't even look around the place. Except when I'm making my way back to the pharmacy counter and pass the boxes showing a thirtysomething woman sitting at her high-luster desk, a phone poised between her ear and shoulder while her fingers dance away at a personal computer. Her hair is bobbed and chestnut, and she looks the perfect junior executive except for the fact that her Brooks Brothers Egyptian-cotton blouse is unbuttoned to her waist while some *Lost in Space*-looking vacuum contraption suckles both breasts dry. What are you smiling about, little Miss Happy Pump? At least I have my dignity. If there is one thing I still have, it's my dignity. I mean, I haven't cried once. Not when the doctor had me in stirrups and told me not to move and left the room—and the door wide open—as he went to get some sort of camera to take a picture of whatever it is that's wrong with me. Not when he told my husband that this was my fault. Not even when I had to give myself my first shot in the abdomen and ended up making dozens of stab marks but never breaking the skin. So, if there is one thing I still have, even if I never have a son or daughter, it's my dignity.

Not that I don't stare at the millions of pregnant women who've suddenly moved into my city, taken over my block, the grocery store, the airwaves. I do. Not that I don't slap the phone pad over and over the moment I put the receiver down after hearing that yet another of my friends is expecting. Again. I do. But God help me, I haven't cried once.

As I sit in the waiting room for the eighth hour this week, I glance around at the other Sarahs and Hannahs sneaking looks at me, too. We don't talk to each other for fear of asking the wrong question, giving too much of ourselves away or misdirecting the good luck that is rightfully ours this month. But I watch them and wonder how long they've been at it, how they're holding up, do *they* ever cry?

There's a woman in denim overalls sitting across from me as we silently vie for the blood technician to call our name. She flips through

Sports Illustrated—no danger of parenting articles there, unless we're talking Shawn Kemp. She has the magazine open to a story on Mia Hamm but keeps glancing up at the door leading out of the anteroom and into the lab. Nobody comes for her so she sits here, with the rest of us, trying to appear calm and natural and interested in the magazine.

I want so badly to talk to her, to tell her it's not her fault, everything will work out in the end. But I don't know that. None of us do. So we keep on sitting here, waiting, until it's finally our turn.

WILL

Min Jin Lee

My husband looked so happy. "That's great," he shouted, then reached over to hug me, but stopped when he saw my face. My sparsely filled eyebrows must have been furrowed again, giving me away. The skin around Christopher's brown eyes crinkled with worry. "What's wrong? Aren't you happy about it?" After all, it wasn't an accident. We'd been married for three years and we'd both agreed recently to start a family.

Christopher removed his suit jacket, having just returned from the office. After spending the entire day at home by myself, I'd pounced on him as soon as he'd opened the front door. Then I'd blurted out the news.

"I am." I glanced at my bare feet, then watched him slip off his brown oxfords. I didn't want to seem ambivalent—so ungrateful. "I just thought it would take longer."

My husband put his arms around me, and I peered over his shoulder, my chin resting on the yoke of his white dress shirt. I stared at the hallway mirror hanging slightly askew on the whitewashed wall. I could smell the clean scent of starch, and I wondered what would become of my life now.

I'd heard a lot about how so many women in New York City were infertile, how difficult it was to conceive. It took us three weeks. I never bought a fertility kit, took my temperature or counted the days of my menstrual cycle. With a snap of the fingers, presto—we were going to have a baby. I was surprised by the speed of it, but more than that, I felt a kind of dread—and this filled me with shame. Children were blessings, everyone knew that.

I would not describe myself as having been a happy child—more like morose and slightly goofy. Far too tall for a Korean girl, I wore my oversized eyeglasses slung low on my rounded nose, my black hair bobbed. My tiny oval eyes bore a pinched expression as if I had lost my way. I was the middle of three girls in an immigrant family. Our parents worked six days a week in their small wholesale jewelry store in midtown Manhattan while my sisters and I went to the local public school, did our homework and waited for them to return safely to our brown brick apartment building in Elmhurst, Queens.

Each night, we'd hear the jangle of keys opening our apartment door; then Mom and Dad would walk in, remove their coats and shoes and separate from one another. Mom marched straight to the kitchen to finish cooking the dinner that my older sister had started preparing, and Dad would go to the living room, collapse into the maroon sectional sofa from Seaman's and read the *shin-mun*. My younger sister would fetch him a clean ashtray from the kitchen counter, and he'd pat her head. The only sounds in our rented one-bedroom apartment were the clinks of pots and pans coming from the narrow galley kitchen and the rustle of Dad's newspapers. The metallic smell of Benson & Hedges filled the air as the three of us, heads down, did our homework and waited for dinner.

Our parents were always tired; my sisters and I felt sorry for them. Though they never said it, we felt like we were an enormous burden— needing lunch money, new sneakers and jeans, and handing them countless school forms having to be read and signed in English. I didn't think about it then, but I can imagine now how scared they must have been to move to a new country, start a small business they knew nothing about and raise three little girls—all with only a modest knowledge of the language.

In Korea, Dad was an account executive who moved from job to job because he fought with his bosses. Mom was a minister's daughter who taught piano to the neighborhood children. Born to well-off families from the opposite sides of a small country, both Mom and Dad had been sheltered from roughness and poverty as children. The war changed everything for them. At age sixteen, Dad left his hometown in the North and never saw his mother again. Unable to shake his fear and hatred of that war, he insisted on bringing us to America—a country, to him, full of romance and possibilities.

I was seven when our family immigrated; my mother was only thirty-five. After just a few months in New York, her white and pink skin faded. Her glossy chestnut hair began to gray. After her bath, I'd occasionally help her pluck the white hairs from her head with a pair of old-fashioned eyebrow tweezers. In the following years when there were too many white hairs to harvest, she turned to Loving Care hair dye from the drugstore.

From the moment she arrived home from work until the rest of us went to bed, Mom was in motion. Her childhood home in Pusan had been filled with servants, and in our home in Seoul, I remember the country girls who lived with us to help Mom with the housework while she earned money as a piano teacher. In America, she worked twelve- or thirteen-hour days, cooked our meals and kept our house tidy. But in those long years in Queens before my parents used their savings to buy a big house in the New Jersey suburbs, I can't recall seeing my mother smile or tease or laugh at a joke, even on holidays. For Mom and Dad, life in America was somber—to succeed, you had to be vigilant, sacrifice pleasure and endure.

As a young girl, I decided that I didn't want to marry or have children. I didn't even like to be around babies or toddlers—they seemed so needy and useless. So I studied very hard, earned gold stars and, when I had spare time, wrote and published essays for a Korean newspaper. My teachers told me that in America you could do anything you wanted. I paid attention to successful people in books and magazines and on television. My favorite writer when I was fifteen was Sinclair Lewis. He had gone to Yale, so I applied and, amazingly, I got in. I formulated a plot for my life: I would be a single professional with money of my own, wear nice clothes and live in a beautiful apartment in Manhattan. I would invest my savings, retire early and write novels and plays. I would not take care of anyone else.

The only thing I never considered was love. I met Christopher when I was twenty-two. After I finished law school two years later, we married. He had come from enormous privilege, the only child of a regal Japanese mother and an American diplomat father. My husband didn't believe that life had to be an unrelenting struggle, filled with difficulties and betrayals of history for which you prepared by sewing gold coins in the lining of your coat. There could be fun and comfort in this life. To me, such ideas were extravagant, exotic, utterly unfamiliar. From the outset, it was obvious to me that I believed in work and he believed in grace.

Right after our honeymoon, I started my job as a corporate lawyer. I was at the office eighty to ninety hours a week, easily billing sixty.

Sometimes I worked forty to fifty hours straight through, without going home to shower or change my clothes. After a year of this, I started to fantasize about selling lipstick at the Bergdorf's counter. At least salesgirls went home when the store closed. I never knew when I could go home. The more work you did, the more work you were given. I was a newlywed—I wanted to go to the movies with my husband on Saturday nights and cook dinner for us now and then. On Sunday nights, I'd cry hopelessly because I'd have to begin another week of endless work, or so it seemed to me. Christopher asked me why. Why would I keep doing something for so many hours if I didn't like it? He said, Quit. We could live on a lot less.

I said no. I couldn't just quit. I'd spent three years in law school. My parents had sacrificed almost twenty years working in that tiny jewelry store to put me through college and law school. As a junior institutional salesman at a Wall Street firm, my husband earned less than I did. I wanted to be a writer, but that wasn't a real job. No one paid you while you wrote a novel, and one book could take years and years. I heard Tolstoy wrote *War and Peace* eight times. I stayed at that firm for another year.

I wondered if I'd enjoy my job more somewhere else, so I changed law firms. The new place was worse: I had to prove myself again. I worked there for fifty days, and after billing my first three-hundred-hour month—a feat I'd once dismissed as urban lawyer myth—I quit. There wasn't enough money in New York for me to work that way, and even so, I didn't care about money enough; I would not endure it anymore.

I had written and published in high school and college, but had stopped in law school and for the two years that I practiced. After I quit my job I bought a computer and a printer. I wrote a very rough draft of a novel. I found an agent. I still needed to learn a great deal about writing, but I felt hopeful—not just about my new career, but about my revised plans for my life. My husband and I talked about having a child.

Perhaps I could be a mother if someone like Christopher was my child's father. He didn't scream, get depressed or fall apart. Not like me. What would a child who was half-Christopher and half-me be like? In my marriage, I felt loved and cared for and attended to. This support made me think that perhaps I could love a child even though I hadn't felt loved as a child. My husband said we would have a wonderful life even if we never had children, but would he always feel this way? I now had doubts about the plot I'd hatched as a young girl. I hadn't planned to get married, yet my marriage had turned out well. Perhaps the same would occur with having a child. I went off the Pill. I primed my body for a baby. I gave up caffeine, exercised in moderation, took prenatal vitamins. We stopped using condoms. Three weeks.

I was pregnant, but I couldn't imagine *my* life as a mother. All I could see was the image of my mother—the whirling dervish—with half a dozen arms spinning in the air, each hand performing a different task. So I tried to focus on the pregnancy itself—on the physical requirements of this life growing in my body. I tried to follow the guidelines of the pregnancy books, but I kept falling short. I could not swallow another glass of grayish skim milk. I never ate any yellow vegetables, and my favorite foods—refined sugar and fat—were clear no-noes. I felt tired all the time, but I resented taking naps. I was so sleepy that I couldn't read anything serious or write anything good. I was angry—my writing schedule was becoming a joke. I knew it would only get worse when the baby came. I was a bad mother, and my baby wasn't even born yet. I got piercing migraines for the first time in my life. Extra Strength Tylenol did nothing for me. I lay across my sofa, wet washcloths on my forehead, and hoped the pain would pass.

During each checkup at the doctor's office, I noticed an increase in my weight. Having previously struggled with a weight problem and lost the extra pounds, I did not want to be fat again, *ever*. The idea of gaining forty pounds was devastating.

I could not admit these feelings which seemed, even to me, grossly superficial and selfish. I did not tell anyone I felt this way. I was too smart, too nice, too with-it, too spiritual to be this vain, this self-conscious, this ungrateful. Everyone was overjoyed that we were having a child. My parents and my in-laws were ecstatic. My sisters were ready to spend a fortune on toys and baby clothes for their future niece or nephew. I was no longer me, I was merely the silent medium for the next generation.

In spite of everyone else's happiness, I grew more terrified. I feared becoming one of those people who talk only about their children, never see films, have a rotten social life, never read history books and live in a toy- and diaper-littered apartment. I had quit being a lawyer, hoping to become a writer, not a mother. And how could I forget that when I was little, my mother never had any time for her piano, her books or for laughter?

Eleven weeks into my pregnancy, my doctor could not find the fetus's heartbeat using a stethoscope with a built-in microphone. She instructed me to get an ultrasound examination at a nearby clinic. There was a slight possibility that something could be wrong: Fibroids could be blocking the fetus's heartbeat, or the fetus could be in a strange position. But she said not to worry, she was explaining these things at length only because she would not be there; another physician, who I didn't know, would see me.

My husband and I went together for the ultrasound. I undressed and lay down on the examining table. The doctor proceeded to project an image of the inside of my uterus on a monitor. In the dim room I tried to be still while a latex-sheathed probe was inserted into me. Christopher held my hand, and I remembered what my mother used to tell me as a child when I went to see the dentist or to church on Sundays: "Be a good girl and don't fidget." It was so quiet in that room, so quiet that I felt dizzy. Minutes later, the doctor mumbled something to his assistant, who turned on the overhead lights. He told me that the fetus had expired. He didn't know why.

After the doctor left the room, Christopher and I cried. He helped me to get dressed and said very little—that it would be all right, that he loved me very much. He was sad, too, but I didn't do much to comfort him. Once again, I felt silenced, not just by my guilt this time, but also by my grief. I wondered if it was possible to have ended a life merely by having doubts about its beginnings.

Christopher returned to the office, and I went home and phoned my best friend to tell her what had happened. Finally, I confided that I hadn't been happy about being pregnant and I wondered if such feelings could have contributed to losing the pregnancy. Next time, I told her, I'd push such negative thoughts from my mind.

What an arrogant thing to think, she said. She repeated it again, *arrogance*.

I was stunned. She might as well have kicked me. My friend was usually a fountain of sympathy. She told me that my fears had nothing to do with it—*I* had nothing to do with it. It was nature, science, God—it wasn't meant to be. Regardless, it wasn't my will that mattered. The truth of her statements wounded me. I told her that I was tired and got off the phone.

When I saw my obstetrician the next day, she said that I needed to have a D&C procedure to clean out my womb and see if everything was all right. Then I should wait at least three months before trying again.

Chris said he would accompany me, but I told him no. I don't know why exactly; a part of me felt that I'd failed him somehow. I was ashamed of another test, another procedure, another required step in the process of one big disappointment. I asked my mother to come with me.

The anesthesiologist told me to count backward. That is all I remember. After it was over, I woke up on a plastic-sheeted operating bed, blood pooling around my hips. My mother held my hand while I sobbed, and though I knew that it didn't make any sense, I felt that I was being punished for my arrogance—for believing that motherhood was elective, not selective.

As a girl, I had asked myself if I ever wanted to be a mother, and I had answered no. I'd assumed that I could be a mother and I could refuse that role because its burdens seemed so great. And I had to ask myself now, as a young, married writer who had just lost a pregnancy: Did I *never* want to be a mother? And my answer was no.

My mother had seemed so sad to me when I was growing up. How can I say this without offense? I didn't want to be like her, and I didn't want her life. I didn't always want to be second or third or fifth. Mom was beyond reproach. She was giving, patient, kind, fair, reliable and extremely competent. I would never be so selfless.

This is even harder to say—I was disappointed with my good mother because she did everything she was supposed to do except to seem happy that I was born. Her sadness and fatigue due to the overwhelming demands on a working mother of three children in a foreign country were without question well justified. But I had needs as her daughter—including the need to see her happy. If my mother wasn't happy, I wondered, then how could I be happy? Nothing I did or could do would ever redeem her sacrifices—this much I was beginning to understand. No lives were equal. She and Dad were far happier now in their retirement, but I still sensed her unarticulated regrets. These were my fears:

One day my child would feel the need to make my life whole through her accomplishments, or worse, as an adult, she would be unable to remember me ever smiling at her as a little girl.

Mom had given up so much—too much, I thought. But I knew that her strength and continued presence had given me the ability to create a better life for myself. Would a life without enough hope and happiness for another generation be a better life—or would it just be a simpler one?

I didn't want to adopt a new plan, hatch a new plot or invoke a new will for my life. Instead I was aware of a wish, a prayer, a hope: in time, to be a decent mother who was happy about being one.

Whether I could be a mother at all was uncertain at that moment; it was simply out of my hands. I had to forget my plans, my fears, my schedule, and just wait and be open to the uncertainty. There was nothing for me to do. In a way, I was relieved.

When I Was Garbage

Allison Crews

Last year, when I was in tenth grade, I skipped a week of school. I was too scared and humiliated, too sick and weak to leave my house. A week away from school earned me two weeks of "in-school suspension." Ten full school days I had to sit in a boxed-in desk, in a six-by-twenty-foot room. Yellowing posters of needles and beer bottles crookedly proclaimed "Just Say No!" from the walls. I was allowed to go to the bathroom only twice daily, for fifteen minutes. When you are five weeks pregnant, thirty minutes a day is hardly adequate for throwing up.

I sat at my desk, fifteen years old, failing in school, pregnant, sick and terrified. I sat at my desk, rubbing my still-flat stomach and clenching my jaw tightly to hold down my vomit. *Two more hours and I can throw up,* I reassured myself. I replayed the moment of truth in my mind millions of times during those two weeks. The moment I saw the second line appear on the pregnancy test stick. Positive. Positive. Positive. But from that moment on, I wasn't positive about anything.

Except the fact that I needed desperately to vomit. I wrote furiously in my blue-velvet-covered journal, tearing the pages with my Hello Kitty pen and smearing the ink with my tears. Fantasies of virgin-white wedding dresses and sponge-painted nurseries unfolded on those blank pages, in the brief moments after bathroom breaks when my fears were purged and flushed away. Incoherent poems and pessimistic single-line entries poured out during the rest of the long days. Many pages read only "No!" in bold letters, traced over and over, the impressions appearing on the next several pages.

I remembered facts about teenage pregnancy I had learned as a freshman in "sex education." Teenage mothers are a burden to society. Their children inevitably become crack-addicted gang members. Teen mothers never successfully complete high school, let alone attend college. These weren't just statistics, I was led to believe, but invariable truths. I had become garbage, worthy only of sitting at my isolated desk, crying to myself and throwing up in a dirty bathroom stall. I was a pregnant teenage girl.

After my two weeks of suspension, I forced my pregnancy into the depths of my mind. Thoughts of my future and of becoming a mother all but disappeared. It was forgotten. My boyfriend and the three friends who knew of my pregnancy assumed I would abort. I was not the type of girl who becomes a mother. Months began to pass, and the only signs of pregnancy were my swollen breasts and an infrequent fluttering in my belly. These signs, undetectable to anyone but me, dredged up the fears that I thought I had buried so well. I was actually pregnant, I began to realize again, more clearly than I had since those two weeks spent in isolation, with only my thoughts and my morning sickness. I continued to hide my pregnancy, even as it became more and more obvious.

School was dismissed during my sixteenth week of pregnancy. My boyfriend and I were engaged in another vicious, mudslinging fight. He threw the lowest blow. At the time, I was so enraged and angry that I could not imagine a more evil act: He told my parents I was pregnant. I realize now what an amazing thing he did for me, although his intent at the time was only to cause me pain. My pregnancy became real. Not only to me, but also to my parents, to my sister, to my relatives, to my newly appointed obstetrician. I was having a baby. There was no turning back. I watched a fuzzy little worm of a baby dance across a television screen as I lay on a long sheet of wax paper, my stomach exposed and covered in chilled jelly. This was what had caused me to vomit. This was what had caused me to outgrow every bra I owned. This was what had caused me so much heartbreak and pain those first few weeks. What appeared to be a hand rose, next to what appeared to be a head. "Hello, Mommy!" my sixtysomething-year-old OB said in a squeaky voice that I assumed was supposed to be a baby's. "I'm a baby boy." I realized then that this little worm that had caused my life to turn upside down in a matter of weeks was no worm at all. He was my son.

It was assumed my son would be given up for adoption, just as a few weeks earlier it had been assumed he would be aborted. I am not sure who made this decision. But it was not me. I wanted to be a good mother. My beautiful, fuzzy black-and-white son, who swam inside me like a fish, deserved only the best. No mother under that magical age of eighteen could provide that, and since I was only fifteen, I would have to let somebody else raise him. That was the "right" thing to do. My boyfriend and I met with a lovely couple. A very rich, childless couple. While I enjoyed their company at dinner, and definitely enjoyed the food that they bought for me, I did not want them to be the parents of my son. I wanted my boyfriend and I to be his parents. We *were* his parents. My boyfriend and I left dinner that night, walking ahead of the lovely couple and my parents.

"We can call your lawyer and work out the rest of the details this week," my mom cooed to the lovely wife.

"I guess we made our decision," my boyfriend whispered. I was trapped.

I did call the lawyer; we did work out the details. I cried myself to sleep every night for the next four months, staining my navy blue pillowcases. I wanted desperately to be a mother, not simply a baby machine for such a lovely couple. The lovely wife, I learned one night after Lamaze class, was pregnant. Relief flooded my swelling body. *I can keep my baby!* I silently rejoiced. *I have diapers to buy, clothes to wash, car seats to find, nursing bras and slings to sew!*

"We still want to adopt though," said the lovely couple. "You know our history of miscarriage."

Oh well. I guess I can't keep my baby after all. I was deflated.

Sure enough, the lovely wife miscarried at twelve weeks. She called me nightly, crying and thanking me for giving her my son. I was, she told me, the only thing that kept her from giving up on life. My son and me. "Our Baby" became his name while she talked to me on the phone. She gave me weekly reports of how the nursery was coming along (complete with a two-thousand-dollar classic Pooh mural, which I am sure would make a world of difference to a newborn), the hundreds of dollars they were spending on clothes, their family's excitement and how much they loved "Our Baby" already. The hole got deeper. I couldn't crawl, scratch or shovel my way out. By law in California, birth mothers must meet with an "adoption facilitator." This mediator "counsels" you and explains the process of adoption to you. I repeatedly told her, over the course of two months, "Lisa, I don't want to do this! I want my baby!"

"Well, I want to take a cruise to the Bahamas. But if I took a cruise to the Bahamas, I wouldn't have money left for rent or food. Sometimes what we want isn't what is best."

Oh, yes, babies and cruises are so similar! How could I have been so blind? I later learned that adoption facilitators, while required by the state, are not employed by the state. Prospective adoptive parents employ adoption facilitators. At the time, I wasn't aware of this. I believed this woman. I was selfish to want to raise my son. How could I be so selfish? she asked me. Pregnant teens are garbage. Once the baby is born, the mother becomes even smellier garbage, dependent on her parents and society's tax dollars to support her children. I had to do something to hoist my son above the metaphorical garbage bin. I had to give him to this lovely couple; they were not garbage, like I was.

I grew during those weeks, not only physically (sixty pounds!) but emotionally and spiritually. I meditated, prayed, screamed, cried, slept, wrote, read and thought. I realized I was more capable than I was led to believe. I made my decision, thirty-eight weeks into my pregnancy. I informed my boyfriend of this decision. "I am keeping the baby. I don't care what anyone says or feels. I will not lose my son. They want any baby, and I only want mine!" My boyfriend and I were going to tell my parents the next evening at dinner. I fell asleep quickly, not sobbing into my pillow as I had grown used to doing during those pain- and growth-filled three months. I was keeping my baby.

I woke up to go to the bathroom at around two o'clock in the morning. As I waddled to the bathroom, I looked down the hallway and saw my boyfriend typing away at the computer, talking to some stranger on the Internet, as he usually did when staying the night. Then came the gush; my water broke. I panted, attempting to jog down the hallway. Then came the pain; I was having contractions already. It wasn't like this in the Lamaze videos! The women in those never got contractions so fast—there must be something wrong with me! I gripped the edge of the kitchen counter and watched the clock on the microwave. Six minutes apart, the orange numbers informed me. I stayed calm, just like I had planned. I packed my bag, brushed my teeth, wrote emails to all of my pregnant friends online, wrote in my journal and cried. I forced my mom to drive me to the hospital at five-fifteen. She didn't believe I was really in labor, but still told me, "Okay, I will call the lovely couple and let them know to start driving down." She said this in the middle of a contraction.

"No! Don't you pick up the phone! This is *my* baby!"

She told me we would talk about it after the baby came.

The baby came at 8:02 A.M., November 20, 1998. My labor was natural, painful and beautiful. I held my tiny infant son in my shaking arms, tears running off my face and onto his still-purple hands. He was so much more than I could have dreamed, so much more than a fuzzy little ultrasound worm. He spent three days in an incubator, on oxygen, as a result of inhaled amniotic fluid. I was terrified of the lovely couple stealing my new son from the nursery, so I woke every hour to walk quickly and quietly down the hall, into the nursery, to see if he was still there.

He was. I checked the machines he was hooked up to, making sure his oxygen saturation levels and heart and breathing rates were what the nurses expected them to be. They were. I padded back down the hallway, into my room, rubbing my soft, wrinkled tummy, and pulled out my new breast pump. I pumped and pumped, watched TV and imagined that it was my tiny baby extracting milk from my breasts. I had an abundance of precious golden milk that only a mother could make. *I was a mother.*

My father told the lovely couple that I decided to keep my son. The lovely husband cursed at him, cursed my boyfriend, told my father I was a piece of trash and hung up. The lovely wife called a few days after I brought the baby home to say that she did not hate us. She also said that when I changed my mind and things got too hard, I could always call them to adopt him. We never spoke again.

Cade Mackenzie is now a happy twenty-four-pound eight-month-old. He sleeps in my bed and is happiest when he is nursing, watching Teletubbies or listening to Bob Marley. I am not a burden on society; my son is not a burden on me. I have received the "Teen Mom Look" from anonymous strangers more times than I can count, and I have learned not to be offended. I turn the other way and hold my son even tighter to my chest. I attend a wonderful homeschool program, which allows me to spend my days at home, raising my son, and I am graduating a semester early. And contrary to what fear-based sex education classes, lovely couples and wonderful counselors had led me to believe, contrary to what I had written so many times in my blue-velvet-covered journal, I am not garbage. I am a mother. I have not yet blown out eighteen candles on a birthday cake, but I am an excellent mother.

Real Moms

Sara Manns

Kids are supposed to happen to you, like a car wreck or bad teeth. There are some who cope gracefully with life's events and some who are less capable, but sooner or later babies happen to all of us. Unless there's something wrong with you or your man, you don't have to plan child-bearing any more than you plan to get a root canal. You're fated to "get yourself pregnant," raise the kids God gave you while complaining about their no-account daddy and crack a molar on a piece of hard candy at Bob Evans after church.

This was my childhood script for how to start a family. I learned the script backward and forward as a child, and I surprised a lot of people by reciting it backward and upside down. I'm certain that any attempt I might have made to read those lines with a straight face would have resulted in disaster. What I know now is, kids are your own once you've fought for them. To make our baby really ours, we had to pass a series of tests. We had to figure out our tolerance for risk, let go of the idea that we were in control and allow strangers to help us. Like the angel Gabriel said to Mary, "Don't worry, God will take care of everything." And she did, just not the way we expected.

We didn't know what we were doing—that's obvious now. We thought that once we had a house, a car and a business that supported the two of us and several pets, we were there. Time for children. The only problem was, we lacked one of the necessary components for achieving pregnancy: sperm. We knew we were all set on the gestation thing, since my wife ovulates as regularly as a tide table and always wanted to bear a child. I would rather floss a hippo than push a healthy baby's skull through my pelvis, so there were no problems on that score. All we needed was to outsource our supplies.

At first we ran an ad for a sperm donor. Weird pothead college students answered, with letters that asked what the baby would call his or her parents and other similar non sequiturs. We burned the whole pile of responses before moving on and calling the sperm bank. They sent a video and catalog. The catalog gave us the chance to select a biological father for our baby based on race, size, education, hobbies and reasons for donation. The video reassured us that using donor sperm could be our secret and no one would ever know that the baby wasn't really mine.

This was the first clue that we might be on the wrong path. The point of the marketing materials was clear: Real parents have kids who look like them. Using technology to have a baby of your own is okay as long as no one knows it's not really your baby. The reflective look and reassuring tone of the dads in the video really set me off. They said things like "I worried about whether I'd be attached to a child who isn't really mine, but believe me, it's just like he was my own son." This is supposed to be a benefit, we sleuthed out after viewing fifty-five minutes of sales pitch.

As we made a party game out of mocking the claims of the fertility industry, it became obvious that our situation deviated from the norm. The child would be more related—legally and biologically—to one of us. Since we're both from all-girl families, we couldn't suggest that a helpful brother provide the genetic material in a paper cup, a technique used successfully by one couple we know. There was also no way for both of us to be legal parents from the start. First Kate would birth the kid, and then we'd move to a state that allowed same-sex adoption. All of this sounded vaguely reasonable at the time. Slowly, as we spun through a year of waiting for Baby, my heart changed and my mind had to follow.

To select a sperm donor, we had to decide whether we cared about the baby resembling both of us. The catalog provided a terrifying level of detail, and based on the video, we guessed that this was intended to reassure. With enough data, we could identify the donor who looks like me and convince ourselves that I'm a real parent too. In our situation, the claim that no one will know I'm not the real daddy was hard to believe. The breasts give it away every time.

I pulled for a donor who was mixed: Irish and Indonesian. My lovely wife felt that we were diverse enough already and insisted on the tall skinny white nerd.

After a few cycles of ordering the sperm, missing the timing and cursing when we paid the bill, we hit it exactly right. One morning after Halloween, Kate called my name from the bathroom while I was in my office. I was irritated at the interruption, and then suddenly I realized the only reason she would ask me to . . . I jumped up and ran. She showed me the plastic stick with its stripes filled in and whispered, "I wanted you to see it before it faded." The fear of no baby was suddenly superseded by fears about pregnancy. We walked the dog in the snow, giggled and glowed with excitement. The morning sickness that made her too nauseous to ride to the Christmas-tree farm was gone when I arrived home with our tree. We hung mistletoe and spun fantasies about next year's Christmas, with the baby.

The fates were against these plans. Some unlucky teenager's Christmas prayers misfired by a little bit, and her hopes became our fears realized. On Christmas Eve morning, Kate was feeling sick. By noon, she began to bleed; by midnight Mass, it was clear that the baby wouldn't live. My sister, a midwife, urged me to take her to the emergency room. I asked what could be done there, and she admitted that an unscheduled abortion in a dirty ER might result in permanent infertility. Kate is a member of the "don't just do something, stand there" school of self-medication, and she insisted that if she were going to lay somewhere and bleed while the baby died, it was going to be her own damn couch. We waited through the night. I took her temperature every few hours and swabbed her down with cool water, forced her to sip warm liquids and tried to hold her head up. In the morning she was confused and irritable, refusing to remember the night's loss.

After the miscarriage we found out that the sperm bank was out of that donor. There was a run on the tall skinny guy's product while we waited for my wife to feel well enough to try again. The crisis hit when it was time to select a new donor. We were somewhat hesitant to put so much effort into the process the second time. After a series of late-night conversations, we made a random selection. Kate described this as the "throw it up there and hope" stage of trying. We had stopped hoping, though, and one month we just forgot to place an order.

Next, we checked out fertility treatment. It seemed clear that no personal or social good could come from spending fifteen thousand dollars on the chance to have a healthy baby. Besides, the videos from the in vitro–fertilization people struck us as parody. "You've waited.

And now you're ready to turn to science for help." Shots of healthy white babies frolicking in the sun. Cut to a doctor in an office lined with leather-bound books. "You understand, of course, that your baby will be yours in every way—legally and biologically." Maybe this approach turned us off because it emphasized what we couldn't have, no matter what crazy money we spent on doctors and lawyers.

Unlike the straight couples we met who adopted after fertility woes, we didn't have to mourn our dream-child or grieve for the baby who looked like both of us. We were never entitled to that baby. Adoption became the only plan that made sense. The fertility specialists' pitch—an effort to convince us that after the failure of our bodies we could be real parents through science—wasn't persuasive.

We thought of domestic adoption. We dredged through pounds of paper and mountains of evidence and were forced to look at other alternatives. Sure, we could have taken a two-year run at the bureaucrats and maybe been rewarded with a seven-year-old boy who sets fires, but we had slim chances of getting approved for public adoption of a baby or toddler.

Then came the whirlwind of considering private adoption: Are we cut out for this? First we have to be approved by the twenty-two-year-old social worker through a series of interviews, inspections and reference checking. Then we would get our photos (or the photo of just one of us, who appears to be a socially stunted weirdo, God knows what she wants with a baby, she must be lonely) in a binder and wait. What would we be waiting for? For a young pregnant woman with limited resources to see what great parents we'd be and choose our family for her unborn child.

Well, of course. The typical birth mother in this country is just dying to have her child raised by lesbians, right? And if she can't get a couple of dykes because the agency doesn't put "unmarried couples" in their book, she's going to be drawn to the single woman with spiked hair who describes herself as an enthusiastic aunt.

Let's say the unlikely happens and we "win" this game. We get to spend fifteen thousand dollars traveling to someplace sexy like El Paso. What if we pay all legal fees and fund the support and medical care, and then the birth mother changes her mind? This "win" also includes on-going contact with birth family who are no doubt thrilled beyond belief about the whole thing. Then at home, we wait a year to see if our local family court feels like finalizing the adoption or if the last laugh goes to the judge who places the baby with a birth-family member who hasn't even asked for her.

Suddenly, international adoption looked affordable and practical. All we had to do was identify the few countries that accept "single" women, and select the one most likely to assign us a child who is actually orphaned. Of course, this too was easier said than done. We assumed that we would adopt from China, until we learned that the Chinese government doesn't want us as parents and asks for a sworn statement from all single mothers to affirm we're not homosexuals.

I woke up early one Saturday, the morning of Halloween. We heard the Halloween parade, led by the marching band, toot up the hill toward downtown. At my insistence, we raced down the driveway dragging our tired old dog. On the way, I explained my secret plan: surely adoptive parents would be there! Parents who had been down this road could tell us what to expect and what agency to use for our home study.

And indeed, the parents of Chinese daughters were there, with their backpacks and juice, following their daughters down the parade route with cameras. They were glad to advise, very excited that we were considering adoption and completely floored by the news that we weren't eligible for China's waiting girls. I got some firm recommendations for agencies to consider.

And the bobsled run began. We raced toward our child, pulled like gravity, no brakes, steering ourselves less than the course directed us. Our only goal was to maintain enough balance to avoid capsizing. Though it felt inevitable that we would reach her, at some moments it felt so far away.

Later, we learned that our daughter was born that Halloween day, the morning I woke up hopeful and ready to do whatever it took to bring our baby home. Seven months later, we pushed through the longest day of our lives carrying the twelve-pound wonder. The three of us woke up in a hotel in Southeast Asia and went to bed forty-seven hours later, on a friend's couch in San Francisco. We were all hungry, smelly and exhausted after that labor, even the baby.

What could be more real than that?

Our baby will never be ours "in every way." She is ours in the ways we hoped for: We care for her, and she kisses us with a mouth full of smashed green beans. She is not-ours in ways we had accepted before we ever ordered the sperm: It's a mystery where she gets that strange yet compelling giggle. We're real moms, she's our real kid. Now that we know her, I'm sure that one of the advantages of adoption is that we are reminded sometimes that she is not ours, really. She is her own, and would have been no matter who had been lucky enough to raise her.

BIRTH

Angela Morrill

My midwife liked to say, "Every woman in labor has a dark night of the soul." But my dark night came during my pregnancy. My midwife and I could not let our power struggle rest. She kept insisting I get an ultrasound to see if my baby was breech. Three other midwives had palpated my belly, and all had agreed my baby was in the position I knew he was in: ass on my right, head lower left. I was impatient. Because I wouldn't get the ultrasound, my midwife asked me to sign a statement regarding the risks.

Our relationship was frustrating in many ways. When I first called my midwife, I told her I was fat—I weighed about 220 pounds and I'm just over five feet tall. I told her that I didn't want to be treated as high risk because of my weight. I practiced tai chi five days a week and was in the best shape of my life. She told me what I wanted to hear: My weight was not inherently a problem and barring other difficulties, I could have a normal home birth. But she always had a hard time finding the heartbeat, and she didn't trust her hands when she palpated my belly.

My midwife knew that I was interested in unassisted birth, and that didn't help our relationship. When I passed seven months, she told me that I had to create a birth plan. As I began reading birth stories voraciously, I let myself daydream about labor and birth. My favorite birth story belonged to my friend Beatrice. She had her baby girl at home, with only her two sons and her husband attending. She got me on an email list for women interested in unassisted birth and I checked out several Internet sites. Here was my way out of the power struggle. For my perfect birth I didn't need to work out my issues with my midwife, my boyfriend, my family. I could do it alone.

Gary and I weren't in a committed relationship when I got pregnant. We were having a very intense friendship that we made more intense by sleeping together. I got pregnant three weeks after we started having sex. We had talked about the possibility, but not very seriously: As he walked me to work one morning after a long night of unprotected sex, I brought up the topic of birth control. He said that he thought most kinds of birth control were unhealthy. I said, "Well, I'd love to have a baby, but I don't think that's what we're in this relationship for." He surprised me by saying, "I'd love it if you got pregnant." We laughed, and I felt relief, joy. I don't know what Gary was feeling. We agreed that we wouldn't try to get pregnant, but it wouldn't be a tragedy if we did.

We did. I had just celebrated my thirty-third birthday. The age of Christ when he died. I knew I wanted to have this baby. Gary said he wanted to travel, he wasn't in love with me, he was scared. Late one night as we talked, he said he didn't want to have anything to do with the baby. The next day he left town to see his father. He came back a few days later and stopped by my work. We sat in a downtown restaurant and he apologized. He said he was going to do his best. He said he loved me.

Four months later he broke up with me. He began dating a woman he worked with. I was devastated. We went to therapy to talk about the baby and the birth. He said he wanted to be a papa, he wanted to be at the birth. We went to birth classes.

I knew I could have the baby alone. I fired my midwife. My due date was July 3. It was July 12.

Gary was spending more time with me; the woman he was dating decided his life was too complicated and ended the relationship. We started having sex again. He pitched his tent in the backyard and said he was staying until the baby came.

Gary wanted to be at the birth, but not alone. I wanted him there. Everyone seemed afraid, and I felt infected by their fear. I wished that I had kept my wishes private. I told my midwife that I wanted her there after all. I gave in. I compromised my wishes, and my position was weaker and weaker as each day passed. I didn't feel ready to have a baby. I wanted everyone to go away.

My midwife suggested again that I have an ultrasound. I finally agreed. I thought it might buy me some time, wipe the worried looks off everyone's faces. Opposite effect. The naturopath we visited said the baby was compromised, the amniotic fluid was very low, the situation was dire. He suggested that I be induced immediately. It was Thursday, July 15. He also told us the sex of our baby—against our wishes. We were having a boy.

My midwife, the supervising midwife and the apprentice met with Gary and me. We discussed the ultrasound and their concerns. I agreed to go to the hospital on Monday if I hadn't had my baby by then.

I couldn't stop crying. I felt so defeated. I had to find peace somehow, find a place to birth as gently and intimately as I had dreamed. If

I went to the hospital, I knew a C-section was in my future. Because I wouldn't go immediately to the hospital, my midwife said I was taking a chance with the baby's health and asked me to state in writing that I knew the risks I was taking and accepted responsibility. How could I create a healthy space while I had to write that? I cried the entire time and gave her the piece of paper on Sunday.

By then I was just scared. I didn't want to go to the hospital. I followed all the recommendations I could find on naturally inducing labor. My fingers were sore from stimulating my nipples. Gary made a spicy Thai dinner. I drank a glass of wine. I played on the swings at the park. I gave myself an enema. I talked to the baby all the time, asking him to please come out and let me see him. I sang to him, "You'd be like heaven to touch/I wanna hold you so much." I became a blowjob queen after reading that ingesting semen worked even better than semen on the cervix. I walked and walked and walked. Gary and I made love. My friend Sue came over to the house Friday night, Saturday morning and Saturday night to try to stimulate labor through acupuncture. Saturday night, her boyfriend, John, played guitar and we sang while she needled me.

Sunday morning, Gary and I had sex. I laughed when he told me to get on top of him. I clambered up and chuckled. Gary said, "That's how he got in there." I felt hopeful.

Later that day, as we met with the midwives, I tried not to cry. I didn't want to go to the hospital yet. They looked at me with concern. I was going to try castor oil.

As soon as they left, I took a dose. Two hours passed quickly and I took another dose, blended with orange juice. We walked to the park to meet some friends—mamas and babies, on blankets, nursing, everywhere. They said I looked ripe. Everyone wished us well. I started feeling crampy, so we left and barely got home before I was on the toilet.

The contractions began with diarrhea. I tried not to get too ex-cited—and failed. The contractions were close together and pretty short. I was able to get up and move around pretty quickly. The phone rang and it was Beatrice, which I took as a very good sign. My contractions had started only an hour before, so I didn't know for sure if I was in labor. But Beatrice sounded excited—she thought this was it!

I grew tired, and Gary and I lay down on the bed. He rubbed massage oil on my belly, thighs and lower back. When two hours had passed, I decided to call my midwife. I left messages for both my midwife and the supervising midwife before reaching the assisting midwife, Patrice, who I loved. I asked her if I could take a short bath and not risk stopping labor. She told me to go for it. We laughed on the phone, so excited.

By nine-thirty that evening, drenched in sweat, I wasn't having such a good time. I had been drinking a lot of water and Recharge, but I hadn't eaten in a long time. Another mom-friend, Pamela, called me, which I took as the second sign that this baby was coming. She offered to come over.

After every contraction, I fell asleep. As the pain ebbed, my eyes closed, and I curled up on my side and slept. Gary checked the heart tones while I rested. Minutes later, a shadow of panic and pain moved me to my hands and knees. I needed Gary to put all of his weight on my lower back. He pressed my hips together while I moaned and breathed into the blanket.

When it really hurt, I said, "Baaaaby, baaaaby, baaaaby" to remind myself that I was a very happy woman and my baby and I would see each other soon. Sometimes I just said, "It huuurts." I thought about the fact that each of my midwives had three children, and it made me angry. I felt inadequate—it was so painful, and I was so tired after only a few hours. But I was happy that I was home and not in a hospital where I would have asked for drugs. By ten o'clock, I'd been in labor almost five hours, and I stopped having linear thoughts. I was either having a contraction or I was asleep. The air seemed thick with energy.

Gary was really amazing, but we were both burning out. I called for my midwife, and for Pamela.

My midwife arrived around midnight. She sat in a chair by my bed while I slept and labored, and she pressed into my back while Gary filled the inflatable pool. "Surrender," she said while I rocked back and forth on the bed. "Breathe." I had hoped she would see me and say, "Oh, you *are* having a baby," but she didn't. After a few more contractions, I felt so much pressure, as if my cervix were totally open. Then I felt a pop and a gush and water ran down my leg. "I feel the head," I said, meaning that the head was in the birth canal. My midwife said she didn't see anything, thinking, I guess, that I meant the baby was crowning. But when she checked me and didn't feel the cervix, *then* she got interested. I remember hearing her on the phone telling the supervising midwife to "come *now*." Pamela was there and though I didn't really see her, I felt her kiss me. Her voice sounded sweet, like a balm.

Someone helped me off the bed and into the inflatable pool that had been mocking me for the last two weeks as I walked past it every day, pregnant and waiting. It was like heaven—I wished I'd labored in it. I loved whoever put a warm wet towel on my lower back. I draped myself over the side of the pool and rested with my knees far apart. Gary had made a nest of blankets under the pool, and I was completely comfortable, eyes closed, drifting. I heard my Aunt Robbie call me "sweetie girl." I felt other people come in the room, and I thought, *That's nice*. It seemed like there was a lot of energy surrounding me, but it also seemed like I was alone.

My baby was filling me up, and when I had my next contraction, I pushed and felt him move down. He didn't pop back up like they tell you babies will do. My boy was so sweet. He just moved gently down with each push, as I roared and felt so strong. I didn't want to tear, but I didn't want to hold back out of fear, so I focused on feeling my baby. My midwife told me the head was crowning, and I felt Gary's hand touching me. "Feel your baby's head," my midwife told me, and I did. *Soon,* I thought. *Maybe I'm not ready. Yes, I am.* And in my next vocalization, I said, "I'm ready." And roared again.

I felt the swift wonderful movement of my baby, shooting out into the water. "Catch him," I said and tried to look around. Gary moved to me, held and stared at our son. His eyes were open and he was crying a little. We spoke softly to him and he calmed down. I asked someone to turn down the lights. Grateful, blessed, amazed, I climbed out of the pool, holding my son, and squatted next to the pool. The placenta came out just a moment later. My midwife caught it in a pan and followed us over to the bed. Someone asked me how I felt, and I replied, "Like I just had sex." Gary got a few "oohs" at that one, but it was true—I felt warm and soul-satisfied and just stimulated down there. I had one small tear inside that didn't bother me, and I chose not to have it sutured. An hour later I amended the sex statement—it felt more like I'd had sex with a football team.

Gary and I were left alone in bed with the baby. Together the three of us were whole. Love was made into flesh and spirit.

Leroy Xavier Wass Morrill was born July 19, 1999, at 1:24 A.M. He weighed seven pounds, six ounces, and from the start had an easily contented, peaceful spirit. He was healthy, not compromised, not in danger, although the cord was narrow and the placenta a little small. It still sits in my freezer. Someday I will go up to Larch Mountain in the Columbia Gorge and plant it deep in the earth. That place is special to Gary and to me.

Leroy turned one last month. Gary left to travel in Southeast Asia for two months—that was more than five months ago. I'm not surprised that I'm a single mom. The day Leroy was born is the day I would live over if given the choice. From sorrow to joy, pain to pleasure, it was the most completely lived day of my life.

When Tito was born, I had a three-month maternity leave. When I went back to work, I planned to keep him on mom's milk—from a bottle during the day and from the breast the rest of the time. I would take my little battery-operated breast pump into the ladies' room (lovely image, eh?) and pump a couple of times a day. Every once in a while I would really get the fish eye from another woman when I emerged. (I had my little bottles in a thermal cooler sack.) I finally found out why. Someone had heard the pump and thought I was in there with a vibrator! (And of course shared her suspicions.) Yeah, you know how we new moms can't get enough. —Corndog

THE PUMP AND I

Alisa Gordaneer

5:30 A.M.

"Chunk-ka whiirr, chunk-ka whiirr, chunk-ka whiirr," goes the breast pump, a soothing, hypnotizing repetition that threatens to send me back to sleep. I'm sitting in the big chair in the living room, with Lizard, my four-month-old baby, on my right breast and his mechanical brother—a space-age contraption of bottle and trumpet and aquarium tubing hooked up to a black box—on my left, each sucking away with all their might.

For a moment, I nod off, lulled by the sound, then jerk awake at the thought I might drop either of them. Eventually, Lizard-boy floats back to snoozeland on a river of milk, and the Medela bottle gets its full-tummied four ounces.

"Sweetie, sleeping dude," I call, and wait a moment. And another moment. And call again, louder, until M stumbles groggily out of bed to deposit baby-dude in the warm spot he's just left.

While M makes coffee, I transfer the fresh milk to one of the bottles I boiled the night before, write the date and time on a Post-it note and put it in the fridge with the bottles I pumped yesterday at work. Then, I wash the pump parts and pack them into the pump. It's six-thirty in the morning.

If we're lucky, we'll get another half-hour or so to eat breakfast together before the Lizard-boy wakes up again, frantic to nurse some more before the Source vanishes, leaving him with nothing but Dad and those chewy bottles. Inevitably, he's awake before I've finished my toast. While I sit with Lizard sucking on me and me sucking on a second cup of coffee, M frantically dresses, shaves, whatever it takes to steel himself for the day. Then he waves the Lizard-dude's hand, bye-bye, as I swing the mechanical kid over my shoulder and take off for work. Corporate mom, stay-at-home dad. Well, sort of.

11:00 A.M.

"Chunk-ka whiirr, chunk-ka whiirr, chunk-ka whiirr," goes the pump, which is one of those fancy ones that looks like a briefcase. "Where'd you get that great purse?" a woman in the office building's elevator once asked. When I explained what it was, she laughed embarrassedly. Too darn weird.

I'm sitting in my boss's office, the door closed and locked, the daily newspaper spread out before me on the table and my shirt open. I've already been pumping for ten minutes of my fifteen-minute break, and I've only collected two and a half ounces on either side. I worry whether it'll be enough. Some of the breast-feeding books recommend gazing at a photo of your baby to stimulate milk production. I'm not into that kind of pump pornography. Besides, it's not like this is downtime. I need to read the papers anyway, and it lets my co-workers truly believe that really all I'm doing in here is gazing at the *Free Press*.

A few drips more than two and a half ounces and it's already time to stop. Maybe it's all the crap in the daily news that's stressing me out, making me less productive today. News about this so-called economic boom (so why am I still struggling to pay my student loans?) and about the future costs of education (baby-dude had better get a job by the time he's three) and about distraught moms who abandon their babies in dumpsters or at the doors of churches (sometimes I can totally relate).

I unhitch myself from the milking machine, cap the bottles and slide them into the pump's ice-pack section. Then I take the pump parts and my little film canister of dish soap to the office kitchen, where I can count on getting at least one curious glance from a co-worker. I might work at an alternative newsweekly, but let's face it, either the staff is too young and hip to have kids, or they're kid-having age but not about to sacrifice their careers or their sanity or their hipness to do so, or they've got wives who stay home and keep the kids from being a threat to their hipness.

In other words, there are not a lot of nursing mamas in our office. Those odd-shaped dishes I keep doing are just too weird not to notice. The guys either ignore it, or ask for a progress report.

"How many ounces?"

"Five, total."

"Whoo, high five! . . . Er, is that good?"

1:00 P.M.

I'm in the middle of editing a story when M strolls in, baby-dude snuggled in a sling onto which M has sewn some rave patches. Lunchtime. I scoop up the dude, who is wearing a pair of blue overalls handed down from my boss's daughter. "I'll go show them off after he's eaten," says M.

Lizard-boy snuggles close, slurping contentedly. Co-workers used to crowd around my cubicle to look at him, but now they're so used to our daily routine they hardly notice. On the days when there's a lunchtime staff meeting, Lizard comes right along, voicing his opinion on stories or pulling away to grin at inopportune moments, forcing me to quickly adjust my shirt. One of the women I work with confesses to having secretly watched to see if she could spot any nipple. The guys pretend nothing is happening. If they have similar confessions, they keep them to themselves.

It was in a staff meeting that I first thought about calling the baby Lizard, whatever its gender. I was sitting there, or rather was propped there, three days away from giving birth, and someone asked about names. "Lizard," I said, repeating the joke we'd teased my mom with for months. "Cool," said someone, and someone else nodded, and I thought, *Yeah, cool. Why the hell not?*

Sure, maybe he'll want to change it when he's older. Sure, certain family members believe with all their hearts that it's a name taken from the French aristocracy, pronounced "Ley-zahhrd." But his name is Lizard, right there on his birth certificate, and the seen-it-all Grosse Pointe hospital clerk even double-checked with me to be sure the spelling was correct.

4:00 P.M.

"Chunk-ka whiirr, chunk-ka whiirr, chunk-ka whiirr."

I tell myself I should write a piece about the challenges of breastfeeding while working full-time. Challenges like how to mop up the milk I splashed on the daily paper before anyone else wants to read it.

Challenges like how to explain, one more time, that I justified the cost of the pump by figuring the cost of formula. In three months, the pump would pay for itself. With only one income, we couldn't afford not to breast-feed. But ultimately, it would have to be a piece that extols the joys of working in an alternative office environment, where the only dress code is you have to be dressed, and the hours are flexible as long as you put them in. A piece that explains how frustrating it is that it only seems possible to live the nursing lifestyle in this kind of alternative environment. Nursing friends who are teachers or corporate flunkies or government hacks seem to have a hard time getting around to pumping on time, or at all, when they're at work. Granted, there's some part determination, and I suppose you could get one hell of a lawsuit going if you were fired for pumping at work, but if you're committed to your career, too, it's hard to fit it in between the emails and v-mails and meetings and . . .

6:00 P.M.

"Slurp, slurp, slurp, slurp, slurp."

Ah, a pumpless feeding. M is relieved that I'm home from work and he can take a break. "He only napped for half an hour," he sighs. "I've got to get some homework done."

Lizard starts crying. "What do I do?" I wail.

"He's been cranky all day," M reassures me. "I think he's teething."

I peer into the Lizard's mouth. No sign of teeth. Still, M ought to know. When stay-at-home dads get in the spotlight, it's usually as though they're some kind of martyr, or some unwitting, cute-but-pathetic Mr. Mom type. Not M. He's a better mom than I.

M's friend D comes over to watch TV. He's one of the few friends we still see because he's willing to come over to our place instead of going out somewhere to play pool, see a movie, drink beer, all those things we used to do.

"Enough with the nipples, already!" he shouts, as Lizard latches on for the umpteenth time this evening. "Get the kid a cheeseburger!"

Like most twentysomething guys, D is more comfortable with breasts in a pornographic context. "You're ruining strip shows for me!" he whines.

"It's not like you can see anything," I say, pointing out that Lizard's head is in the way.

"No, but the thought is freaking me out!"

11:00 P.M.

Silence.

Lizard's just drifted off to sleep on our futon, and I've pulled myself from his mouth. I creep out into the living room, where M is half reading, half dozing. I transfer the refrigerated milk into bottles for tomorrow and scrub the used bottles from today. I dismantle and wash the pump parts, and then all of the plastic—so much plastic!—goes into a big stainless-steel pot I used to make lentil soup in, back when I had time to do things like make soup.

I sit, exhausted, flipping through a mail-order catalog of fancy baby items I'll never be able to afford. I'm too tired to read the descriptions, but the pictures, accented with smiling happy babies, are nice to look at.

When it comes to a boil, I don oven mitts, carry the pot to the sink, pour out the water. The steam rises.

I sleep, and we start all over again.

The Piano Tuner

Andrea Buchanan

Mister Rogers' Neighborhood is on television. My daughter seems more interested in her blocks at the moment, but I have turned on the TV anyway, a bad habit, I'm sure. I remember my younger sister liking Mr. Rogers so much she asked my mother if he could be her dad. Maybe I, too, liked him way back when, but now Mr. Rogers creeps me out with his lite jazz piano and his blue sweater and all that Christian niceness. Yesterday when I turned it on for my daughter, who didn't pay attention then either, the story was all about how Mr. Rogers had to go somewhere and how his "good friend" would stay with us. Mr. Rogers' friend was so perfectly coifed and eager and they talked so much about being special friends and doing very interesting things together that I couldn't help but snicker, thinking of the comments my sister would make now, watching that.

I am half watching TV, half supervising my daughter as I try to straighten things up before the piano tuner arrives. My little girl is clearly not interested in the television, and I am about to turn it off when Mr. Rogers mentions yesterday's departure and holds up a poster of André Watts. "I had to go to a meeting," he tells us, "and that meeting was about arranging a visit with another very good friend of mine, André Watts. He's a very famous pianist." I know this. I have many recordings of his. I have been to his concerts. I have even performed for him in a master class. And here he is on *Mister Rogers'*. I am transfixed, and even though I find Mr. Rogers and his fake-sounding puppet voices creepy, I want to keep watching. I want to see what André Watts will do. I want a glimpse into the world I used to inhabit: not Mr. Rogers' neighborhood, but Mr. Watts'. The phone rings; it is the piano tuner. I turn off the TV and pick up my daughter, who is excited by the noise of the phone and wants to see who is coming to visit.

The last time the piano was tuned she still had two months left in the womb. I was already huge and lumbering, and I remember watching the piano tuner wince as he heard my twangy, sadly out-of-tune Yamaha. "Make another appointment for June," he scolded me. "I'll need to come back then and fix it, since I doubt this tuning will hold long." I nodded, and probably even said yes. But my baby was born that June, and it has taken until now, thirteen months later, for me to have the luxury of a moment to remember to have the piano tuned and to actually call a tuner. I called a different piano tuner this time, embarrassed by yet another lapse in piano maintenance.

When he arrives, I think he looks less like a piano tuner than like one of Mr. Rogers' "good friends." He has that 1970s look about him: the polyester tan of his pants, the part in his hair so far on the side that it seems to start below his ear. He looks scrubbed clean, no wrinkles in his shirt. He introduces himself, and my daughter clings to me, unsure of what to make of this stranger I seem to welcome. I warn him about the piano, almost as if I am bragging when I tell him how long it has been since it's been tuned. I catch him glancing at the framed advertisement for my last recital hanging on the wall. He plays a few octaves. "It's really bad up top," I tell him, apologizing. He noodles around and then says, "Well, you must have a really good ear. I've heard a lot worse." This does not inspire confidence. "Are you a pianist?" he asks. I hesitate. "Yes and no," I tell him. I nod at my daughter. "Not a whole lot of time for practicing these days." And then we are off to the park, leaving the piano tuner to his tuning, the hour or so of tweaking open fourths and fifths.

Truthfully, it has been a while since I thought of myself as a pianist, although I suppose even when I did qualify as one, I always felt uncomfortable admitting it. It felt a little fraudulent: I had no CDs, no major competition titles to my name, no international concertizing. But people always took me at my word. I think they wanted to buy into the romance of it, the nineteenth-century aura of it: a pianist! And the world I lived in for so long did seem romantic on the surface: Telling people on airplanes or blind dates about my life at the conservatory, in the practice rooms, on the stage, always seemed to enhance our time together and give me an air of sophistication and mystery I otherwise lacked. But the reality of it was constant, lonely work, the result of which depended on the mood of whoever was listening and judging. When I first arrived at music school and saw that even the graffiti in the bathroom was music related ("Liszt piszt here and miszt"), I vowed never to become like that, swore I'd never lose my perspective on the rest of the world. But soon my conversations were about music, my dreams at night were about music—even, sadly, my jokes were about music. Back then I was immersed in it, the language of tone and balance and phrasing and color. Now I hear of former classmates performing around the world. Now I fumble through basic Mozart sonatas for my daughter. Now I see André Watts on *Mister Rogers'*.

I was out the other day with a friend, taking our babies for a walk. As we passed the dry-cleaning place a few blocks from my apartment, my friend stopped and embraced the proprietor. I heard them exclaim how long it had been; the woman marveled at my friend's baby and brought the entire Korean clan from behind the counter to see what their former customer had created.

When we left, my friend told me she and her husband used to go there all the time back when they lived in my neighborhood. "She's really nice," my friend said. "Actually, she's a pianist." And then: "She's like you." She saw the look on my face and stopped short. "She was really serious, I mean, for a while," she said by way of apology. I started to feel defensive but realized she was right. The Korean dry-cleaning lady is like me: serious about something I couldn't sustain, serious until I was forced to be serious about other things.

My teacher at the conservatory was a taciturn Korean woman, who with her broken and improvised English was somehow able to communicate beyond what her language capacity should have allowed. She was small and seemingly frail, but I spent our first year together terrified of her, terrified of her silence, her judgment, her fierceness at the keyboard. The student whose lesson was before mine always emerged from the studio red-eyed and puffy-faced, and I greeted the student after me the same way. I would get headaches from trying to concentrate so hard during my lessons, trying to please her, trying to match her sound. She would demonstrate something; I would try it. She would tell me I didn't do it right; I would try again. She would tell me I did it right that time; I would have no idea what the difference was between the time it was right and the time it was wrong. Sometime during our second year things clicked a little and I began to understand what she meant when she'd use words like "color" and "breath" and "timing." I didn't cry so much during my lessons. I made progress, and I could tell when she would say "good" afterward that she was pleased with my playing.

Once, during my third year she talked about her daughter, who, she said, was about my age. "She is like you," she told me. "She is a writer." I modified her statement by protesting that I merely liked to write. But she told me about her daughter, who wanted to be a writer, and showed me the story her daughter had written about her. It was beautiful and touching, and in reading it I saw a side of my teacher I had never seen in the studio. I was honored that she had let me read it, that she had let me see her, for a moment, the way her daughter saw her. I was secretly proud that on some level she equated me with her daughter. Part of the story was about her daughter's own battles with the piano, and I asked my teacher if her daughter still played, if she was serious, if she was considering music school. "Oh no," my teacher replied, without hesitation. "My daughter is very good, she is good. But she is not quite good enough. I encouraged her to do other things." She suddenly stopped and looked at me as if she were only just remembering I was there. She saw my face change, as I'm sure it must have, despite my efforts to mask my feelings. "Perhaps," she said after a moment, "we should return to our lesson." I understood then that she was a teacher of students she knew would probably never reach the level of understanding she had of music. She was a teacher of students she would rather encourage to do other things, knowing as she did their limitations before those liabilities could be discovered by the students themselves.

At my last recital under her tutelage, she broke character and said in front of everyone at the reception what a joy it was to attend a concert of mine, since she knew I would be playing with intelligence and passion and that I would always be aware of the music and have something to say. But what broke me inside was when she whispered to me privately, "You deserve a better place." I knew she meant I had done a good job and deserved to be recognized for it; but I also knew she meant I deserved to be a few years younger, with bigger hands and more disposable income, about to graduate from a school like Juilliard instead of the one where she taught. She meant I deserved to be able to explore music at the piano in a way she knew I could not.

I did not attend Juilliard for graduate school, despite her lukewarm encouragement; instead, I opted for an easier ride at a low-pressure conservatory on the West Coast. A few years later I gave a recital in New York, and she was able to attend the second half. I knew as I was playing that it would be my last real performance, and she told me afterward, before she flitted away, "You made some beautiful moments."

My daughter and I return from the park, and before I even enter the apartment I can hear the piano tuner plunking chords, a sure sign that his work is done. I wonder what ended up happening on *Mister Rogers'*, whether André Watts performed, whether he patiently explained to everyone things I already know. And I wonder too about my former teacher: What made her encourage me in a profession she wouldn't choose for her own daughter? What made her urge me to continue in the face of uncertain success? And what am I supposed to do now with my useless ability and knowledge?

Back inside, the piano tuner compliments me on the piano, telling me how mellow it is, how big it sounds for such a small grand, how the tone is comparable to much bigger, much better pianos. I agree and I tell him how I fell in love with its personality in the store, how glad I am it hasn't become bright and brittle sounding, like most Yamahas do after a few years. "Oh, yeah," he tells me, "this is a beauty. The bass on this could bring tears to your eyes." He plays a few more chords and then yields the bench to me, offering me a chance to test his handiwork. "Oh, no," I say, "it sounds great, I can tell." But he urges me to play. He points to the advertisement of my last concert. "That's you, right? Well, come on!" Embarrassed, I put down my daughter and try to think of what piece I remember the most. The Brahms, I guess; I've performed it at almost every recital since I was eighteen. But before I can sit to the keys, my daughter rushes over and stands on her tiptoes, her fingers barely reaching the keyboard. She whines until she finally plays a few notes, then smiles a broad grin.

"Oh, look," says the piano tuner. "She really wants to play."

My Secret Weapon

Phaedra Hise

My daughter is only three, but already I'm working on her self-image. My goal is to start fortifying it early, so that by the time she hits adolescence her ego will be strong enough to withstand the punishments of peer pressure. For this job, I have a secret weapon: an airplane.

Face it, girls' little egos are particularly at risk during the perils of adolescence. A girl with a wimpy ego is primed to be taken advantage of. What parent of a boy worries about date rape? Anorexia or bulimia? The simple truth is that girls, more often than boys, grow up to become victims—of others or of their own grotesque self-images. But a girl who grows up feeling powerful, intelligent, skilled, a girl who knows her value—won't that girl be less likely to be victimized?

I sure hope so. That's why I take my daughter flying. My husband and I are pilots, and we use our single-engine plane in much the same way other people use their boats, RVs or comfortable sedan cars—to sightsee on weekends, visit the grandparents, take a short vacation.

While we're doing that, I'm encouraging my daughter to "help," playing up her strength and ability to do a tricky and complicated job. While the autopilot flies the plane, I let her sit in my lap and hold the "yoke," or steering wheel. I ask her to unfold the maps and help spot other airplanes below and above us. Before we start the engine, her special job is to holler "Clear!" out the window. She knows these are important tasks in the operation of an airplane and takes pride in doing them.

Compared to my daughter, I came to flying late in life. I learned at age seventeen, the tail end of adolescence. Flying quickly became my reliable ego boost, my fix in the face of self-doubt. Maybe you've felt that skin-crawling sensation of hating yourself. The taunting voice inside your head that points out how fat your thighs are, soft and white like dimpled marshmallows. The voice that laughs when you wear the wrong outfit to a party or lose a borrowed book. The voice that builds into a crescendo of accusations, demanding, *Who do you think you are, anyway? Why should anyone like you? What makes you think you're accomplishing anything worthwhile?*

The climb back to normalcy from this fear-and-loathing frenzy is slow. I reassure and forgive myself, listing the things that I do, and do well. At the top of the list is always the same big thing: I am a pilot. I can take a heavy chunk of metal up into the air and float it back down again safely. The complex and dangerous machine does what I tell it. Only a tiny fraction of people in this world can accomplish that, I remind myself, and only a handful are women. So what if I have bad hair, no Manolo Blahnik shoes. Those tiny transgressions pale in the face of what I can do.

Flying is the biggest gun in my ego's arsenal. It's what made me downright arrogant in college. I didn't doubt that I was absolutely cool, so interesting and intelligent that only dull and stupid people wouldn't like me. That soaring self-confidence ensured that I made friends, smiled, tried out for sports, smacked guys that made passes and was happy.

I hope it will work for my daughter as well, boosting her self-image when her creepy peers or the little voice inside her head stick it to her. Today she sits in the cockpit with me and confidently turns a radio dial. Tomorrow she might boldly raise her hand to try out for the role of Juliet in the school play. If she fails in some of adolescence's high dramas, she'll already have one strong accomplishment to fall back on. If she doesn't make the cheerleading squad, maybe she can console herself with the thought that none of those girls ever flew her mom's airplane.

Hoping this, I point out the occasional woman pilot at airports. I give my daughter books with titles like *Ann Can Fly* and *Amelia [Earhart] and Eleanor Go for a Ride*. I'm seizing the little window of opportunity while she's still gripped with a child's enthusiasm for all things Mom does. As she grows older and starts necessarily growing apart from me, flying might not hold the same attraction for her.

That's okay. I don't need to teach her to fly, although I'll have my instructor's rating by the time she's old enough to solo, just in case. My father gave me the gift of flight. Despite his many sins, his fumbles at parenting, his outright insults and injuries, when I think of him, I think first of flying. The joy of flying together pushed aside some of our problems.

As I do, I'm sure my child will remember the bad parenting moments—that I always got water in her eyes when I rinsed out the shampoo, that I forgot to pack her lunch for the summer-camp picnic, or that I missed her high-school track meet. Added to those insults are the genetic problems I've likely already given her—the arthritis, the anemia. Naturally I also want to pass along something good, something fun and happy for her to remember later when she starts tallying up her childhood scores. Maybe when she thinks of me while she's someday bossing around her own airplane, she'll think kindly.

Even if I don't teach her to fly solo, I think it will be enough for her to have helped. She will grow up understanding the mysteries of aviation, knowing that girls can master something so tricky. Whatever it is that she wants to do later—program a computer, try out for pole-vaulting or simply ask someone on a date—I want to give her the confidence to try. By allowing her to help fly the plane now, I'm handing her a powerful weapon for facing the battles of adolescence and beyond.

MOTHER TONGUE

Sherry Thompson

I cringed when I walked into the venue. It was a beautiful place, an old boathouse converted into a tearoom complete with battered, comfortable chairs and the exposed wooden beams of the building's first incarnation. But it was all one room. I looked doubtfully at my husband, and we both glanced at the tiny baby girl in my arms, our week-old bundle of id. With very little hope for her being good at the poetry reading, we had planned to shuffle her out into a lobby during the inevitable crying. "The acoustics are great," my husband said and smiled as he brought the sling out of our black diaper bag. We would just have to try her out in this environment of sipped coffee and heady words. There was no question of leaving: I was a featured poet.

The evening turned out well in all respects. The baby was remarkably quiet, nursing herself in and out of sleep for three hours of poetry and song. During my set, my sister rocked her in the sling as my words floated over the crowd. Even the clothes I had purchased after hunting through half a dozen thrift stores ("Got anything that will cover my postpartum tummy, will be easy to nurse in, is fairly dressy and preferably black?") were not uncomfortable and even looked rather funky. It was one of the best performances I have ever given, and the sweetness of the evening was, I am certain, partly due to the scent of new baby tickling my nostrils as I made my way through the crowd to center stage.

It is not always so easy to integrate my artistic aspirations with my regular mama life. It is difficult to write with a small boy and an infant daughter. I sometimes catch a glimpse of myself: a woman digging around for a pen and paper, balancing a baby on her hip, calling frantically for her son to climb down off the counter "and leave the peanut butter alone, please!" striving to remember that one perfect poetic line as the dirty dishes breed in the sink. And I wonder why I don't let something go, lighten my load and make the journey a little easier. Of course, it couldn't be the baby, who would tumble to the ground without my arm securely around her. And it couldn't be my son, who would surely kill himself if not for my vigilant watch. I know the only *something* I could get rid of would be my oddly strung bits of words and rhythm; yet I cling to them like a drowning woman. (The dishes, however, get the shaft.)

I have always told stories. My childhood was filled with little booklets, one-year diaries and, as I aged, plain black journals filled with eager teen-angst scribbling. When I entered university as an adult, I channeled my writing into clever essays that spun into decent grades before my very eyes. During this period of my life I wrote very little "for pleasure." With my toddler son in care three mornings a week so I could take a course load of six classes and still see him through much of the day, I was too tired to do much more than study, eat and sleep. At the end of that exhilarating and grueling year, I took a creative-writing class and began to work with words again. We were told one night that a small coffee house in the area held an open-mike night for poets once a week. I let the thought linger, not acted upon for months until one rare evening at the end of the school year when we paid for the luxury of a baby sitter. I didn't bring my poems (I thought at the time it was too arrogant and too obvious a gesture), but after an hour or so I begged my husband to run home and grab my folder for me. I was hooked.

The spoken-word scene is varied. I have been asked to read at little coffee shops where the audience consisted mainly of farmers with thirty years more life experience than I. I have also read at folk festivals, smoky bars, parks and once in a damp, cavernous summer hockey arena cleared of ice. The poets themselves are as different as the shifting backdrops: those published in respected literary journals, sweet and angry boys still in high school, folk singers struggling to make a living, the self-published, the inspired, the academic, the loud, the shy, the banal and the stunningly original. But there are very few mothers of small children. I often get the same reaction, especially from women: "How do you find the time?"

It is an extraordinarily difficult question to answer. Truthfully, I do not have the time, or at least time in long, unbroken, leisurely blocks that I think might lead to good poems. There are always things that I ought to be doing other than writing. (As I write this, the baby snoozes in the buzz of an oscillating fan under the weight of her first summer heat wave. My husband and son are out getting haircuts. I squint with concentration, not only in an effort to write with purpose, but to shut out the unmade bed behind me, the plastic blocks strewn in every room of the apartment, the towering pile of unpaid bills, and the kitchen— well, I would rather not comment on the state of the kitchen.) I scatter the apartment with blank spiral notebooks and black felt-tipped pens and try to catch the words that occur to me. It might be days or weeks before I can sit down at my desk and attempt to turn them into something other than black marks on a page. When I must finish a piece, I send the children to the park under their father's parental eye. Sometimes this turns out badly. I sit staring at my computer screen, knowing that they will burst in at any minute, unable to clear the thought from my head so that I can work. There are also times when my inspiration sputters and dies because it had the ill fortune to show up at two in the afternoon rather than a much more convenient nine o'clock in the evening. As most parents do, I look back over the period when I did not yet have children and exclaim at the months I could have used for working: The time I wasted! How much easier things would be if I had used that time to my advantage!

Like a lot of simplistic laments, this one, too, is flawed.

Although it is true that I do not have the time I would like to spend pursuing my creative path, it is also true that I am an artist *because* I have children. My skill as an orator has grown in direct proportion to my son's delight in auditory stimulation. Only after giving birth was I able to follow the old adage "write what you know." It is only here—in the midst of sandwich crusts, dirty diapers, trips to the doctor, bedtime stories, lost sandals, baby lotion, wooden trains, the whorl of hair on my baby's head, piles of laundry, my son's songs and the endless trips to the grocery store—that I have found my poetic voice.

This is not to say that all, or even most, of my work is about my children. I write very little directly about them. Often I find my love for them too difficult, too raw a wound still, to put into words. My children appear just under the surface of the poems: the echo of the color of my son's hair, for example, or the sound my daughter makes when she's enthralled. However small my body of work, due to time constraints, I know that the quality of the work is only possible because of the authentic, transformative experience of motherhood.

It is this truth I call upon when I hunch over my desk, one ear strained for the baby's cry, the other tuned to the inner rhythm I attend to when I write. The pull between these desires creates a powerful tension within which I am able to work and to live. I can give myself to my children because I write. I can give myself to my writing because of the power I draw from mothering.

Last summer, heavily pregnant and bloated from the heat, I took my husband and son to a folk festival where I was reading. Amid drumbeats and dancing, we grooved all weekend long, stopping only for complimentary snacks in the performers' tent. On Sunday, clutching the microphone, about to read my work, I looked out over the audience to the smiling face of my two-year-old son. Sun-browned and happy, he sat on the lap of one of my friends. He had heard his first punk band that weekend, shared bagels and bananas with a troop of folk singers and danced with a tiny girl in the middle of a drum circle. I took a deep breath and in that space my son squealed, "Hi, Mommy!" The crowd laughed and my friend whispered that it was time to listen. "But it's my mommy! My mommy's a poet!" And he laughed some more, delighted with his perception.

I began to read, delighted with him.

PROGRESS

Coleen Murphy

My children are holding up progress. It's true. I know they appear to be merely going about their daily business of eating, sleeping, playing, crying, laughing, drooling and peeing all over the place, but their underlying purpose in life is to hold me back. Or so I'm told. I was the first among my friends to have a baby, but one of the last in my extended family. Opting out of teenage parenthood yet unable to wait for true financial stability, I fall into some kind of working-class middle ground. I began my mothering career in a climate of mixed emotions, hearing, "It's about time!" from my relatives, and witnessing stunned, we're-trying-not-to-show-our-utter-horror stares from my peers. With their looks, my friends tell me what few of them dare to say out loud: that were it not for my insistence on bringing more children into this already overcrowded world (let alone my already overcrowded life), I could join them in more television-perfect pursuits, such as buying a home, finishing a degree or two and maintaining a one-car-per-adult household.

I started college nearly two years before my first son came into the picture. School was something I had long considered doing, and after getting married, finding a part-time job that I enjoyed and just generally feeling kind of purposeful, I threw myself into it with thoughts of an eventual career in law. I was twenty-seven, and it wasn't the first time for me. I attended a semester and a half at a small, alternative college at the age of eighteen, back in 1986. It was an interesting place that attracted interesting people, and there were good times, but I burned out quickly, came down with a series of baffling symptoms that added up to chronic fatigue syndrome and went back home to regroup. Nine years, a dozen crappy waitressing jobs and countless disastrous relationships later, I was back in school and doing well.

It was unsettling how well I was doing. I felt restless and found no joy in the daily grind of school, but the sense of accomplishment pleased me. Unschooled by my parents from the age of ten on, I have little patience for hoop-jumping, test-taking and red tape. I have joked at times that I have a bad attitude about school—and certainly, when faced with authority that I find meaningless, I wind up feeling like a bona fide Sweathog. As a teenager, I counted myself lucky to have parents who embraced child-led learning as a way of life, and I imagined that anyone in my shoes would feel the same. My days varied from getting up at dawn to assist with necessary repairs on our house to sleeping until noon after reading all night. I cared for our chickens, ducks and lone pig. I went through a bread-baking phase, an embroidery phase, an Atari phase and numerous journaling phases. I had pen pals all over North America and regularly pored over my atlas.

My interactions with other teens were limited until I took a job at a local ice-cream parlor. Excited to have a closer look at "regular" folks, I was amazed to encounter people my age who seemed to be my exact opposite. Envying me my freedom not one bit, these kids were on the fast track to overachievement, and expressed concern about the fate of an uneducated soul like me. During the years since my liberated adolescence, numerous friends have joined the chorus, chiding me for refusing to "play the game." "You have to give in sometimes," they have told me. "You can't always just do what you want." Another popular refrain is, "There are certain things people have to be made to do, whether they like it or not."

The fact that there are some things in life that simply must be done was at the forefront of my home education. I still beam a little when I tell someone about how I helped my father build a seventy-foot-long steel-hulled shrimp boat, or the way I used to fearlessly walk along the floor joists that made up the framework of our second-story back porch—the one that my older brother and I screened in all by ourselves. The summer I was sixteen, I went with a Unitarian Universalist youth delegation to the Soviet Union, using money that I had raised single-handedly at churches all over Florida. When my great-grandmother was ill, my siblings and I took turns caring for her. In my mother's home daycare, I was in the trenches with a rowdy bunch of two-year-olds, honing skills that I now use every day.

Maybe it was my old scoop-shop friends I was trying to impress with my breakneck course schedule. Certainly, the news that I was back in school prompted an outpouring of approval from everyone I knew. Finally, I was getting it together, putting my brains to good use—insert your favorite cliché here. Three days a week I waited in the dark for the bus that would take me to my 7:45 A.M. classes, took the train to work in the afternoon and back to school again, after which the same bus brought me home to do homework and fall asleep in front of *Seinfeld* reruns by eleven o'clock. Even my parents were proud of me; they knew I was working hard for something I valued. A home movie from that period shows me laughing in the kitchen at my parents' thirtieth wedding anniversary party, my father teasing me about my mode of dress (what else is new?). I told him that as a judge I would wear whatever I wanted.

Somewhere during that time, I got in touch with my desire to have children. No, that's not exactly true—my desire to have children had been out in the open all along. It was my desire to have children before exiting my twenties that reared its head, and I started reconsidering everything that I was doing. My husband, six years my junior, was uneasy about the prospect of parenthood, but after a few months of negotiations we tossed the birth control pills and jumped headfirst into baby making.

In theory, it would be simple. We would conceive in the fall in order to avoid missing out on work or school when I delivered in late spring. I would recuperate over the summer and be back on track the following fall quarter. In reality, it was even simpler: We conceived the very first time that we ceased being obsessively cautious. By the time school started at the beginning of what I had envisioned as my childbearing year, I was well acquainted with the ins and outs of public vomiting.

For nearly four months, I worked thirty-hour weeks in a kindergarten and carried a full load of classes while hauling around my pregnant body. Ever achy and always exhausted, I ambled through each day just waiting for my next opportunity to rest. Two years later when I read birth activist Sheila Kitzinger's comment that the first trimester is often the most physically and emotionally draining time of pregnancy, I wept at the sheer validation of it. I remember an afternoon at the kindergarten when I lay my head down on the tiny, crayon-stained table after the children had gone home and cried, "These children are sucking the life out of me." At the time, I didn't realize that the child inside me played a larger role in my mental state than any external forces could, even the mighty army of three-year-olds that filled my days.

With the onset of the third trimester my sleep schedule expanded as I gave up my job but stuck with school. Most of my pregnancy rendered me invisible around campus, a rumpled and pasty-faced woman with crusty stuff in the corners of her eyes. Unless you count the day in my sixth month when a classmate approached to let me know that my skirt was tucked rather revealingly into the back of my underwear, my days of being singled out for my fashion sense were apparently over. I marveled at the energy my fellow students had as I navigated the hallways overflowing with women who were impeccably turned out, dressed up, done up and made up. A novelty in all of my classes as "the pregnant lady," I sat near the door so that I could race out when my bladder sounded the alarm, and stuffed my face to combat nausea.

My due date fell on the last day of finals, and everyone, including me, watched eagerly to see if I would to make it to the end of the quarter. I hoped that I wouldn't, but I did. March 17, a day that had been circled on my wall calendar for the past six months, became just one more day that I waddled out of the classroom, onto the train and then the bus, a mile down the street and finally up the flight of stairs (stopping to rest in the middle) that led me home. I spent the next two weeks waiting for baby, sleeping, reading, taking long baths and then sleeping some more. In my idealized recollections of my life before motherhood, it is those two weeks that come to mind more often than any others—those two weeks and the delicious slumber that dominated that little chapter of my life. Were it not for the fact that I spent most of my waking moments gripped by fear and anxiety about the impending labor and birth, it really would have been a lovely time.

The much-anticipated labor and birth came, and it was a horror, but worthwhile. The first few weeks of life with a newborn were shockingly hard, but I adjusted. I was tired and I was shell-shocked, but I was happy with my baby. I kept school in the back of my mind, though, and imagined that baby Nash would start daycare in the fall. It was important to me to stay on task. On one of the crazy, sleep-deprived days just after I gave birth, my mother and a friend helped me ransack my house in search of my financial aid application. It took us three hours to find all of the paperwork, but we sent it off in time, and I allowed myself to relax a little. A little, but not much. At a family wedding, a friend in his mid-twenties asked me as I stood with my nine-week-old child in my arms, "So, what are you doing with yourself these days?" When I finally stopped laughing and caught my breath, he repeated the question, because he really wanted to know.

It was in this climate that I began to assure those around me that I would return to school, that I had not lost track of my goals. Fall quarter found me front and center in all of my classes, crammed one after the other into two days a week in order to cut down on our need for childcare. My husband and I had chickened out on daycare for our five-month-old, choosing instead a hectic schedule for me, and daddy-care for little Nash. On my school days, I spent my breaks breast-feeding wherever I could find a quiet spot: the couch in the women's room, park benches, empty classrooms. I said at the time that it felt like some sort of a conjugal jailhouse visit. While we nursed, Nash's dad would get me a sandwich at Subway or stand nearby like a sentry.

When I look back on it, that year in school sends bittersweet images through my mind. It was perhaps the most accelerated learning period of my adult life, but very little of my newfound knowledge was part of the school curriculum. It was a time of milk-stained shirts and endless cups of decaf. It was planning my days down to the minute and then realizing that I had left no time to study, eat or bathe. It was knowing that my baby son scrambled for the front door when he heard my bus stop at the corner to let me out. It was stumbling into a fervent debate on welfare issues in response to a classmate's assertion that "the poor should just give up their children," and finding myself on the verge of tears. I discovered the Internet and learned that I was not entirely alone as a passionate, misfit parent. I became acquainted with terms like "stay-at-home mom" and "attachment parent," and heard them used in reference to me. By springtime, I often used coveted computer lab time to chat online with other women balancing motherhood with personhood, and through our discussions I felt myself taking shape as a parent and as a mother, rather than just a girl who had a baby.

It was two weeks before finals that I confirmed that I was pregnant with my second child, and everything around me seemed to unravel. Twenty-month-old Nash and I both came down with a wicked flu, and I coughed my way through my exams. I managed to get extensions on my two term papers, but only finished one of them. My unfinished paper was to address the legal aspects of the death penalty, a topic that had become insurmountable somehow. Each day I would drag out my overdue library books, review my research, write a few lines and wind up sobbing. Unable to face my professor, I communicated with him through a series of despairing email messages. My life as I knew it was falling apart, and I told him so.

By the time winter break was over, morning sickness had set in, bringing with it bone-crushing fatigue. My death-penalty paper got set aside as something to do as soon as I felt up to it, an occasion that never arrived. A new semester was upon me, and each day I got up, threw up, went to class and threw up some more. I made valiant attempt to stay focused, reminding myself that I had continued with school all through my pregnancy with Nash. I had done it then, surely I could do it now. If only I could stay the course, if only I could be strong enough . . . It was here that my argument wore thin. *Strong enough for what,* I had to ask. I was tired every day, tired all over, and the prospect of spending the next several months so impossibly tired was too much for me.

Feeling that I faced a choice between my future and my present, I withdrew from my classes.

As my baby grew, and my toddler grew up, the year wore on. Although it continued to be a trial physically, I made peace with my pregnancy and spent sweet bathtub hours with Nash scrubbing my giant belly. Genuinely thrilled to be expecting a new baby, I felt a pride in my appearance that had been conspicuously absent throughout my mothering experience thus far. I immersed myself in yoga, yogurt, toddler days and online nights, and it was good. Not always, of course; not when I tripped over the dog and had to spend hours on a fetal monitor in the middle of the night, not when we found out that our new car had actually been recalled a decade earlier, and not when I found myself being rushed into the operating room for my second cesarean section after wanting so badly to "do it right" this time around. But there was calm in between the drama, and the relief that came with my liberation from deadlines and schedules was so great as to be indescribable.

So great, in fact, that I can scarcely imagine going back. A friend nearly twice my age visited just a month before the birth of my second son and broached the subject, giving me a look of great concern. "When do you think you will go back? I mean, you have so much more to go, really, years of school ahead of you, you know . . . " I did know. I do know. But—and this is the part that seems just impossible to convey—I don't care. "My children are only going to be little for a short time," I told my friend, and he looked hopeful. "Well," he said, "that's true. So, you'll take a year off, maybe, and then get back to it?" I sighed. I wasn't sure how to break it to him. "The thing is, right at this moment, I have no interest in school. None whatsoever. So that isn't the place for me right now. School will always be there. I can go back whenever I want. If I want." My friend looked disappointed, but not defeated. Teaching high school for a living, he eats bad attitudes for breakfast. "So," he said brightly, "when these two little guys are a few years older, you'll be thinking of school again, and you can go finish up and head on to law school."

I hesitated. *What the hell,* I thought, *might as well be honest.* "The thing is," I said again, "the thing is, I'm pretty sure I want to have more children." You could have heard a pin drop.

If I graduate from college, I will be the first in my family to do so. If I graduate from college, I will have a degree. If I graduate from college, I will be eligible to apply for the opportunity to go to graduate school. If I graduate from college, I will be pronounced formally educated. If I graduate from college, I will be expected to pay back my student loans. If I graduate from college, I will do it at my own pace and in my own time. If I graduate from college, I will throw a huge party and everyone will be invited.

Until then, I have babies to nurse without glancing at the clock, dishes to wash whenever I get around to it, stories to tell all day long and dinner to cook when we get hungry. My education has not been put on hold; on the contrary, I am a full-time student in an accelerated toddler studies program. My three-year-old is experimenting with wet-on-wet watercolors, and the baby will be walking soon. Now that's what I call progress.

MOVEMENTS

June Day

Allegro

I worry about stretch marks because I have to.

I worry about them in between worrying about Daughter not crawling yet, the teeth poking painfully through her gums, her refusal to eat, her need to always be held, the wet diapers, Armageddon, the cold weather, the laundry I haven't done and the bad taste in my mouth.

Secretly, I love the marks on my breasts. I watched them form with more wonder than dread. They are an intricate tattoo, a testament to our mother-daughter relationship. I often rub the deeper ones with my finger while I nurse Daughter. I like the thick impression they have left on my skin.

It's beauty.

I love my potbelly, too. It's round, small, just the right shape.

I exercise, but not because I want to.

I exercise because I have to prepare my body for display. It's ironic that the first time in my life that I truly love my body—I mean, really respect and adore my body—it won't be acceptable in the club.

I feel that I must always be ready for the stage. The threat of welfare closing its doors on me before I'm ready, or a factory job being forced on me and my English B.A., keeps me doing stomach crunches during those beloved naptimes.

I was an excellent dancer. I worked through the early months of my pregnancy. I made a lot of money. But I had hoped that part of my life was over.

I think that I no longer crave the stage.

For a long time I was addicted to the smell of sweat, money and cheap cigarettes. The stage was a place where, not quite eighteen, I learned to be a chameleon. I could seduce a credit card from a bum. I was like a shapeshifter. Any man could look at me and see whatever he wanted most. I was an airhead, an intellectual, a dog, a mistress. I was every kind of pervert and dominatrix and girl next door he could imagine. Sliding and spinning on the stage, I could ultimately have the whole room, women and men, in a trance, in love.

Even more than the stage, I loved the dressing room. In that tiny, sweaty little space full of mirrors and cigarette smoke, women in all stages of costume made love to one another. Well, we didn't literally make love, but I see it that way in my memory. We flirted. We were naked. We were beautiful. I loved them all in some way. For me, each of them represented a little piece of reality. And for a small-town middle-class girl, their realness was enough to leave me smitten for life.

I thought, in that tiny, smoky dressing room, that I was learning not to be a girl anymore. I was learning to be a woman. I loved all of the dancers—their voices, their ideas, their freedom, their complexities. I even loved Paloma the night she came running off the stage and into the dressing room where I sat, five months pregnant. A handful of girls around me, I was applying makeup, a combination of habit and art. Paloma was holding a knife and screaming to the air, "And you just sat there and let them do it to me," with lipstick colors streaming down her chin. I saw her bleeding, her knife, her distress and insanity.

Normally, I found Paloma entertaining, an enigma. That night I thought only of her blood, my blood inside my body, my baby, her bad habits . . . AIDS. I ran for the only safe place, center stage. That, in or out of love, was my last night of work.

As I lay in bed, four months after that night, I heard a funny sort of click and felt an internal shift.

Suddenly I was laying in a puddle. Water poured out of me and onto the bed. And when the contractions started, I finally felt all woman.

I was all woman in the hospital later when my mother and my girlfriend held me and I gave birth to Daughter. And now when I see my breasts, as I pull them out to feed my child, I don't think, *I've got to save up for those implants.*

I'm all woman; tiny, sagging, stretched breasts and all. And if I should find myself inclined, either by choice or necessity, to return to the stage, these breasts will go with me just the way they are.

Molto

It's like bad sex. During the fearsome episode I'm frustrated, pained. I consider saying, "Okay—get out. This just isn't working." Would he take it too personally? The next morning I feel sick, misunderstood, sore and molested. The steaming shower barely helps, and the cup of coffee and Cocoa Krispies just feel like an empty and tiring routine. I know that only time can dull the feeling of disgust. The problem is, as sure as my menses, he'll be back next month.

His visits are short, supervised (by me), and monthly. Why should I complain? I complain because he doesn't pay child support; because when I wouldn't take then-illegal RU-486 ("the abortion pill") five months into my pregnancy, he punched me in the stomach; because he calls the child "our daughter," and he bought her tiny infant booties for her first birthday. He comes on strong during his one visit a month and holds her too tightly. When she cries, he holds her tighter. When she escapes or starts yelling for Mama, he sulks in the corner. He frightens me when he sulks. Before baby, I was petrified by that look. Postbaby, I am more petrified. He is capable of anything.

What are a girl and a smaller girl to do? First, we moved to the opposite side of the state. The state is small, so he still visits, but I figure we've cut out any casual, unplanned meetings. Second, I fantasize. I imagine that Daughter was immaculately conceived. God must have . . . Then I blush from such a goofy thought. I also entertain a series of elaborate daydreams. I imagine this "father" moving to another country, or staying forever in the States while Daughter and I move to a foreign country. I imagine him getting married and having a family someday and being humbled by the array of awesome responsibilities. I imagine him hurt and sick.

Other days I imagine him healthy, generous and kindhearted.

What are mother and daughter to do with Dad for a Day?

We have the best deal we can expect from the courts. All we can do legally is try to wait him out, hope that he gets bored and tired of trying. Until then, it's lots of Cocoa Krispies and two or three sleepless nights a month.

Daughter and I can feel strong, loved and secure because we have each other. We also have concealed weapons and 911 (just in case).

Adagio

My daughter is almost two. I have not produced any significant art or writing since her birth. I no longer call myself a writer, even in secret. I catch myself confessing to old friends at galleries and independent films, "I'm just being a mother right now. She's still so little . . . " Their looks confirm my own suspicions: I'm a lame, white-trash welfare-leech.

For the last three mornings my daughter has been getting up before three o'clock, instead of her usual six; I'm developing a twitch in my right eye. During her two-hour nap, I do the dishes, clean, pay bills and brainstorm how to make lunch out of one can of government-issue corn and three gallons of WIC milk. I spend my creativity with this can of corn, not a paintbrush. Most days, when I try to hold my daughter's hand or help her with a puzzle or a utensil, she cries, "No, Mommy, I dood it!" More energy spent trying to stay grown-up when I want to scream, "Mine!"

The thing is, I feel awful all around. When I try to work on my art, I'm not present with it. I love being a full-time mom, but mothering is really, really hard: I never get enough sleep; I'm always stressed; I have zits; I can't afford a haircut, gas for my car, fresh fruit or Band-Aids.

My guilt over being "unproductive" tires me out. I shouldn't feel this guilt. I shouldn't have to. Cultural expectations are the source of my problem. It isn't enough just to be a mother, even though it's difficult and important work. Good mothering isn't considered successful or even sufficient. One must have a MotherPlus Plan—maybe have the MotherPlus law career or be a MotherPlus novelist. It fills me with guilt, always coming up short.

I have to remind myself that giving a little person a fabulous life is enough. Sometimes my daughter reminds me herself by pretending to be a small sheep and saying, "Baaaa," while she nudges her cheek against mine. Suddenly everything shifts, writing is some distant hobby, and my girl is a sweet little fairy that has chosen me to follow and lead through life. I stop pressuring her to eat fried, microwaved or broiled corn, and we skip about the apartment laughing hysterically. When she's older, she may choose not to behave like a drunken monkey, so I'd better hang out with her now.

Presto

Darling,

I have returned to the stage at last. This is not Broadway, of course. This is no tiny opera house or even the hay-littered stage of rural theater. This is the city at its best. Stripped of decadence and pretense. Stripped of all the tiny lies and expectations of ordinary life.

I have returned to the stage. With theatrics, I expose the truth. With movement, I quell the frustrations of the crowd. With kindness, I listen to the stories of strange and average men as they try to understand how it is they have fallen into their lives. With envy or disgust, or both, they watch me. With envy or disgust, or both, I watch them.

With my locker full of costumes, the top shelf overflowing with one-dollar bills, I choose some music that moves me. I know that when I am moved, they are moved. I choose the music, the costume, the mood. On this street, the seediest street in the city, in the smallest of all possible strip clubs, on the most neglected of stages, I perform magic for dozens of men and women: I move them. My reflection on the streaked mirror chases me around the stage, intimate as a lover at dawn.

And I am free.

True love doesn't start out as true love. Like a hailstone, it starts as a particle and builds layer by layer, each one making it harder and stronger than the one before. But true love is also slippery. It will disintegrate if crushed underfoot and will melt away if not given what it needs to maintain its integrity.

True love is a work in progress, never complete. —Katmoonblue

I didn't really believe in true love until I had my children. It's a wide-open thing, which leaves you open to devastation, but from which the light of the universe can flow. It's a blessing, like rain after a drought. And it's circular, because my love for my children enables me to love myself, which enables me to love them more. —LivingNappy

PARALLEL PARENTING

Kara Gall

Lydia began her naked phase. I saw no harm in letting her run around the house sans clothes. Coincidentally, she was also watching *Kiki's Delivery Service,* the anime movie about a young witch who rode the proverbial witch's broom. These two pursuits collided in a moment of unhygienic behavior when I found Lydia riding our kitchen broom with no clothes on. Enter my roommate, Kate, noting in the most casual of voices, "Witches' Rule Number One, Lydia: Always wear panties when riding the broom."

Living with another mother is a godsend. Living with another child is challenging. For almost a year, I have shared a three-bedroom apartment with my roommate, Kate, and her six-year-old daughter, Eden. My own daughter is three. Both Eden and Lydia had previously spent their entire lives as only children. Both Kate and I are single mothers.

There are undeniable advantages to living with another parent. Kate and I have a little bit more freedom to pursue social lives because we are willing to provide last-minute (i.e., free) baby-sitting for each other. We give each other coupons for free afternoons away from our children. She reassures me that Lydia's actions are on par with three-year-old development: "Eden used to do that all the time. It's completely normal that Lydia wants waffles as soon as you pour the milk on the Cheerios," or "I remember when Eden drew a sun just like that. She was about three."

The similarities ended when Lydia started touching her private parts in public. Casting my eyes hopefully toward Kate, I asked, "Eden went through this stage, right?" "Oh, no. She never did that." Two out of three ain't bad.

We take turns making the morning coffee. We hug each other when our own mothers make us feel like incompetent fools. We write each other notes on the mirror. "WARNING: Dead fish in toilet—Operation Replacement begins at 0900 hours." Sometimes Kate even wipes up potty-training messes while I run to the bookstore to purchase the latest toilet-training/toddler-rearing book, which ultimately only reinforces my mother's belief that I am a bungling ogre of a parent. We attend each other's work-sponsored parties. We sit on the deck on hot summer evenings, sipping red wine and listening to the harsh cries of bedtime rebellion.

"Is that your child?"

"Sounds more like yours."

"Ya know . . . you just might be right."

There is always one of us who is not so emotionally invested in an experience that she can't find great humor in it. Most couples I know are too tired, too strung out in their personal battles to deal with crap from a kid with any humor at all. But when you parallel parent, you have a personal comedian on board, extracting the comedy from all the mundane details of your life.

"It's hot, so put on a T-shirt for bed," Kate instructs her daughter. Eden is wearing an interesting combination of dress-up clothes, resulting in a cryptic cross between Deadhead and Vegas starlet. "But I'm not hot," Eden retorts, sticking a six-year-old hand on a six-year-old hip.

"Well, I insist you wear a T-shirt." One eyebrow raises.

"It's not that hot." Other hand. Other hip.

"Put it on!"

At this point, Eden stomps to the bathroom, grumbling a litany of injustice. When she is safely out of earshot, I utter the malediction I am sure is passing through Kate's mind: "Well, it's hot in hell, and that's where little girls who don't listen to their mommies go!"

Sometimes the camaraderie goes beyond the Mommy-to-Mommy connection and we find ourselves interacting as a family. Our dinnertime ritual is to go around the table and talk about the parts of our days we enjoyed and the parts that were not so easy. One evening, when it was my turn, I talked about how strong I felt in my yoga class that day. Eden chimed in about how strong she was, too. Before you know it, all four of us were showing each other our bulging muscles. It may not be the family Norman Rockwell had in mind, but I envied the girls at that moment. Two little girls and their mommies showing off their muscles at the dinner table.

Then there are the nature shows. When the rains came in the dead of winter we found ourselves consistently sitting around the television on Saturday afternoons, watching a PBS series of wildlife documentaries. While ominous music played over scenes of the predacious polar bear, the British-accented narrator droned, "Spring is a dangerous time for the baby harp seal." An hour later, black-beaked orioles nose-dived into a swarm of butterflies while the previous narrator's female equivalent warned, "Winter in Mexico is a dangerous time for the monarch butterfly." It is now our household catch phrase. "Eight o'clock on

Sunday morning is a dangerous time for the children," I'll mutter while trying to remember where I put the coffee filters.

Addressing the "Daddy" issue has become a household project. Eden and Lydia both have birth fathers. Though Eden has an adopted daddy involved in her life, Lydia does not. Early on in our household experiment, Eden wanted to know the whereabouts of Lydia's daddy. Uncomfortable at first, I wasn't prepared to talk about it with either Lydia or Eden, whose questions, while well meant, felt like an evil inquisition. Kate and I had both been involved with substance abusers who were unable to stay sober, let alone act as parents.

Since both girls had similar birth-father stories, Kate explained Lydia's story to Eden in terms she understood. Hearing Kate's explanation prepared me for the time when Lydia would ask me about her daddy; by then, I was accustomed to explaining, "Your daddy lives far away and he loves you very much, but he's sick and can't take care of you."

There is a flip side. Coordinating morning and bedtime routines requires a precision usually reserved for air-traffic controllers. Halve the space, double the noise level. The slightest miscalculation, and chaos and pandemonium ensue.

Ours is not a large apartment. There are technically only two bedrooms. We turned the office into a third. Initially, the girls shared a room. The first night involved hitting, crying, name-calling and an alleged bite, though no physical evidence was found. We decided to give it a week. After all, everybody needs an adjustment period, right? Eventually, we found that there were excessive squabbles over toy ownership and ultimately too many distractions at bedtime. Deciding who would share a room with her child was difficult. Since my daughter is younger, we decided it would be best for Lydia and me to share a room. This situation must change as time goes by, but for now it suits us well.

All across the country, parents are attempting some variation of parallel parenting. "Guess what *your* child did today," a mother will say to a father, after said child washes her hair in a very tempting mud puddle in the driveway. In the true parallel parenting household, however, it is clear whose kid is whose. Sometimes uncomfortably so. Disciplining someone else's child requires a fine blend of standing your ground and being sensitive to the other parent's values.

I woke up one Saturday morning to hear Eden whispering something to Lydia. Lydia then ran into my room crying. It was six-forty-five in the morning. I was tired. I was grumpy. I was certainly not in touch with my problem-solving skills.

"How long has this been going on?" I yelled at Eden from my doorway.

"I . . . I don't know," she stammered.

"Well, it better not happen again!"

Enter Kate. Not knowing what had just happened, and wanting to hear the whole story, she asked Eden what happened.

"I don't know," she whined, tears streaming down her face.

Crap. What did just happen? I didn't have any actual evidence of a junior-roommate misdemeanor. What I did have was a knee-jerk reaction to a rude predawn awakening.

We have had to create some rules to minimize the conflicts and make living together a little more bearable. All screaming, jumping and general theatrical gymnastics must cease at seven in the evening. All toys, books and general child paraphernalia left in the living room, kitchen, hallway or bathroom are subject to community use. Ergo, anything you don't want anyone to touch must be kept in your room. You must knock on the door and ask to enter anyone's room but your own. The door of the room you are playing in must remain open (a rule instituted after Eden informed us, "Sometimes I take Lydia to my room and teach her things"). We installed a six-foot-high lock on the door to

Lydia's and my room after she wandered out in the middle of the night and ate all of Eden's Halloween candy.

Adjusting my expectations has been the hardest part of parallel parenting. When I was young and ignorant, I had the typical American fantasy: I'm going to grow up, get married, buy a house, have a family and live happily ever after. Apparently, I couldn't even make it to the altar before things fell apart. After Lydia was born, I kept telling myself roommates were part of college history. Then again, maybe not. While the four of us dance around the living room in circles, our tiaras bouncing, skirts flying and bracelets jangling, the neighbor downstairs knocking on the ceiling and screaming for us to please stop stomping, I think to myself, *we are re-creating family. We are developing a support network.* There are conflicts. There are compromises. There is little personal space, overfilled refrigerators and no parking. Most of all, though, there is love, laughter and a family-sized bottle of disinfectant for the broom.

BELLY OF THE WHALE

Beth Lucht

Miles asks my boyfriend, "Why don't you like my daddy?" John tries to explain to Miles that he does like his daddy. I'm not so sure it's true, but it sounds good. Miles asks John, "Why doesn't Daddy like you?" John says that it's not that Daddy dislikes him, but rather that he makes Daddy feel sad. That's not quite true, either. Daddy probably doesn't like John, though he pretty much did before I started sleeping with John. This is all too much to explain to Miles.

I am sitting on the couch with Miles, writing this. It would be easier to write at the computer, but Miles doesn't want to let me out of his sight. We are watching *Pinocchio*. Right now, Geppetto and Figaro are stuck in the belly of Monstro, the whale. Every time I try to leave the room, Miles presses stop on the VCR and comes to get me. He says he's afraid I'll miss the movie. When I sneak out to the computer to check on something, he follows. "I'm mad at you, Mom," he says, feigning fierceness. "You're not paying 'tention."

Miles asks me if Phil is dead. He asks when he's going to see "my friend Phil" again, and why we don't see him. He asks me why I don't like Phil, and asks if it is maybe that Phil doesn't like him.

All of this is terrible, and I am the only person to blame. My life is confusing and it has confused my two-year-old. I have put him in the position to view my confusing life, to know and love the players in it. They are all good people, kind people, people who love children. I am glad to have the people in my life know my son, and glad to have him know them. Boyfriends are the problem. There have been two since my separation. It's a goddamn soap opera, truthfully. Miles has known both boyfriends. They would make great dads, though neither has tried to replace the one he already has. Miles lives with his dad half the time and with me half the time. His dad loves him and is a great dad. Everyone in Miles' life loves him and cares for him. Most of the time he seems perfectly happy with the arrangement, though I worry about what will happen in a year, in two years, in ten years. I can already hear the adolescent recriminations: "If only you hadn't gotten divorced . . . "

I wonder also why the comings and goings of boyfriends bother me. I don't worry, introducing Miles to friends, whether they will be around in six months or a year. I figure most of them will be, but friends have fallings-out and people leave town. He likes my friends, talks about them and enjoys seeing them, but I don't worry that if one of them leaves my (and his) life, he will be scarred forever. I don't understand what it is about that connection—Mom's boyfriend—that marks the relationship as more significant.

Some moms clearly make mistakes in choosing partners. Last fall in my area, two thirteen-year-old girls were murdered, in the space of a few days. They were both killed by their mothers' boyfriends. In one case, the girl had apparently been sexually abused by the boyfriend before he strangled her and hid the body. In the other case, the boyfriend was fighting with the mother, and the girl got in the way. The cause of death was blunt trauma to the head. I wonder about these mothers. They probably reassured themselves that they were making good choices, loving good men, though in hindsight, they clearly were not. What separates me from them? What blind spot stopped them from seeing their lovers in a realistic light? Could I have a similar spot, lurking somewhere, hidden? And why is it that I blame these mothers for their daughters' deaths, almost more than I blame the men who actually did the killing?

Pinocchio and Geppetto have just been reunited, and Geppetto has noticed Pinocchio's donkey ears. He is horrified. Miles is staring straight ahead at the TV screen, a blank look on his face.

I lived with my father, but I didn't know him. He was robbed from me by school and work and alcohol and his own terror of getting close to the people he loved. Perhaps that terror is genetic. Perhaps I will continue to careen from relationship to relationship, withdrawing every time I fear that the true me will be revealed to someone. Perhaps someday I will also hide myself from Miles. I don't remember if my father hid from me when I was two, or if that day didn't come until I was five or ten. All I remember is not knowing him, feeling as if there were a chasm between us that I could dimly perceive and certainly never span. Even as an adult, after undergoing years of therapy and completing my own training as a therapist, I have no idea where to start.

Now Pinocchio has died protecting his father. He awakens to find himself a real boy. Miles is grinning widely. It is Thursday afternoon. He will be with me until Saturday, go to his father's, return on Tuesday. He has two bedrooms, two toothbrushes, two sets of little sippy cups with lids to guard against spills. He splits himself between two sets of people who love him. He hasn't yet learned to feel guilty about loving anyone back, but I know he will soon. He already tells his father, "Daddy, you should like John. He doesn't kick or hit." He tells me, on the phone from his father's house, "You should come and stay here. We have a lot of room." I can't let him dictate all of my decisions; I need a life of my own. Yet he has to dictate some; I think of the mothers of the dead girls and know that there must have come a time when their children did not dictate the decisions that they should have. Somewhere, a bad choice was made, which led to more and more bad choices. On bad days, I tell myself I should be celibate until he is eighteen, but I know that this is nothing more than a joke. I teeter, and I will continue teetering, on the line between Miles's best interest and mine. His life is in the balance; I hold him in my arms. I only hope that I never fall.

BECOMING HIS MOTHER

Yantra Bertelli

I never asked myself when I became my daughter's mother. No quest to declare a defining moment. No frantic search through memories, analyzing each interaction. My belly swelled with her movement. Months passed as I familiarized myself with the soft curves of her coiled being. In anticipation, I grappled with her developing temperament and rehearsed our future embraces. We shared flesh, blood, dream, and breath. I tended the seed of motherhood planted deep within my body, nurturing it toward sunlight. My roots instinctively spread thick in their soil to anchor my changing womanhood. I cultivated the mother I would become. She grew from my realizations, my work, myself.

My son's body did not grow under my skin, though his soul visited me from time to time. He grew inside my lover, but he tickled my daydreams. I witnessed the motion of long arms and tiny toes rolling underneath someone else's skin. I watched him stretch, confined in her body. Through layers of flesh, the sound of his beating heart reached for me. I ached for the familiarity of his rhythm. I agonized that my love would not match the intensity I held for his sister, that I would not live up to what he deserved. I feared that my insecurities would seep into his skin as I held him. I hoped he would accept me. I wondered when I would become his mom.

Was I his mom during the insemination, the conception? The hours following, in those anxious moments of unyielding hope? The instant when that one pale pink line crossed the other? The months I waited to meet him, wondering who he would be? Was I his mom during his birth, those timeless hours when two mothers looked into each other's eyes and worlds connected? Was I his mom when he poured into the light of the bedroom, small, wet, bright-eyed, peeing everywhere and singing that shallow, weepy song? When he lay in my arms for the first time and I marveled at his gaze? Was I his mom the first night that I brought him to my own breast, begging for relief from his colic and my own sleep deprivation? When he called me "Mama"? When my lover moved away from us?

What about now, today, this minute—am I his mom now? Is there evidence in our nightly dance, exchanging song for sleep? He seeks reassurance within my chest, burrowing his head, his hands, the cool bite of his trepidations. His face brightens as I sneak around the corner. His giggles tickle the bottoms of my feet. Our bodies intermingle with tight grasps and the whisper of blown kisses. I am present to console him in troubled moments. I am here to encourage him to push past his inhibitions. I read to him, idle over him, dream of him. I am consumed in the details that every day demands. Have my instincts underlined the reality of my role, or does their urgency reveal a neurotic effort to conceal a lacking piece of our life's puzzle?

I dread that I am his mom merely in her absence, that biological authenticity will denounce our bond. I am panicked in my efforts to remain centered. I can sense my hopes falling away when she reappears. My energies are lost in the air separating our bodies. I am afraid to meet his glance and face a reality where he finds less comfort in my reflection. His eyes glisten for her, and I search for a sign of dullness when we stand face to face. Every pore of my body rages for him. My fire does not fade. My gut pangs for a glimmer of his affection. I loathe my sunken heart, and my inability to love and anticipate nothing in return. I have searched for selflessness and continue to collide with tears. Am I just a temporary fix, a decent substitute?

Why does my heart look to a child, to a young boy, for such validation? How can I ignore the reality that he cannot define "mother"? I do not hang on my daughter's actions. I label her rejections as blossoming independence. I know that looking to him for proof of my importance robs him of the unconditional love that a parent and child deserve to share. Yet I remain unsettled. I fear that he will know my ache. He will see through me. I fear that I will paint a picture of my adoration, and he will peel it away. I fear that I will indulge myself in the revelation of my love for him, and he will be ripped from my arms. If she were to come back for him, how could I go on? How can I protect myself from the real possibility that our futures may not intertwine, and at the same time devote my heart to him?

There are diapers to change, meals to prepare, toys to gather and minds to inspire, but the real work of motherhood seethes within. I struggle to prove my worthiness, and I cower in my insecurities. Instead of settling into who I am, I churn over the qualities I am lacking. When four became three in our family bed, nights of sadness and anger followed.

We share the same silence in sleep, we breathe the same breath; he rides my hip, his hands find warmth between my breasts, we flow as one. I have succumbed to this motherly passion. It is impossible to shield myself from the torment that our uncertain future conjures. It is done. I have given myself and I am learning to ask for no other moment than the one in which we stand.

My own body yielded a daughter, the wind offered a son; the delicacies of motherhood flourish. I labor to create our lush garden. I deliberate daily over the height of its border. I coax their roots to find hold in my rich soil. I fuss over their depth. I tend to their needs and shine over them with love. I stand guard, ready to pluck my own doubts from our soft earth. I challenge myself to search for peace rather than meaning. We have grown together, mother, daughter, son. And in our steady creep toward the sky, I am finding my answers.

BIG MAMA

Kai Ro

I'm a big mama now, and my baby girl's grandparents drive me crazy. Every once in a long while I get sentimental and wish we all got along. I wish I liked them enough to hang out every weekend, I wish they didn't make me contemplate jumping on a Greyhound bus with a one-way ticket to Boise, Idaho. Most of the time I want to move two thousand miles back out west where I was for six good years far away from family. But I moved back here to try to improve my relationship with my mom and dad. It has backfired, and now that I'm closer to home they're even more disappointed in the lack of Christianity in my life. My lifestyle makes me a sinner in their eyes, but if this is sinning, well, sign me up, sister! After all, my three-month-old baby girl is a result of this return trip to Florida, and I think she's the crème de la crème. I should scram while I still have my sanity.

I've also scored my second husband, the best boy to come along since my first. Oddly enough, they're both punk, skinny Pisceans who are considered mildly offensive by the majority of their peers. That must be what I look for in a spouse. I found my future second husband dressed as a kissing booth at a Halloween party three years ago, and dared him to earn change for a ten. It was easy money for him, getting kisses from the grown boys and girls of our neighborhood. That night after a kiss that changed the way I'd previously thought of my neuter next-door neighbor, we went home together and got severely naked for hours. Midnight trysts bicycling to his house together and getting busy till the sun rose led to days of antique shopping and nights of going to shows together. We spent New Year's Eve in Chicago and took a summer trip to Iceland. We left things open and fun. When he told me he always fell for women in pairs, I bought him Deborah Anapol's book *Polyamory: The New Love without Limits*. He bought me *The Ethical Slut* when I told him about the overlapping relationships of my past.

Some people say they just like the practice, but we decided all this great fooling around would be the perfect way to start a nontraditional family. Maybe it was the hormones or the ripe egg or a sign of good fortune, but my orgasm the morning we made Ember . . . well, I was sure I would have to call in sick due to fatigue. Three weeks later when my nipples turned brown, the smell of food made me ill, and the blue line showed up on the EPT stick, our life as a married couple began.

Husband number two and I shouldn't have married—if we had stayed single, I would have qualified for public assistance after getting knocked up, and our little sweet pea would have had health insurance until she was three years old. But our parents flipped about my pregnancy, and in a panic, we got hitched at the courthouse. Now Dad makes too much money for us to be on WIC, but has too much debt for us not to be scraping by. And I've acquired a second set of in-laws who drive me absolutely crazy.

When husband number two—let's call him Bean—told his parents we were having a baby, they said, "We love you and the baby, and oh yeah, we love your girlfriend too." Two days later Bean's Rush Limbaugh–worshipping dad freaked out and called my house to yell at me. It was the beginning of a nine-month string of anecdotal gems:

"I don't understand how this could have happened if you were on birth control."

"You're not going to have an abortion or give this baby up for adoption. You're going to get married—no illegitimate children in our family!"

"Bean has been the perfect son, and we don't want to see his future ruined."

"You need to go to a Jewish doctor—they're smart, clean people who know what they're doing."

"Having a midwife sounds so medieval."

"Why don't you just get some poor immigrant for a nanny after the baby's born and go back to work in two weeks. If you don't trust her you can buy a security camera."

"I can't believe your lack of drive, not wanting to go back to work or school after the baby is born."

"Your kid is going to be weird if it sleeps in bed with you."

"I don't know why anyone would want to be there when his wife has a baby. My wife never asked me to be there and I'm glad she didn't."

And, after watching the *Gentle Birth Choices* video: "We've decided we want to be there when you have the baby."

I fantasize about sitting down with my in-laws and calmly explaining, "Your son is a polyamorist with genital piercings. We have an open relationship, and he asks me if it's okay (and usually gets me flowers) before he goes on dates with other women. He's hidden his tattoos from you for years, since before he met me. He told me he wanted to have babies with me before I ever contemplated the idea.

"And me, I'm queer and very lonely for a girlfriend right now. I feel a billion years older at age twenty-six than all the girls here in collegeland. The twenty-year-old I was hanging out with disappeared after I got pregnant and married her ex-boyfriend. (It's a small town, what can I say?) Yeah, I have a degree in molecular biology, but every research project I've worked on has compromised my principles—and being a mama doesn't. I don't need to make money to have a sense of accomplishment and self-worth. I don't want to "grow up" to be square, hide my tattoos, grow out my hair and live in the suburbs. And your son, my husband and lover—and more importantly, the dad of this little baby girl who is making me work harder and love harder than ever before in my life—totally supports me in this."

But that conversation is never going to happen because husband number two likes the façade he's built for his folks. I like mine, too. My parents know I've slept around and dated women in the past—both unacceptable behaviors in their eyes—but they assume everything is different now that I'm hitched and "settled down." Though the pretense distances us from our folks, it's worth it. I never want to deal with some family court trying to take my baby away because they think we're unfit punk-as-fuck parents.

My daughter is teething and screaming upstairs with her dad, who is trying to put her in a fresh cloth diaper. When her tooth hurts, she spits out the nip and screams. My boob isn't the universal pacifier it used to be. My poor little lady only wants us to carry her in the "colic hold" and walk around to distract her from her painful mouth. Even then, she lets out small yells, telling us how much it sucks to be getting her first tooth when she's so little. Sometimes the ceiling fan or a toy catches her eye, and she smiles and starts a conversation with it.

Bean and I are attachment parents: Ember drinks only her mama's breast milk. She sleeps in bed with us, wears cloth diapers in the house and Tushies when we're on the road. At three months old, she still has no immunizations. Bean and I hold Ember almost all of the time, until she freaks and needs her space. The first time I recognized that her crying meant she just wanted to be put down, I was both heartbroken and a little relieved. At fifteen pounds, she's killing my back, so it's nice to know that Ember doesn't mind a break as well.

Ember takes a shower with her dad or me once a week, and we don't use soap—just warm water and a cloth to wipe her down. I like her natural smell. It's pure breast-milk goodness now: fresh milk-breath from her mouth, fermented feta-smelling milk in her neck rolls and armpits, mustardy milk gas from her bottom. After my daughter was born, my armpit smell changed to a strong goat musk. I don't wear deodorant anymore so that Ember can recognize her big mama with her eyes closed. I pick the cradle cap off her little bald scalp, and trim her fingernails with my teeth when they are too tiny to cut with clippers.

Bean walks her around on the porch during the hot days when he's home, and lulls her to sleep with songs on those late nights when I've crashed out and she's still alert. When Ember has tummy pains, Bean becomes Colic Man and rubs her belly, walks her up and down the stairs a hundred times and brings her to me to put her on the nip until she and I sleep side by side, with her dreaming of endless nursing.

My little baby is still very sensitive; she startles at the smallest noises. I've even seen Ember scare herself by lip-smacking too loudly when she's nursing. Yesterday a little hippie girl told me, "That's okay. It's just because she's new to this world." Perfect wisdom from the mouth of a seven-year-old. Ember is new to this world, and yes, everything is okay.

I'm so in love with my little Ember that I'm moved to tears several times a week. It saddens me to think that someday Ember may want to escape me the way I want to escape her grandparents, to live out her life in anonymity far away from her biological family. Maybe Ember will make herself a new family, as I am. Maybe someday I'll disapprove of my daughter's lifestyle, of her beliefs, of who and how she loves, as my parents do. Maybe I'll boss her around, expect her to consult me before every decision, show my disappointment and throw guilt trips at her when she doesn't, as her dad's parents do to him. I hope I don't and I pray I won't, because Ember may not remember these days when we spend at least twenty out of twenty-four hours together, touching, cuddling, just looking at each other and smiling. She probably will not remember our long talks of consonants and vowels transcending words in the stillness between a serious, wide-eyed baby girl and her wide-eyed big mama. But big mama will remember and big mama wonders if this is how her own mama felt about her.

BREAD AND ROSES

Bee Lavender

I was twenty-one years old, my life sorted and tidy; it was the first day of graduate school, the first morning at daycare for my daughter. My husband was just home after two years of military service in Alaska. Working my way through school and taking care of a baby alone had ended any romantic illusions I might have once held. I was not going to let my teenage marriage derail me from my goal of being politically active. I didn't really care that my husband was opposed to my plans. I wanted a degree in a practical subject, public administration, which would allow me to earn a living and still be involved in a radical social movement. I was sitting on a bench near the library with autumnal foliage all around, watching crows hop at my feet, when a tall boy wearing a rugby shirt walked up to talk to my friend. He was wheezing. As I looked at him, all of my random thoughts and worries about life suddenly connected. For the first time, I realized that I didn't want to be married. It wasn't his appearance or anything else I knew about him at the time; it was just a zapping sensation straight out of a bad romance novel.

I didn't break up with my husband to be with that asthmatic boy—though the marriage did end within a week of that encounter. I had been involved in committed relationships for five years, and my restless interest in a stranger convinced me that I should make an attempt to be single. The asthmatic boy, Byron, became a good friend. We studied at cafes, played aggressive board games and went out to movies or shows when my daughter stayed the night with her grandparents. I gave him rides to the airport, and he accompanied me to the military hospital when I had the final test to prove my remission from childhood cancer.

Byron held my attention with his intellect and clean room, his guitar playing and outrageous lies, his charm and social ease. I held his attention, too, and an interesting tension developed between us, though we both resisted further involvement. I didn't want to be in love or use my finite emotional resources to deal with a boyfriend who wanted something permanent, particularly not a boyfriend still figuring out his identity and his plans for the future. Graduate school, community organizing and an active, happy toddler occupied my time. I was competent, focused, with a child to raise. He had picked his academic subject based on the choices of the cute girl in front of him in the registration line. Byron had a romantic and idealized affection for me, but he knew that he was too young to take on the responsibility that comes with dating a mother. He wasn't ready to give up his youth in exchange for a stable relationship and family.

For all these reasons, we didn't begin dating until much later, after we became roommates, after his love affair with another roommate turned bad and she convinced me to evict him. After he lived in the driveway in his van and I kept unplugging his extension cord. After we both had relationships with other people and worked through ideas about responsibility and family and independence.

But then one weekend my daughter was out of town. I went over to Byron's to watch videos, and the next thing I knew, we were a couple—against our mutual better judgment. We would rather have had an affair. We resisted becoming a unit; we didn't want to live together, continued to try to see other people. But we just couldn't; we were magnetically drawn toward an overwhelming and imperative exclusivity. We felt almost persecuted by the complete and honest perfection of our emotional connection.

Changing my life again wasn't all that easy. When my husband (who I had misplaced but not divorced) showed up periodically to introduce me to his new girlfriends, he would tell me that Byron was a fine and honorable choice as a life partner to help raise our child. However, Byron's friends were not nearly as understanding. Their reactions ranged from reflexively horrified to casually cruel. He was living with girl rugby players who disliked my work wardrobe and cautious, safety-first attitude. I would wade through their piercing parties, indicating their poor needle sterilization practices and talking about universal precautions. It was silly for him to continue to pay rent on a room when he was at my house all the time, so we defaulted into living together.

In a little cabin on the outskirts of town, we set up a household with my best friend. We shared resources and responsibilities, like childcare and rides and cooking. We struggled with student poverty and dealing with our friends and not having enough time. My extended family (including my husband and in-laws) was involved in our lives and provided a great deal of help with childcare and emotional support. We had other friends and mentors, professors and colleagues, who adopted our little family and helped us eke out an existence and stay in school. I started to work on my thesis and became increasingly involved in disability activism, finding an intellectual home, real friends and a way to have a career that was both salaried and based on radical political ideology. Byron switched to a new major, logic and math, with no previous experience in the subject. We all worked incredibly hard to be present, get along, do well at school and work, take care of each other.

At twenty-three, I finished my master's degree and officially started my career. My daughter was four years old. I had very little difficulty implementing plans to achieve my goals because of my near-pathological conviction that I had no time to waste. I planned and scheduled and acted correctly in each individual role: mother, student, worker, girlfriend. Each came easily to me. The tricky part was figuring out what I actually wanted to do, and who I wanted to do it with. As a teenager it had been easy to put out zines, organize protests, work in nonprofits, study, have fun, even have a baby. But adding a real job on top of all the other commitments tipped the balance. I envisioned the grand scheme but forgot the part about enjoying myself. I made a series of compromises for the career—from giving up my preferred clothes and shoes to being away from my child for sixty hours each week—that inexorably destroyed my ideals and optimism about political work. It took about a year to realize that the pain I felt while working was not acceptable.

Byron decided to go to graduate school in Oregon. My choices were to stay with the career and professional network and community I had worked hard to develop, or move on. But if I moved, it would not be with Byron. It would be to Washington, D.C., to take a better job, improve my financial situation, continue advancing, adhere to my activist goals. I wasn't interested in sacrificing my career to follow someone, no matter how much I cared for him or enjoyed our life together.

But then I had an epiphany. I realized that I didn't want to be a single parent. I was sick of working so hard and endlessly for material advances. I was compromising my values, and I was unhappy. I had never had so much as a summer off from school or work. It seemed to me that if I wanted to continue my career, I would have to be drugged.

I quit and announced that I would never again work for money. I would in fact move with Byron, as an act of personal defiance, and we would worry about the technical details later. I took the biggest risk of my life and walked away from everything familiar, without a plan or resources.

It takes practice to be idle. After a lifetime where the demands of others defined my schedule, I struggled to figure out what to do with my time. I thought too much. When my daughter started school, I found myself pacing around the apartment. I felt that without work I lacked an identity, a community, a purpose.

So I decided to have another baby. I forced a divorce out of my first husband to simplify the situation and then decided I needed to get married again for health insurance. Byron and I went to the 24 Hour Church of Elvis on January 8—an oversight on our part, since that is the high holy birthday. Our plan for a private, funny little evening together was interrupted by an uninvited television news crew cracking jokes about blue suede shoes and taking gratuitous shots of the street troubadour who serenaded the ceremony. The minister of the church dressed as a benevolent fairy godmother, and our vows consisted of only one promise: that we would always remain friends. The evening news promo of our wedding was shown more times than the promo for Keiko's (the *Free Willy* whale) departure for Iceland.

Three months of pregnancy bed rest and bleeding in a new city left me aching for my old friends, old community, any kind of contact. I was alone all day, then unable to care for my daughter when she came home from school. I was too tired for much of anything. Then I was hospitalized for a dismal month before an unavoidable emergency cesarean section. My only friend or ally in town was Byron. He came into the operating room with me and chatted with the doctor about the music on the PA system, charmed the nurses, talked about the wallpaper and acted his usual cheery part despite his reluctance to be exposed to the gore of the procedure. The anesthesiologist blustered through the epidural, insisting that the medication was effective when, in fact, it was not. I felt the scalpel split me open, but because I remained calm the doctor didn't believe that the anesthesia had failed. Byron came to my rescue. He forced the surgery staff to listen to me as I clinically analyzed for them the feeling of being cut in half. He held my hand when I passed out from the new drugs and the panic, and he watched my blood gush out of my belly and onto the floor. He held our tiny premature son for me to look at when I achieved a moment of clarity, and then protected us from hospital staff intrusions in the hours following the surgery.

At age twenty-five we had a six-year-old and a fragile newborn to parent. In contrast to the years of our courtship, we were separated from friends and family, with no money and no community to call on in times of crisis. We realized that it was necessary to build something again, to identify the values that were most important to us, find friends and become involved with a group larger than our small family. I decided to set aside my cynicism about work and activism, and deliberately set out to find people who would accept and love us. People who were political, with similar lifestyle values. I gradually started to give more of my time to community organizing and realized that I needed that kind of involvement in order to stay connected to my own needs and those of my family.

At age thirty, I have been a parent for eleven years. I have been in a stable relationship for eight years. Byron and I have learned that we both need to work and be involved in things outside of our roles as parents, and that we must do so without sacrificing anything else. We unschool the children and split our responsibilities in half. We divide childcare, education and cleaning equally, and barter for the less desirable tasks (I'll pay bills if you make appointments). We both work full-time, but I protect my library time, writing time, road trips, costumes, the nuclear-red stripe in my hair. Byron writes in his journals, travels the world, barters his mathematical skills and started a Take a Punk to Work program. The whole family sings in a radical protest chorus. We have figured out a way to earn our keep without destroying the integrity of our personalities.

In this relationship, we try both to achieve our goals and honor the love—and family—we share. We work hard to avoid unjust expectations of each other. Neither of us would sacrifice an important goal or dream for the other person. We support the desire of one or the other to move away or stay in one place, finish a doctorate, have babies, start a business, paint the house orange, learn to sing or go roller-skating. Neither of us would lay claim to all the creative energy and forward-thinking of the relationship. We do not value each other more or less based on the nature of our work, or the monetary value of our careers. The fact that we want to do something is enough to put it on the agenda, and the relationship balances on that principle. Our decision to create a shared life does not limit us, it gives us the stability necessary to find freedom.

I believe in true love. In my life, true love is expressed through the creation of family, friendship, community. True love requires commitment: the kind that means you are available to rescue your friends; the kind that you are willing to take risks for, like raising children; the kind that means you devote years to nurturing a community, never asking for more thanks than the joy of participation. True love also means protecting your own self and choosing friends and lovers who share your ideals. Our marriage is my ultimate expression of this belief—we are unified in our admiration of each other, yes, but we are also committed to raising children and participating in our chosen community.

True love is hope and defiance, persistence and hard work.

SIMILARITIES AND DIFFERENCES

Kimberly Bright

Toddler	*Bad Boyfriend*
• Throws tantrums	• Throws tantrums
• Embarrasses you in public and in front of childless yuppie friends and hipper-than-thou total strangers, unless he's being a perfect angel in public that day and saving his bad behavior for when you get him home	• Embarrasses you in public and at most social gatherings, mainly in front of your yuppie friends and parents
• Bullies you often	• Bullies you often
• Self-centered; learning empathy	• Self-centered; no empathy

- Wakes you in the middle of the night with weird nightmares, requests for drinks, demands to watch his *Winnie-the-Pooh* video again, or general refusal to sleep

- Opinionated and tyrannical; likes to argue

- Weird sleeping habits; wakes up at the crack of dawn

- Gets up between five and six in the morning

- No table manners

- Must be taught that it is not okay to hit people

- Angst-ridden, moody

- Usually repentant after tantrums, fights and outbursts

- You miss him when he is not around, as you should

- Sociopathic tendencies; is capable of displaying devastating charm and irresistible smiles

- No willpower with regard to candy, ice cream or soft drinks

- Wakes you in the middle of the night with demands for sex or calls from jail with requests that you bring bail money and a change of clothes

- Opinionated and tyrannical; likes to argue

- Weird sleeping habits; won't wake up before noon

- Is just coming home between five and six in the morning

- No table manners

- Was never taught that it is not okay to hit people

- Angst-ridden, moody

- Rarely repentant after tantrums, fights and outbursts

- You sometimes miss him when he is not around, even though you shouldn't

- Sociopathic tendencies; is capable of displaying devastating charm and irresistible smiles

- No willpower with regard to alcohol, other women or drugs of any kind

- Jealous of your attention; hates to let you out of his sight

- Interrupts you when you're speaking

- Bad fashion sense

- Often affectionate

- Loves you with all his heart

- Jealous when you hold and play with other children

- Jealous of your attention; hates to let you out of his sight, except when he disappears for days on end without warning

- Interrupts you when you're speaking

- Bad fashion sense

- Often affectionate in order to obtain something from you

- Only claims to love you with all his heart

- Jealous when you do just about anything

Therapy is great, but screaming obscenities is cheaper. —Lexcessa

I don't need real disasters; I have enough imagined ones to keep me miserable. —Maxmama

The worst thing about being a mother is not sleepless nights, or dirty diapers, or less money, or whatever. It's just the fear. I don't know how to keep both of them safe every second of the day! —MadCuteMama

CALLS FROM ANOTHER PLANET

Australia Sims

I.

Unborn baby boy-child nudges me in the ribs, eliciting a grin that probably seems inappropriate to the social worker. We are talking about options for my mother. Where will she go after this hospitalization? As we talk, I lean against the wall outside Mom's room, as I have many times over the past years. Mom's overdoses and suicide attempts are coming closer together and leaving her more damaged. In combination with her disabling mental illness and her other medical diagnoses, these episodes are edging her closer to institutionalization. She is fifty-eight. Hospital duty sucks, but baby boy doesn't know that yet. He kicks and swims and pulls me back into the rest of my life, where I have a husband who can justly be described as my soul mate, a good job and a new home with room for the baby and our studios. The sweetest and toughest moments of my life are happening all at once, and I wonder if this is the universe's way of tickling me with the highs and lows of motherhood.

While waiting for doctors and nurses, I read magazines. My ratty bookbag is filled with *Mothering, Government Technology*, a local political weekly and a quarterly about outsider art. Mom sleeps on. Wrapped in a white hospital gown with a tiny blue pattern, she is propped up slightly by the angle of the bed. Her small body lies heavy with exhaustion. The IV pours some measure of comfort into her. I stay frozen for a minute, staring at her.

My first emotion is anger. I can't believe she has done this again. Then I'm distracted by her appearance. Her hair hasn't been washed in a while and is pressed against her head like a doll's hair after it's been stored in the attic. Her teeth are caked with yellow-brown ick, and her lips crack with dried saliva.

I move through compassion, trying to linger there, but it is drowned out in a few moments by the numbness of shock. I want to disappear completely, but go to the hospital cafeteria for lousy chicken salad instead. I check my messages at work and call some people back. I feel like I'm returning calls from another planet. Pressed and fragile, I wonder what's next.

II.

At least she's not tied to the bed like last time she swallowed a bottle of sleeping pills. The nurses kept trying to give Mom the chance to be unrestrained, but she kept kicking them when they unleashed her. For two days she screamed. I remember the two phrases she repeated most often: "I don't want to die lying," and "Mother, Mother, it hurts, it hurts!" She looked me in the eye at one point and yelled, "Get that fish off my bicycle!" That day, I walked from Mom's ICU room to my OB/GYN's office in another part of the hospital complex to get some test results of my own. I was pregnant for the first time. Despite this huge and happy news, I remained completely mesmerized by my incapacitated and violent mother. This woman was not my mother. She was my mother's illnesses. I could not take my eyes off her. This weak woman was tied to a hospital bed surrounded by three nurses. She posed no threat to me.

A few hours later, she kicked me as I was helping the nurses move her. A few days later, I miscarried. Cause and effect? Probably not.

III.

Now it is me, the social workers and the discharge plan. These conversations are strenuous in a special way because I still try to be completely present for every nuance. This vigilance is exhausting, but it is part of the confusion of Mom's world. Her situation doesn't entirely fit in the "just leave 'em where God dropped 'em" frame, although that's my default mode when I can't think or feel anymore. Nor can she be simplified into the "sweet, unfortunate sick lady who just needs some help managing her medications." Most of her friends, five husbands and her sister have found reasons not to be a part of Mom's life. I spend time trying to figure out how to be less involved, too. Reviewing Mom's options for care, I'm reminded we live in Texas, home of the crap of the crop of social benefits. Because Mom owns a car worth more than four thousand dollars, and she's tied to the income of her estranged-for-ten-years husband, she can't qualify for Medicaid. Which doesn't really matter, because the kind of care that would work for her, assisted living, falls into a gap in Medicaid services. Medicaid might pay for a nursing home, but Mom can't receive hospital-prescribed home health services because her home is an "unsafe environment" due to her history of overmedicating. Mom refuses the one option insurance would pay for, chemical dependency treatment. In her words, she's "been there, done that." I think I understand her refusal. The meds she's supposed to take give her tremors and make her feel like a forgotten Styrofoam box of takeout food baking in the hot sun in the back seat. The meds she'd be denied at a treatment center are the ones that make her feel great. And the hospital visits that cause me disruption and pain don't seem to upset her much, as long as there's coffee in the morning and the TV works. Once she's lucid enough to dislike the hospital, she's released and sent home. Mom is the one person who doesn't express worry about her debilitation. She wants to be left alone with her pills. Being discharged and home is fine with her.

I drive her home and tell her I'll call later to check on her.

IV.

At home I sink into the couch and check out the nightly belly show, watching my abdomen contort and flicker as the boy completes his evening of watery interpretive dance. I sip decaf coffee wishing for a full-fledged latte. I visualize doing my pregnancy yoga. I carry my little Boston terrier around in the baby sling for practice. My thoughts spin around work and money and painting and writing and asking my boss to let me take a six-month leave of absence.

People ask me what I'm going to do after the baby comes, as if I should be preparing for the apocalypse. Finally I've learned to say, "I don't know." I imagine I'll take fewer long baths and spend a lot less time in coffee shops thinking big thoughts. I'll spend less time at corporate work and more time in nurturing work. I'll feel more vulnerable. I'll earn less money. I'll have a view into love I've never experienced before. Maybe I'll learn to keep my house neat, or at least free of pieces of fuzz that could prove toxic. I don't know. I do know how I feel now. I feel great about the prospect of being a mom. I am learning to breathe and walk slowly away after flipping through *Martha Stewart Baby* at the checkout stand.

V.

She's in the hospital again. Out of town for a couple of days, I return to phone messages saying where she is, and would I please call. I burst into tears, not part of my usual hospital routine. She sounds lucid on the phone, very lucid. No real surprises in the story of the hospitalization: She couldn't move. She called her friend. Her friend brought her to the hospital a couple of days ago. The doctors think there is something wrong with her medications.

"Maybe something wrong with my lithium," she says. "Can you believe that? . . . And I was wondering if you could bring me some clothes, and my dental floss, and the rest of my purse, and some underwear. I don't have any underwear." Her no-underwear situation bores into me. My tough-love resolve—*Let her deal with the hospital on her own,* I was thinking, *maybe my attending her hospital visits is enabling her*—dissolves in the face of her being without the simple dignity of underwear.

"I'll come visit tonight after my childbirth class."

Now I'm tired and passionless. It is ten o'clock when I get to the hospital. Mom greets me like we're reuniting over a nice lunch. It is as if one of us has been in Europe for a month.

"Oh honey, let me see you," she says, arms outstretched. I walk toward her, but back away from letting her touch me. She wants to pat the belly, and I don't let her. My withdrawal surprises me.

"Are you mad at me?" Mom asks. "I want this baby to know me. Let me give him a grandmotherly pat."

More tears. "This baby does know you," I say. "He knows you as the woman who upsets his mother, the woman who we visit in the hospital over and over again, the woman who makes his mom cry."

I feel distinctly out of my mind.

"I cannot do this anymore. I have been living with your crazy life for at least twenty-five years now, and I'm not going to drag this boy through it, too. I'm at the bottom of my well for being able to deal with the pain you create in your life with your bizarre choices. And then you expect me to be a caregiver and supporter.

"I want you to take some responsibility for your life, and to see that these hospitalizations are a pattern. It's always some medication problem, either admittedly a suicide attempt or some mysterious medication interaction. I want you to admit you can't manage your own medications. I want you to get some help, and to set up a situation where the people who care about you don't have to always be wondering if you're lying in your own vomit in your house. Or even worse, that those people don't have to get to the point where they think they don't care if you're lying in your own vomit in your house. I want you to get some help. Either treatment, or at least set up some in-home care or an assisted living situation where there is some supervision. I am not on call for you anymore."

"You don't trust me with my medications?" she asks quietly, after a pause.

I hold back the urge to laugh at what seems like a ridiculous question. Then I swing over to feeling like I've said too much, hit too hard. "No, I don't."

"Well, I'll think about that. The doctors are going to tell me what's wrong tomorrow and then it'll be fixed."

"Do you really think that's true, Mom? That this time the doctors will have some insight into your situation that will change things and stop these hospitalizations? Is that what you've thought at the end of every hospitalization for the last twenty-five years? That doctors will

come to some conclusions that will lead to you getting better and re-
suming life?"

After a long pause, she says yes, that is how she sees it. I retreat from
the dialogue, defeated by the weight of her denial. I extract a promise
from her to get one of those 911 necklaces so she can call an ambulance
from anywhere in her house if she feels unable to move again. I know
she won't do it. We part cordially, and I go home.

Mom goes home the next day, with the doctors ruling the cause of
hospitalization as lithium overdose.

"I was taking it as prescribed," Mom says.

VI.

Mom's kept herself out of the hospital for a few weeks now, long enough
for me to realize that what felt like a cruel outburst at her was probably
a long-overdue truth-telling. We talked the other day. She said it must
be frustrating dealing with someone like her. "I know you're going to be
a great mom, unlike me," she said.

"I'm reading a book on manic-depression, and hoping I can stay
flat enough between now and when your baby's born that you'll let me
hold him," she continues. I try to let myself hear her words without
suspicion or cynicism.

We've had similar periods of insight. They've always been short-
lived, and coming down off them is so hard. But maybe this time . . . I
read somewhere that mental illnesses can actually calm as a person ages.

"I'd say there's a pretty good probability of that." I try to sound like
I believe it.

How it must be to live life like Mom does, full of unconnected
scenes, inexplicable betrayals dished out and taken in and then these
sharp moments of understanding how much has been lost. Instinctively,

the little girl inside me starts making plans to help Mommy feel better. Then my maternal side intervenes to keep that little girl from getting her hopes up.

VII.

I am terrified of carrying my mom's world into my baby's life. I wonder if I am already broken as a mom. Clearly I received little mothering; can I expect to be capable of giving it? These questions pry open whole rooms of sadness, showing my own lost hopes of a happy childhood. I wilt with grief as I poke around the scenes of lonely impotence. I ache under the disappointment of broken promises. The more I feel passionate love for my child, the more I mourn receiving so little of it myself. Yet I was loved by my mother, however imperfectly. There were times when Mom acted like a mom. And perhaps more importantly, I continue to love her. However imperfectly. I have a great marriage, close friends, and now there is the loving presence of my husband's family. I have a track record of doggedly pressing myself, through therapy and inner exploration, to stay open to love. I so passionately want to meet and hold my baby. I draw his tiny face in the air with my hands, tracing the shape of his eyes and the curves of his soft body. I imagine looking in my husband's eyes after we have each felt this boy made of us. I can't wait to show all the sweetness of this life to him. I fiercely want to protect him from everything else.

The other day I was finishing up the dinner dishes after my husband had gone out for the evening. Standing at the sink, I became aware of the distinct sensation of being watched. Frightened at first, I soon relaxed and smiled, realizing I wasn't being watched, but rather joined, by the spirit of the boy in my belly. It was as if he were standing on a chair beside me, helping. I laughed and welcomed him in.

Bᴏᴍʙ Tʜʀᴇᴀᴛ

Alex McCall

When the call came in, I didn't immediately recognize my daughter's preschool director on the phone line, as her normally booming, authoritative voice was reduced to a panicked stutter: "*A bomb . . . daycare center . . . come now!*" I dropped the phone, knocking over my mug of vile office coffee onto the stupid memo I was reading. I took flight, pausing only to screech, "I have to go—bomb—at the daycare!" in the direction of my boss's office. Heads popped over cubicle walls, shouting questions: "Is this for real, Alex?" and "Where's the bomb?" but I did not stop to listen. I burst through the door and out onto the street, trying to remember to breathe.

Sprinting the ten blocks to Sarah's daycare, I tried to talk myself out of believing this was really happening: Denver is a sleepy cow town, not a Middle-Eastern demilitarized zone. It must be a prank—who would bomb a cruddy old government building, and why? It simply cannot happen here, it can't.

For three years, my life had been devoted to my daughter, my every thought to her safety and well-being. I had chosen this daycare for all the right reasons: small class size and individual attention, the close proximity to my office. Sarah loved this school because we ride the 16th Street Mall shuttle to get there. That her daycare was in a mammoth, neoclassical building housing some heavy-duty federal government offices did not make much of an impression on me, aside from my occasional surreptitious drooling over the cute uniformed types traipsing in and out of the recruiting offices.

I hurtled up the city streets, yelling "Move it!" at people, cars, dogs, street signs and lampposts in my way. Lights flashed, and sirens could be heard two blocks away from the Federal Building. When I rounded the corner, I saw a sea of cops, firemen, EMTs and federal marshals, bellowing through bullhorns and trying to organize a screaming stream of office workers out of the building. TV news crews were out in force, the reporters and cameramen jostling and jockeying for interviews with hassled cops and fleeing workers. A crowd of random people gathered behind police tape, necks craning for a clear view. Police stood in the streets, directing traffic away from the area and people out of the way of the fire trucks and SWAT vehicles. A news helicopter circled overhead, giving the whole scene a surreal, Hollywood feel—except for the palpably real terror on the faces of men and women rushing by.

Panicked, anxious and dizzy with adrenaline, I pushed through the crowd, searching for faces of kids, teachers, anyone recognizable. I made my way up the steep front stairs to the main doors, where I stood in line to present ID and go through a metal detector. As precious minutes passed while I stood outside waiting, my efforts to appear calm and collected quickly dissolved. Pleading for information, demanding information, brought forth no help: "There's been a threat on the building" was the only answer I could get from the officers standing sentry at the entrance like cowboy sheriffs, hands on their gun belts.

Hoping to make an end run around the security measures, I mentioned my employer, a popular Denver alternative newspaper, to the officer inspecting my ID. He reddened, handed my wallet back and yelled at the impatient line for all press to wait outside. Shaking now, my breathing thin and labored, I lost my shit. *"My kid is in there! Let me in! Get out of my damn way!"* I felt a cold dread start in the roots of my hair, my brain screaming in my ears. What had I done? "Please, I'm sorry. Just let me in!" After a tense renegotiation and some angry shouting from the people behind me in line, I proceeded quietly through the metal detector and pat-down, wisely electing not to respond to the muttered comments and accusatory glances beamed my way. It occurred to me that broadcasting my affiliation with a left-wing newspaper known for its radical politics was maybe not such a good idea, under the circumstances.

Down a long, empty hallway I ran to the ancient elevator at the far end and jumped in, startling the FBI agent inside. When all you want to do is go apeshit, just breathing in and out becomes a difficult imperative. I stared at the gap in the door, willing the elevator to move at light speed, instead of its usual molasses-slow. *Come on, come on, come on!* The Fed cleared his throat and shifted his weight from foot to foot, causing the floor to creak loudly. I asked him what the hell he thought was going on. "A bomb threat was called in," he quietly replied, looking me over suspiciously.

Somebody better give me my kid, or I'll show you threats, I thought to myself, as I sprinted out of the elevator and through the daycare's door. The basement was jarringly calm and quiet. The only indication of the chaos outside was the presence of several armed policemen milling around the daycare office with walkie-talkies pressed to their ears. The director looked like she might spontaneously combust. She saw me, cocked her head toward a closed door and made a check on her clipboard. The kids were in the lunchroom, their teachers leading them in loud, silly songs. I caught the tail end of "The Wheels on the Bus." By the first refrain of "The Itsy Bitsy Spider," I found Sarah sitting cross-legged on the floor. She jumped in my arms and we hugged, tightly. A great sigh whooshed out of me. *By God, if there is a bomb, we'll go together. We're together now. It's okay, we're together.*

Sarah stared wide-eyed at the policemen directing us through another gauntlet of metal detectors and ID-flashing at the building's rear entrance. When I lifted her onto my back, I heard her gasp at the spectacle unfolding outside. We managed to avoid most of the commotion, and walked slowly back to my office. I tried to remain calm, for her sake. Sarah wanted to know what was going on, so we talked about the policemen and the excitement going on around her school. "Remember when that kid pulled the fire alarm by accident a while back, and the firemen came in their trucks?" I asked her. "Someone played a very bad trick at your school today, honey." I wondered if there really was a bomb in Denver, if we could get away in time. A bomb in the centrally located Federal Building would surely wipe out the whole city, I guessed. We walked on, wandering through masses of suits and secretaries emptying out of high-rise buildings along the way.

People on the street were talking about Oklahoma City, about a bomb and dead babies at a preschool there. A pit of fire opened in me, and everything inside tried to whirlpool out. *What kind of person bombs a preschool? Denver, or Oklahoma City, ain't Beirut, for Chrissakes. What the fuck is going on in this world?*

Back at the newspaper's office, my co-workers gathered around my desk. Our reporters were anxious to hear about the scene I'd witnessed: Was there a bomb in Denver? What was the connection with Oklahoma

City? Were any arrests imminent? What were the Feds doing to find the terrorists responsible? Were they locals? A militia? I didn't know, didn't care. My mind was focused on retrieving my precious soul, my kid. My reporter's instincts went out the window. My boss, the incredibly fabulous editor and fellow working mom, understood: I would be going home for the day.

I splurged on the way home, McDonald's and beer. Everywhere, people were talking about Oklahoma City. The liquor store clerk barely registered our existence, so engrossed was he in listening to his radio, listening to reports of casualties, theories being bandied about. Back at our little duplex, I tucked Sarah into bed for a nap with a forced-cheerful reading of *Lyle, Lyle, Crocodile* and an extra-long hug. I grabbed a beer and sat on the sofa. I was still jumpy, too anxious to focus on day-to-day stuff, like the *"past due," "final notice," "law offices of"* letters piled on my coffee table. I wanted to shut it all out, but couldn't. I flipped on the TV.

Tom Brokaw, his face a map of furrows, was cuing footage from Oklahoma City. The scene was a slow-pan of a building, looking very much like the Federal Building here in Denver, only ripped in half, its guts of drywall and steel beams hanging in shreds. My belly tightened into a knot. The camera traveled over firefighters and other workers there, sifting through massive piles of concrete rubble and twisted steel, carrying dust-covered and bloody bodies out of the wreckage. Dozens of families were shown, screaming, crying, railing at the sky. Then, a close-up shot of a young mother, white with shock, waiting in unimaginable desperation for news of her two little boys. Over and over, the talking heads muttered words like "terrorist act," "tragedy," "senseless" and "dead." I turned off the set and curled up into a ball on the sofa, sobbing quietly so as not to wake my baby.

LINEAGE

Jessica Rigney

The day my ten-month-old son woke from his nap and didn't want to settle back down to nurse as he had been doing for the past weeks, something in me snapped. I tried to coax him down, holding him gently near, pulling his face close to my breast. He kept getting up, walking off from the napping place I'd made for him on the floor. I don't remember how many times I retrieved him. He cried out of frustration, I out of exhaustion and confusion. I wept, surprisingly loud by his side, unable to cope with his refusal to stay down for a nap. My crying came forcefully, for I believe it was ten months and several years in coming.

My thoughts turned from my own self-pity to sadness for my son. How could he be given a mother like me? How could I manage to raise him without crumbling into a sobbing mess at the slightest change in his development? What saved us that day alone was the late-summer wind moving over our country plot. We lived in an old, converted schoolhouse planted in the middle of corn and soybean fields. Doubled over with sobs, and my son's scared cries in my ear, I carried him. I carried us both through the fields, down to the creek and all over our land. I walked to save myself. I walked until my husband came home from another long day, for in the back of my mind I held my grandmother's suicide and my mother's contemplation of suicide. I feared it could grip me, too.

Some things, you figure, are as they are because of where you came from. I had assumed I would be a good mother because I wanted so badly to be a good mother, but I knew where I came from. Soon after that day with my son, I found myself crying again in the bathroom with my husband. I pleaded in his arms, "What's wrong with me?" Daily, my son's cries set off a chain reaction: I tried to stop the cries, feeling guilty for not knowing exactly what to do, wished for him to stop and then felt sorry for myself and ashamed that I couldn't simply allow him his own set of emotions. I entered therapy and cried the entire first session. Slowly I began to piece together my mothering lineage. With my therapist, I turned over events in my memory. I started asking my mother questions. I examined nightmares that still woke me from my sleep with a struggle for breath. And with my son playing by my side during therapy sessions, I started climbing out from under the story. This is how it goes.

My grandmother, Lillian, married Frank at nineteen. They both came from Polish families. Seven months later my mother was born, the first of five children. On March 28, 1948, when Frank came home late at night from his job as a Chicago police officer, he put his gun away in the bedroom closet. By the time he'd walked to the kitchen, Lillian had climbed out of bed, pointed at her abdomen and shot once. She was twenty-six. My mother, in the bedroom down the hall with her sister and brothers, was a few months shy of six.

My mother doesn't remember hearing the gunshot; she does remember hearing voices in her parents' bedroom and knowing her mother was dead. Still in bed, she began crying. An uncle entered her bedroom and asked, "What are you crying about?" She answered him, "I'm crying because my mommy's dead." The uncle simply said, "Don't be silly, go back to sleep." This is just the beginning of what was not said to my mother. At Lillian's funeral my mother was slapped with the truth of that night when a neighborhood kid came up to her and asked, "Is it true your mom shot herself in the stomach?" She looked at her mother lying in the coffin in a long pink gown with pink shoes to match. Someone had painted her fingernails. My mother remembers the polish in clear detail and is still saddened by it, placed on her mother's hands by people who did not know her, did not know her nails were never polished.

My mother, her sister and two of her three brothers were taken into Frank's mother's care while her infant brother, Tom, was given to a cousin for a year. Frank remarried a year after Lillian's death. During that time, my mother played outside and looked for a new mother. She watched and talked to a woman who walked down their street every day on her way to work. One day my mother was brave enough to tell the woman, "You look a lot like my mommy." The woman walked on the other side of the street from that day on, as if suicide were contagious. I wonder if this is where the legacy of silence began, though surely it was earlier, otherwise Lillian might have found a way to speak about her desire to leave this world and might have been saved. These days such avoidance is called denial, but back then it was considered normal: "We just don't talk about these things." Who can say why Lillian killed herself?

When I entered therapy, not only did I have to overcome the habit of keeping my feelings to myself, I also needed to rid myself of a serious "perfect mother" affliction. Though I chose to stay home with my son, a decision I considered ultra-feminist, I also believed I had to be with him at all times. In my mind, leaving him for even an hour would constitute abandonment. I had visions of my own toddler days in the 1970s when I was left to cry myself to sleep. I can recall the exact dimensions of my playpen with its off-white vinyl bottom covered in funky gold-star and glitter graphics. The nylon mesh had holes large enough for me to hang my fingers and toes along the sides as I changed positions, oddly comforted by the feel of the fabric touching my skin.

As a new mother, I read Jean Liedloff's *The Continuum Concept* with recognition. She describes the ache new mothers feel in their chest when their babies cry—an ache most intense in women who were left to cry as infants themselves. I felt that ache in my chest like an enormous boulder crushing my breath. I carried my son in a sling to prevent him from crying. I nursed him at the slightest whimper and changed his diaper at the first sign of wetness. My determination was fueled by the desire to secure for him a childhood free of emotional want. I worked desperately to "fix" things so my family's life could be idyllic, but I had never been taught how to integrate my emotions into my life. With little to draw from in her own experience, my mother was unable to instill this ability in her children. After her own mother's death, her life's silences multiplied.

When my mother was thirteen, she began waitressing and by sixteen she was a floor girl at Woolworth's, handling the day's cash and register tapes. During this time, she attended church and "sex education" classes with small groups of other girls. Taught by a new, young priest who felt the teenagers weren't getting the information they needed, separate classes were held for the boys and girls. The classes later became individualized and physical. My mother "learned" from the priest but also loved him. The children in these classes didn't discuss them, and the parents, of course, knew nothing about them. By the time my mother was eighteen she'd switched jobs again but had managed to save over six hundred dollars to move away from home. Living the single life, all she really wanted was to marry and have children. After a couple of years, she turned to the priest for comfort, and they began dating. No longer her teacher, he took her to fine restaurants, bought her clothes, paid for weekend stints in hotels but when pressed for marriage, he claimed he could never leave the church. He had the perfect excuse to avoid commitment, but my mother became pregnant. She told the priest it was his baby, and it very well could have been—she didn't know for sure.

My mother told her family she was being sent to New York to receive job training for a year. Instead, she packed, bleached her dark hair blond and moved five miles away to carry the baby. The priest helped out now and then, but my mother found herself alone at home partway through her pregnancy with incredible back pains, watching the news of JFK's assassination. She gave birth a few months later in a hospital where the nurses called her Goldilocks and made sure she knew that giving birth out of wedlock was unforgivable. The priest did not come to the hospital. Instead, he sent a friend to give her a blessing and communion, and helped arrange a gray-market adoption for her baby boy.

Accompanied by a friend of the adopting parents, she checked out of the hospital with the baby. She relinquished her baby in the middle of an unrecognizable parking lot. Two weeks later she had to sign the adoption papers at a lawyer's office. Still full with milk, her breasts began leaking as she signed, saturating her blouse and the cheap fur coat she wore that day. She tossed the coat away, not even bothering to try to clean it. The adoption papers specified six month's time for her to change her mind. She never did.

Shortly after, when my mother finally did marry and settle into one of the brand-new suburbs north of Chicago, she had three more children, me being the middle one. She was told she'd pass on her allergies if she breast-fed, so all of us were given bottles. She heard from her doctor, from the "experts," how we would learn to self-soothe if left to cry in our cribs, so we were. This was how it was done, she tells me as she recalls having to leave the house to sit and cry on the front stoop while I wailed away inside in my crib. But in that small country town, she gave us a childhood with potential to be more than what she had been, growing up in Chicago. We woke on summer mornings to don bathing suits, head out the back door and explore the lake in our backyard. We learned about bluegills, turtles, crayfish and blue herons. I marked my own triumphs over fear by mucking around knee-deep in seaweed and mud to look for clams, while my mother never attempted to learn to swim. I rode my bike barefoot to the park without worry and reveled in the pure laziness of watering the garden with the hose while seated high up on a sturdy tree branch nearby.

As I approached age twelve, my mother gave my sister and me her version of a sex talk: She told us about the priest. She wasn't so much concerned that we'd have sex and get pregnant—though that was understood to be bad—but that we would perhaps, in some weird and twisted way, meet up with our half brother and end up dating him. Maybe even falling in love with him, marrying and bearing his children.

This was my most memorable conversation with my mother. I sat there, coping with prepubescent hormones, my greatest worry being how often I changed my tampon to avoid the newly discovered toxic shock syndrome, as my mother spoke the truth about her life for once. I ate it up as I finger-spooned Cheez Whiz from a jar into my mouth. I wanted to know so many details at the time, but it was one of those moments when you just sit there and listen, knowing if you dare speak the conversation will be abandoned. It has taken my mother fifteen years to let it unfold over glasses of vodka and ice, and I'm not so sure I've heard it all.

Following my mother's example, I kept my own brand of secrets. How could I not? In the home my parents created for us, emotions were downplayed or ignored and when fights broke out between siblings or parent and child; hurtful words soaked into the walls, never to be washed away by apology. Once over, it was done. From my mother's perspective, it's easy to understand how this evolved—things were just too painful to discuss.

When I was nineteen and pregnant, I never considered having the baby, never considered telling my mother. I never told her of the abortion either, for then everyone in the family would know but nothing would be said, and I'd still be dealing with it alone. I cried alone in my room and began writing down what was inside me so it would have a place to go.

Setting goals for myself was confusing as I waded through a mishmash of hidden truths, leftover female expectations from my mother's era and a desire to live comfortably yet independently. I went to college because it was assumed I would, though I chose to take an hour-long train ride into Chicago each day to attend a college with an urban mix of students. This is where time seemed to fold back over itself. I had seen photos of my mother in her years before marriage and children, outfitted finely in work dresses and pumps, walking along the sidewalks of Chicago. I found the face of my grandmother, Lillian, on her wedding day and recognized the curve of her nose and eyebrows in my own. As I walked between classes, my shoes click-clacking along the sidewalk, I was my mother in her city sophistication; I was my grandmother in her innocent beauty. At home one night, my mother brought out old seventy-eight-speed records that Lillian had recorded and sent to Frank during World War II. I had never heard my grandmother's voice before. In the instant the needle of the Victrola player rested on the record, her young voice poured out singing "I'm Nobody's Baby" and I felt time compress. Lillian's voice, my mother's voice and my voice were all the same in tone and masked sadness.

But it wasn't until years later, in the moment when I birthed my own baby at home in a pool of warm water, that I began to feel the true weight of our intertwining stories. The very real pain during the birth of my son felt like a kind of truth that I craved. I had never before felt "heard." In the moments I spent up on my knees in the water, pushing my son down into this world, my grunts and moans took on a deep, guttural quality that could only signify great change. Even so, I like to tell pregnant friends expecting their first, "That was the easy part."

By the time my son's first birthday arrived, I'd had a good dozen sessions of therapy; I was ready to make the first, miniscule reintegration of our family's heritage into my life. Passed down from my parents' families is an Eastern European ritual so old no one remembers its origin. On a baby's first birthday, after the cake, gifts and other routine celebrations, the baby is placed in a highchair and presented with three objects: a dollar bill, a shot glass and a rosary. Sometimes a book is added to the collection. The child's future is told by which object he picks up. The money tells of a future full of material riches; the shot glass foretells a troubled life of addiction; the rosary predicts a life serving God on a spiritual path. A photograph shows me at my first birthday with the rosary clenched between fists and mouth. Given my mother's experience with the priest, I have always had mixed feelings about this tradition.

My mother came to my son's birthday party with a dollar, a shot glass and a rosary in her purse. In a brave and shaky voice, I announced a new twist on the old tradition. I wanted to preserve the ritual but change the somewhat confining possibilities offered by the traditional objects by replacing them with more life-affirming items. My sister and I placed my son atop two pillows on a dining-room chair. In a circle before him we positioned a rock, a feather, a shell and a piece of wood fallen from a tree.

To disbelieving stares I described the four elements of the universe and the great powers they possess: "The rock is earth and patience. It is forgiving, dependable and always enduring. The feather is air, the realm of the mind, always curious to understand the true nature of things. The shell is water, fluid, accepting and tolerant. The wood represents fire's passion and the ability to foster love of life." My son reached out with delight and grasped the feather tight in his small hand. In an almost perceptible whoosh of air, time expanded and my chest filled with a deep, boulder-lifting breath.

Days earlier I had remarked to my therapist in one particularly difficult session that I was so tired of doing the work, that I realized the true breadth of my task was to overcome two generations, perhaps three, of emotionally distant mothering. I told her that once, when I was a teenager, my mother admitted to me that she'd contemplated suicide when my younger brother was an infant. She faced his severe allergies, illnesses and learning disabilities while also caring for my sister and me. Just like her mother, she found herself alone the better part of most days while my father worked long hours. She had planned to kill both herself and my brother. How was I supposed to ingest that information?

On another day, I came to therapy with the news that my uncle had just shot himself in the head. He was the infant son that Lillian had left behind. I wondered out loud what she would think of this ironic twist in her children's lives. Though I barely knew my uncle, I wasn't shocked at all. Oddly enough, I think everyone in our extended family was just waiting to see who would do it next.

I didn't want to be next. I wanted change. And I wanted to be able to speak openly about the reality of my life. Turning over the events that made up my mothering lineage helped me see more clearly how my grandmother and mother had made their own choices. Instead of feeling the pattern of familial suicide as an inevitable doom hovering in the back of my mind, I could see my life as separate from theirs. During trying moments with my son, I could hold him, telling him I loved him over and over, crying with him. Even if he didn't understand what I was saying, I could tell him what I was feeling.

Perhaps the most painful part of my transformation included the realization that if I wanted to change how I interacted with my son, I had to change how I interacted with my mother. If you asked her when this occurred, she would probably speak of the sudden lack of phone calls and our confrontations about events in my childhood. I clung to anger for a time and refused to keep my mouth shut. Miraculously, she began talking more, telling me more about her feelings, asking me more about mine. Somehow, after a couple of years, we found a way back to each other, but I am a different daughter than before. I can't pinpoint the day I felt free of my neurotic, suicidal lineage; it lifted a little at a time, and only because I did the work to push it off.

EDGING

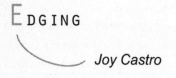

Joy Castro

When the baby was born, Jeff and I were living in a barrio in San Antonio. I was a year from graduating, and he worked nights as a security guard at a power plant. Two hundred dollars a month rented a makeshift apartment in an old two-story house, with a chin-high General Electric refrigerator that needed weekly defrosting and an oven you could only light with a rolled-up newspaper. This is not nostalgia for decades ago; I am not that old. It was 1990, and we were dirt poor.

The most pervasive memory I have of that time is the sense of insecurity—the screaming and slamming in the apartment below—Adam and Diana, nineteen and eighteen, with a two-year-old daughter and a newborn son, all wedged into a kitchen, bath and bedroom with no air conditioning, just one rattling fan. Or the night Jeff ran into the street with his gun tucked into his jeans while I stood on the terrace dialing 911 and hushing Grey on my hip—a woman screaming rape down the block (and shrieking at the cops, "Don't leave me here! Don't *leave* me!" after they had taken her report; the car pulled slowly from the curb, the officer's profile flashing red and blue as he shook his thick face at her). Not being able to play in the yard with Grey—scraps of metal embedded in the dirt, hidden beneath grass, beer can shims silvering the driveway, broken glass lacing the sidewalk cracks, old rubbers shimmering under the stairs. The tense conversations every two weeks when we decided which bills to pay and which to put off with a token five dollars. In line at the checkout counter, waiting until the last possible moment to pull out the food stamps, not looking in anyone's face. The pathetic guilt when we borrowed coins from the baby's piggy bank to do the laundry.

I remember at Christmas we visited friends just for the evening, and when we returned our pipes had frozen, had broken. Icy slush across the torn linoleum. (Two old gas heaters, neither with a grate; we had to turn them off when we left for fear of fire. Eleven houses burned down in the two years we lived in that neighborhood.) We stayed for three nights in one of the guest rooms of a fellow student and friend. Alexis had a whole house to herself in Alamo Heights while she finished at St. Mary's, a seventh-year junior, living off her father. She looked not quite at me, but at a spot above the wide-screen TV: "I mean, it's nothing about *you* guys, it's just the *baby*, you know. He just gets on my—well, he's just so *active*, you know. I mean, I guess one more night would be okay, but after that—well, I mean, I'm sure y'all have lots of other friends that wouldn't mind . . . " We had sixty-four cents between us and no family on this side. She left to buy a quarter bag and rent a couple of movies, and the two of us sat numbly on the sofa, holding hands and saying nothing, until Grey toddled over and we felt guilty at the worry in his little face.

Insecurity, yes, and bitterness, too. And fear like an old coin in the side of your mouth—so familiar you forget, and then a wash of metal floods your tongue.

A block up and a block over was the Stop-N-Go, where we'd some-times buy milk, and every payday two cold lemonades, and sit on the curb with all the *vatos* and their beer, laughing at the funny things Grey did. And next door was the laundromat where we did wash on Sundays.

It happened on a miserably hot, bright, humid day around a hun-dred and eight. We had lingered over the folding that morning for the air conditioning, taking turns pushing the baby around in the wheeled baskets between the rows of washers, the faded plastic plants. It had been quiet when we left.

We saw it on the news that night and in the *Light* the next day. A little boy, three, and his father (a nondescript Latino male, is how the papers always put it) were standing together on the sidewalk with their paper cups of Coke, talking. A woman pulled in to get iced tea. Did her foot slip from the brake to the accelerator? Did a sudden spasm in her leg make her slam it down? She couldn't say. She couldn't speak to the microphone waving in her face. She couldn't speak; her car jumped the curb and severed the child in half against the lower shelf edge of a pay phone. His father was less than two feet away.

A bulletin board has hung over my desk through four or five moves now, and the clipping about the boy and his father hung there for about three years, slowly yellowing and curling. "'We were just talking about tadpoles, how they grow up to be frogs,' he told reporters. 'I was so close, I had just patted him on the head, and then—'" I would read it and read it, imagining that helplessness, the emptiness of the arms that weren't fast enough. The punishment that would never end; the edges would rub and rub and one day be soft, but soft like the shape of a mouth that opens to moan, and smeared the way edges of objects blur just before tears. A grief like the fish in the bottom of the boat that won't stop gasping long enough to die, and you hate it for not dying, for making you watch it helplessly flopping. And then when it dies, you double up on the floor of the boat and wail.

Some truths, I think, can wait. I took the clipping down when Grey started reading and pinned in its place a blank white sheet from a memo pad. I would look at it and hear the words roll by in my inner ear.

This morning in the predawn hours after bringing my son home from the hospital, I am staring at that clean white square, so precise and sterile amid the surrounding jumble. I'd been brushing my teeth before bed, and he'd rushed in to show me a drawing. I turned to look, and instead I saw him spin and fall and smash his face on the rim of the porcelain tub. Saw the chin, the neck, the chest drenching blood, the gape of mouth, the bewildered eyes and terror. The long scream down the highway, Grey terrified of the lights, the strangers, the blood, of my fear. But he's safe, *safe*—my son is safe in his bed at last with painkillers and small stitches. And the beauty of medical insurance tolls like a soft, sweet chime at three in the morning as I stare at that empty white square and hear his light breathing in the next room. I'm living the inescapable wrench in the stomach, the cavern in the chest, the breaths that bring no air, knowing that the difference between that empty whiteness and the one he'd leave behind is that there would be no edges, no boundaries, no place my hands would not keep reaching out in search of him.

NEONATAL SWEET POTATO

Ayun Halliday

Salad Bin

My baby's bassinet in the neonatal intensive care unit looks like one of the large plastic bins we used to store lettuce at Dave's Italian Kitchen in Evanston, Illinois. It is lined with a number of hospital-issue baby blankets, expertly folded to perform a variety of functions—anchor the crib sheets, warm the tiny occupant, form a horseshoe around the eggshell head. The burgundy and turquoise stripes that edge the white blanket make me think of Mother Teresa's order, nuns in homespun saris. I steal one of the blankets to cuddle and cling to on the nights when I am in bed on the maternity ward and baby is in her salad bin one flight below. But I don't think blanket stealing is limited to the parents of intensive care babies. Ever since I became a mother, not a week goes by that I don't notice some other woman carrying one of Mother Teresa's baby novices. There are too many for all of them to have passed through the neonatal intensive care unit. But just in case,

I search the parent's face, veteran to veteran, to find out if they've seen combat too.

Grandparents
I am sitting beside my baby's salad bin, watching her sleep, when Baby Wickline's grandparents arrive. Baby Wickline is not looking so good; he's been put in an incubator, the same kind that house the tiny shaved monkey preemies. Somehow, this looks more grim, his strapping ten-pound form encased in this plastic box. He is asleep when his grandparents arrive unescorted from upstate New York. They look healthy, cultured. I guess they look like my parents, who don't look like grandparents to me. Not the way grandparents looked when I was a little kid.

The new grandparents stand shoulder to shoulder, gazing at Baby Wickline through the plastic walls of his box. They look like the couple who doesn't know anyone else at the party, standing awkwardly by the punch bowl, trying to think of things to say to each other.

"Well, there he is," the grandfather announces in a bluff, uncertain voice.

They can't touch him. Twin portholes in the sides of the box allow the nurses to reach in and do their business, but this is a hospital and Baby Wickline's grandparents don't want to touch anything without permission. They're unsure of how to proceed. They look but there's no one to congratulate, no mommy who's looking wonderful, no daddy to tease, no baby to hold, give him to me, come here you, hello, hello, I'm your grandma, that's who I am, yes, I am, yes I am.

They just look at him. And finally, without speaking, Baby Wickline's grandfather pulls a tiny camera out of his windbreaker and bends his knees so that the incubator won't obstruct the view. You can tell he's the kind of man who once embarrassed the hell out of his kids, making them pose in front of the Grand Canyon and Cinderella's Castle for what seemed like hours while he tried to figure out the workings of his pocket Instamatic. He makes his way around the incubator, shooting from every conceivable angle.

His wife has been looking around the NICU, hoping that no one is watching her husband's lumbering efforts. A dozen or so frames, and she can't take it anymore. "That's enough!" she hisses. "Put that camera away! Put it away!"

Her husband is confused. "What?" he says, blinking as he pulls the little camera away from his eye.

"I don't want Sherry to see him like this!" Baby Wickline's grandmother glares at her husband while gesturing angrily at the baby in the bin. "Put it away! You've got enough! Put it away!"

Her husband straightens back up to his full height and says, with great dignity, "I'm not taking them for Sherry. I want them for myself."

This story chokes me up every time, even though a few days later I witnessed the triumphant departure of Baby Wickline, who exited the NICU in six-month-sized shorts.

Bless you, Grandfather of Baby Wickline. Bless you and your shameless Instamatic. Bless you for reaching into your wallet and fishing out a picture with your big bearlike paws, a picture of a large baby looking pale and disoriented in a covered plastic salad bin. Bless you and bless your wife and give her strength when the soufflés fall and hems come unstitched and the mail gets returned and the pictures don't come out right and something is wrong with the baby.

It's okay. It's okay. Everything's going to be okay.

Jung

At night, the fluorescent overheads are switched off and each baby's bin is spotlit. A few parents camp in scattered rocking chairs. Baby Wickline's father reads to his son from *How Proust Can Change Your Life*. The luckiest mothers get to rock their babies in their arms, their faces ecstatic, drunk from contact.

The nurses pad between the bins on their gum-soled, white nurse feet, bending to the babies like seraphim. The banks of monitors click and whir.

The babies lie still, their eyes closed, even the crack babies, breathing together, in and out, their tiny hearts pattering like the hearts of mice. Sleeping. Probably sleeping. Or maybe they're born knowing everything, and this is the time when they're busy erasing the tapes.

Jeremiah

I recognize one of the other intensive care mothers from the East Village. She is a tall, striking woman, about my age, her red hair wrapped in an enormous turban. She appears in the afternoons, holding the hand of her other child, a wild, corkscrew-haired two-year-old. I've seen her before, definitely, doing her groovy mother thing up and down First Avenue. I introduce myself and we become friendly right off the bat, jawing away like bunkmates at summer camp. She tells me how she planted her older son's placenta in her patch of the community garden at Sixth and B. She tells me how with this second birth, she'd been looking forward to delivering the placenta because it had felt sooooo good coming out the first time. Mm-hmmm! I remember the cool flop of the placenta, like a nice cold T-bone over a cartoon black eye. My friend didn't get to keep the placenta with this birth. They needed it in pathology.

"Do you know how much money hospitals make selling placentas?" my friend demands, not caring if the nurses hear.

Wow! I am thrilled to know this experienced, groovy single mother. Like me, she was transferred from the birthing center to the hospital when her labor slowed way down. Unlike me, who obediently dressed and climbed into a taxicab for the two-block ride, my friend was taken shouting, "Fuck you! Get away from me! I'm going home! I'll have this baby at home!"

Well, of course, that wasn't an option, and her birthing story ends with a doctor charging into the delivery room, shouting, "Hold on!" as he flipped her over like a pancake and reached up inside her with what my friend refers to with a shudder as "these hands," yanking the baby out. When she reached for her son, the nurses all shouted, "No! Don't touch him!" and whisked the baby away. Now the baby is here in intensive care and my friend visits every day, sometimes with her toddler, sometimes with her mother or father, who live on Long Island.

Her mother makes a big fuss over my baby, who lived for six days as Baby Girl Halliday before receiving a name. We had been so certain we were having a boy. "Oh India, what a lovely name! What a beautiful baby! I could tell she was a girl, even before you told me. She's very feminine, you see. Oh, let me hold her!"

My friend's mother holds India for almost an hour, very glad, I think, to be holding a baby, any baby. Her baby, my friend's baby, her grandson, lies on his back in his salad bin, and there are rules against picking him up. His head is carpeted with lush black fur, and he has big legs and big arms and a big wide nose. Strong cheekbones. He looks like he should be out cutting wood.

"Jeremiah," my friend's mother chirps, approaching his incubator with my baby in her arms, "this is India. Do you think they might grow up and marry each other? I had friends who did just that. 'How did you two meet?' I asked and they said to me, 'We met on the day we were born.' Well, not really you know, but they were born at the same hospital, and they were in the nursery at the same time, you see. So perhaps Jeremiah and India . . . "

Jeremiah, big Jeremiah, lies helplessly on his back, his limbs swollen from antibiotics, his eyelids puffed shut. India is on antibiotics, too, but she remains delicate, feminine, solemnly regarding Jeremiah's grandmother from her nest of hospital blankets. Jeremiah is nude. The nurses will not let my friend diaper him. Instead, he wears a washcloth folded over his penis and every few hours, the washcloth is removed and weighed to determine his urine output, a homespun test in this high-tech world. Every so often he twitches as if he is having a seizure. He looks like he is being electrocuted. His mother and I don't talk about this. We talk about Asian healing therapies and restaurants we both like in the East Village.

One morning when my friend isn't there, I hear Jeremiah crying as a nurse tends to him. I am shocked. He is so big and hairy lying there without a diaper, his swollen limbs look so dense with muscle that I had forgotten he is a baby.

My friend tells me that she dreamed of Jeremiah before he was born. She dreamed of a big, strong baby with dark hair. She decided that if she had that baby she would name him Jeremiah. If she had another baby, she would name him something else.

I guess she had that baby.

Dawn of the Dead

Those of us on the maternity ward with babies in the neonatal intensive care unit are awakened several times a night to go feed our babies. I don't complain. For the first few days after India was born, I wasn't allowed to feed her. Instead, they woke me up three times a night to pump the milk out of my breasts with a hulking metal contraption that looked like a ticker-tape machine from 1929. Sometimes, pumping in the middle of the night, I would fall asleep, the hand holding the suctioning device against my body would slip, and I'd wake up to find a big red hickey on one of my boobs. So, now when they come for me, I bounce right up. I feel like I'm in *The Sound of Music,* the nuns gently shaking me awake so I can escape the Nazis.

At this time of night, there's not much going on. Sometimes I catch sight of a maintenance man swabbing the halls with a dirty-looking mop. Once, while waiting for the elevator at three in the morning, I hear the piteous groans of a woman in labor and burst into tears.

Other mothers glide into the intensive care unit rubbing their eyes. We don't speak. We sit in rockers, the shyer ones behind screens. We smile blissed-out, zombie smiles when the nurses deposit the swaddled packages in our arms. We make up nicknames for our babies, murmur encouragements in the hopes that they will eat up, that things will improve and we can go home. It hurts at first, but it's good, those little gums clamping on to our defenseless nipples.

What does it feel like? It feels like packing a snowball with your bare hands.

Hand Knit by Volunteers

One of the nurses, when her chores are finished, amuses herself by dressing her patients in baby clothes hand knit by volunteers. She stores them in a white plastic bag in a cupboard near the crack babies. Every so often, she dips into it for a fresh supply of shapeless booties and flesh-colored crocheted skullcaps that look so much like human breasts it's hard not to blush as she works them over the babies' heads. They're horrible, these baby clothes knit by volunteers. They stink of swap-meet handicrafts, plastic Southern-belle dolls in lumpy acrylic skirts,

Budweiser cans flattened and scalloped together with yarn to form vests.

How easy it is to conjure a mental image of the volunteer workforce. Kindly, soft-lapped grannies throwing their Social Security checks at the church offertory plate and the Woolworth's crafts counter. As the parent of an ailing baby, I must receive their output gracefully. I accept every flesh-colored booby hat, every unbearable afghan square, with a smile, cotton-mouthed. We all do.

This is how the two-pound, incubated preemie parked next to the wall comes to resemble a Q-tip, her twiglike legs poking out of clumsy pastel boots, her lemon-sized head trapped in a fluffy formless tam-o-shanter, its synthetic fibers glinting ominously under the bilirubin lights. This is a nurse's doing, not the parents'. Actually, this baby doesn't seem to have parents. I wonder what happened to them. Do they live too far away to visit, or are they teenagers who never wanted a baby to begin with? Do they work round-the-clock, or do they have so many children they can barely stay afloat? Or is it just too much for them? Where are this baby's parents? This baby doesn't have parents. She has a nurse—who enjoys dressing her up, and even changes her outfits sometimes, throwing the worn ones into the trash without ceremony. It's probably some health regulation, but even if it isn't, who'd want second-hand baby clothes from the neonatal intensive care unit? Especially these clothes, hand knit by volunteers.

Perspective

People always ask me if any of the babies in the ICU died. And the answer is no. Not while I was there. The babies lived, kept alive by some of the most sophisticated medical technology money can buy. Babies like the Q-tip would die without it. India would've died without antibiotics.

"Do you know how sick your baby was when she was brought in here?" one of the graveyard-shift nurses asks curiously as we stand shoulder to shoulder over India's bin late one night.

And the answer again is no. I didn't know. I guess if we'd had her in a cabin in Vermont, she would've died. Greg likes to remind me that I would've died, too. A hundred years ago, I would've died. But not now. The babies in the ICU didn't die. The isolation room where I lived had wall switches labeled "oxygen" and "vacuum" and an observation window, as if it were an operating theater. I slept like a baby in there away from the phones and the visitors and the trays of hospital food, and none of the babies died, no.

Four babies died in August in a neonatal intensive care unit in Boston. They were contaminated by a virus from outside. And they died. The unit was closed down when they saw, too late, what was happening. I can't imagine but I do.

A couple of months before India was born, a family friend gave birth to a baby with three holes in her heart. Kathleen. Kate. She's still alive today. They let her parents take her home after teaching them how to hook her up to a portable oxygen kit and insert a feeding tube down her throat. The doctors are amazed. Everybody thinks she's lived as long as she has because her parents are so loving. But even with that, she won't live. I can't imagine but I do.

Some nights, crying alongside India's salad bin, I'd look up to see another mother crying across from me, still another crying down the way.

"It isn't fair! It isn't fair!" one sobbed to a sympathetic nurse. She went home with her baby two days later.

Trying to be a good sport as well as a good parent, I said to the same nurse, "I can't complain. I know there are other people here whose situations are much more grim than mine. I have a friend whose baby has three holes in her heart."

"Well," she replied, "it's a place of broken dreams. No matter what the situation is, it boils down to somebody's dream being shattered."

After she said that, I felt like I could relax. Yeah, my dream was shattered but my baby is alive.

PINWORM PATROL

Gayle Brandeis

Shining a flashlight into my sleeping child's butt crack is not my favorite way to pass the time. Especially when a worm pokes out and undulates, like a tiny tongue giving me the raspberry. Pinworm patrol is a dirty stinking job, but there are times when a mama has to bend to the occasion.

I remember my first pinworm expedition. When my son was two, an article about parasites appeared in *Mothering* magazine. Symptoms of pinworm infestation, the piece mentioned, include irritability, restlessness and a general out-of-sorts attitude. After reading this, every mother I knew was convinced her child had pinworms.

We hunted for the clammy creatures in the dead of night—the best time to find them, the article said, since they come out to deposit their eggs nocturnally. My friends and I weren't sure why any creature would want to birth its offspring in an anal fold, but hey, all birth is messy. We didn't have time to judge the evolution of parasite life; we were on a simple mission to search and destroy.

Picture us, a far-flung battalion of reconnaissance mamas. We crawled into our children's bedrooms, flashlights in our mouths, magnifying glasses in our fists. We stealthily pulled back sheets, lifted nightgowns, eased down pajama bottoms. We gently tugged aside diapers and underpants. We looked for signs of life—translucent white threads, ten millimeters long, or tiny luminous eggs. We were all a bit disappointed when we didn't find anything.

Time went by, and the article faded from my mind. My son seemed happily parasite free. After my daughter was born, I never once considered she might be full of nematodes, even during her most trying toddler times. We dealt with chicken pox, hand-foot-and-mouth disease, warts and head lice, but pinworms never entered the picture. The closest we came, in name, was ringworm, but that turned out to be a fungus, not a true worm at all.

Then a neighbor friend found a pile of wriggly beasties in her daughter's panties. I embarked on another midnight butt-spelunking mission, sure I'd hit the worm motherlode this time. My search was in vain, though; not a parasite could be found. I began to wonder if we were strangely immune.

No one is immune to pinworms, I discovered. Pinworms are the most common intestinal parasite in the United States, affecting twenty to forty million people each year. Two years ago, my family finally joined the ranks of the infested.

My daughter, then three, started to complain about an itchy butt. It had slipped my mind that this was the main symptom of pinworms. At first, I thought I wasn't wiping her well enough. Maybe she needed more baths. I stepped up on the anal hygiene, but the itching didn't go away. Maybe it's a yeast infection, I thought. I gave her yogurt and garlic and bought some antifungal cream. No use. Then my seven-year-old son started to complain about itchiness, as well. He also woke up with wet sheets a few mornings in a row, which had never happened in the past. Both kids seemed awfully cranky, too. My husband and I were baffled. What in the world was going on?

I didn't put two and two together until the mother of a girl I occasionally baby-sat called. Her children had been diagnosed with pinworms. Maybe I should check my own kids, she said. Did I know how to check for pinworms?

Did I know how to check for pinworms?

I should have a pinworm patrol badge, I told her.

That night, I pulled out the flashlight and the magnifying glass yet again. I approached my sleeping daughter first. She twisted around lightly as I slid her nightgown up her tummy. I waited until she settled before I pulled a leghole of her underpants aside and shined the light at her butt. Her anus looked perfectly normal, maybe a little bit shiny. I figured it was sweat. I was certainly sweating. There was no worm evidence around, as far as I could tell. Confused, I waited a while longer. Nothing changed.

I was about to turn off the flashlight when a tiny white thread suddenly poked out from my daughter's puckered orifice. I watched the worm slide out a bit further and wiggle around as if checking to see if the coast was clear. It stared right in my direction, then sent me a Bronx cheer before it slithered back inside. I quickly snapped the leg of my daughter's underwear back into place, then ran around the house shaking my hands and yelling "Ewwwwwwww!"

I decided not to check my son's butt. The itching and the bedwetting—not to mention the worm crawling out of his sister—were all the proof I needed.

In the morning, we bought some over-the-counter pinworm medicine—Pin-X, which sounded more like a piercing salon to me than a parasite remedy. We also got some pumpkin seeds, which are supposed to help flush worms out naturally, some homeopathic Cina pellets, a tincture of black walnut and wormwood, and lots of garlic.

When even one member of a family gets pinworms, everyone has to be treated. The four of us gathered for a communal deworming session. The box of medicine promised a "pleasant caramel flavor"—pleasant, we discovered, if you like your caramel bitter and mixed with chalk dust. We each drank a shot of the stuff from a little plastic measuring cup, followed by a stiff cranberry-hibiscus-juice chaser. As we waited for the worms to drop dead, my husband and I washed all the sheets and towels and underwear in the house, and had a little talk with the kids about washing their hands.

The most frequent mode of pinworm transmission is anus to mouth, the knowledge of which makes me more than a little queasy. Worms can also be spread when people bite their nails or suck their fingers after touching infected sheets or toilet seats or the ground where wormy animals have pooped. The creatures can travel a fairly circuitous route— say one child scratches her butt, then uses a pencil; another child borrows the pencil and later sticks his finger in his mouth while he looks over his writing. Voila! Instant worms!

The best way to avoid pinworms is by thorough hand washing, especially before eating and after going to the bathroom or petting animals. Unfortunately, it's impossible to guard against the parasites entirely.

The tiny eggs can also become airborne, so you can get worms simply by inhaling them. Unless you want to walk around wearing a surgical mask, there's not much you can do about this particular mode of transmission.

I'm not sure how, exactly, my kids ended up with their case of worms. We were certainly happy to see them go, though. A few days after we quaffed the gritty liquid, the kids became considerably less crabby, their butts stopped itching, and my son's sheets stayed dry every morning. Our house remained blissfully uninfested for a couple of years.

Then, last September, my kids started to act like beasts. I attributed this to back-to-school excitement and anxiety, and tried to be patient with them. They were horrible well beyond reason, though—whining and fighting, acting rude and moody and irritable and mean. My husband and I felt like total failures as parents. Our bright, creative kids were turning into juvenile delinquents before our eyes. There seemed to be nothing we could do about it. Then my daughter came up to me and said, "Mom, my butt really, really itches."

Aha, I thought. Of course. I made a mental note to find the flashlight, and steeled myself for another nighttime mission. Pinworm patrol mama, back in action. Ready to save the world.

When our daughter was six months old, my husband and I set off on a road trip in an old cop car painted flat black with tinted windows. The plan was to go to British Columbia to visit my family and show off my daughter. Along the way we stopped off in Vegas to get married at the Graceland Chapel. We decided to get matching tattoos instead of rings. I waited until I got to my hometown and then had a scarab beetle with wings tattooed across my lower back. —Trixie

I decided to get a tattoo to honor my son Carson, who died of SIDS when he was fifty-five days old. Just a simple blue heart on my ankle, with his name inside. —Rachelle

Baby Vibe

Julie Jamison

It is always alarming when a woman's vibrator quits working. I know there are those among you who know this feeling of panic. It seems to happen at the most inconvenient times. You shake it, you bang it, you even flip the switch back and forth repeatedly. New batteries are of no use. Eventually you have to accept it. It is over. That faithful friend will never hum again.

My favored vibrator was red. It was medium sized and its case created the illusion of a giant lipstick. It had a certain degree of class. Acquired in 1989, it was my first, so it held a special place in my heart. After examining and poking at the wires within, I reluctantly accepted its demise. Replacing it would not be easy.

I was not all that concerned because I still had an alternate vibrating bullet, a Joni's butterfly, a detachable massaging shower head and my hand. I was in no great hurry. Accommodations could be made. I assumed eventually I would click my way to an online sex shop and select an updated version.

The town I live in has no liquor stores. It also has no sex shops. You can get a copy of *Penthouse* at one particular gas station, which keeps them covered up behind the counter. That is the extent of porn in this small Kansas town. Pitiful. If I had been aware of this at the time, I never would have accepted employment in such a backward 'burb.

As I drove home from an out-of-town meeting last week, I decided to stop at my usual X-rated video store, conveniently located at an intersection I passed right through on the way back into town. Though about seven cars were parked in the lot, no one was in the store. They must have all been in the twenty-four-hour theater. On Tuesdays women get in free. I had often wondered about this free Tuesday thing and had made a mental note to check it out, for research purposes. Unfortunately, it was a Thursday.

I was relieved to see I had privacy for browsing. I was in a bit of a rush, so I headed straight for the vibrators. The first objects that caught my eye were enormous penis-shaped versions. I ruled them out almost immediately. First of all, they seemed quite large. Where would you store such a thing? It certainly wouldn't fit in my wooden jewelry box on the nightstand. Plus, they were tacky. Some had attachments that actually frightened me.

Next I saw a nice-looking silver one, aerodynamic, with a sleek case. I was impressed, but it was a bit pricey. I am nothing if not cheap. I also worried it would be cold against my naked flesh. While I do enjoy the ice cube trick, this was not what I was looking for in a vibrator.

There was a whole rack of what were termed "personal vibrators" (as opposed to public vibrators, I assume). They came in many pleasing colors. I was tempted. They were very small though, four inches maybe. What if it got . . . well . . . lost? Despite a vigorous regimen of kegels, I've often wondered if perhaps I'm not just a little roomy. My ego might not be able to take such a humiliating event. I'd just as soon avoid *that* conversation with an ER nurse.

At this point I started to panic. The salesclerk gave me a look from behind the counter. I wasn't sure if it was an annoyed look or a lecherous look. Perhaps there was nothing there for me. Maybe I needed to retreat to the safety of online anonymity and limitless comparison shopping.

Then a lilac-colored object caught my eye. The package boasted it was made from a "realistic gel." It had a rubbery, flexible tip with enough stiffness to get the job done. It was a nice size and had that element of charm I was looking for. I snatched it up and headed for the cashier. As usual, I fumed, silently asking myself why the counter was so damn high. I had to reach up to pay the man, as if I were in some intimidating secret booth. He looked down and asked, "Do you need me to put a battery in that?" I suppose in case I needed to use it immediately, perhaps in the car on the drive home. I thanked him for his kindness and let him slip it in. The battery, I mean.

I drove back into town, picked up my son and headed for home. Once I was able to relax, I took the new toy from my purse and opened it so I could check out this alleged realistic feel. I was pinching it when the phone rang.

It was my mother. We chatted for a minute and soon I heard a happy squeal coming from the baby. I looked up to smile at my thirteen-month-old charmer, and then I saw a sight that made my heart drop.

He was happily chewing on the vibrator and sucking on its tip. Apparently, the realistic texture made a great teether. I dashed across the room and snatched it from his innocent lips. He reacted as any child would. He let out a high-pitched, ear-shattering shriek. I offered him several other options, but he was fixated on the pretty purple thing. What's a mother to do?

So I turned it on. If he had thought it was a cool toy before, he was enraptured then. He giggled with glee and even made a type of vibrating babble noise—eh eh eh eh eh. I allowed him a few moments of joy before slyly substituting an oatmeal cookie in its place.

Obviously, now I can never use it. It is far too bizarre on so many levels. I'd hate to settle in for a nice masturbating session and suddenly flash on my son's grinning face. To use it now would lead to therapy later, I am certain. I am thankful he discovered it when it was fresh from the package and not after . . . well . . . after I'd had it a while. The horror.

Perhaps I could exchange it for a new one. But how would I explain the teeth marks?

Teelee Talks

Megan Lambert

My son, Jason, is one of the few uncircumcised boys in his preschool. His teachers often take children to the bathroom in small groups, so I knew that he had seen other little boys' circumcised penises. But Jason never mentioned noticing that his "teelee" was different from theirs. Then, shortly after his third birthday, Jason retracted his foreskin for the first time while taking a bath.

"It looks just like Tommy's!" he happily exclaimed, referring to one of his circumcised friends. Then he slipped his foreskin back down and said, "I want to do it again!" And so, he did. Repeatedly.

Jason was quite impressed by this new trick, and its discovery led to many discussions about circumcision—or "teelee talks," as we came to refer to them in our household, "teelee" being the Jamaican Patois word for a little boy's penis. One of Jason's first questions was, "Where did Tommy's foreskin go?" Trying to answer him honestly and gently was a challenge for me because, being three years old and heavily into the "whys," Jason did not buy the statement that Tommy's body was simply different from his. So, I told him, "When Tommy was a very tiny baby, his parents decided that it would be best to have a doctor cut off his foreskin."

Furrowing his brow he said, "And Tommy didn't like that!"

When my partner told this story to Tommy's mom, she laughed and good-naturedly said, "He's right, Tommy didn't like that one bit!"

I was rather selfishly relieved that Jason's incessant "whys" did not lead him to ask me *why* Tommy's parents thought it would be best for him to have a doctor cut off his foreskin. I would not have known how to answer this question because, to put it mildly, I do not think it is best for boys to be circumcised. I would feel uncomfortable defending the procedure—even in casual conversation with my son. While I don't think that routine male circumcision ranks up there with the worst of human atrocities, I do see it as an often ill-considered act that leads to unnecessary risks and pain. I am not Jewish or Muslim, so I do not have a cultural or religious tie to the practice. Many parents who are of these faiths deeply value the tradition of male circumcision, and other members of these communities question these practices and even work against them.

Jason also stopped short of asking me why I decided not to have him circumcised. Wanting to offer him only as much information as he requested so that he could set the pace of the discussion, I did not fill him in on my reasons. But, if he were to ask this question, I could give him a very thorough and passionate answer, which would begin with the statement that I did not think that it was right for me to make this decision for him. After all, there is no medical reason for circumcision. As Jason's mother, I make many health-related decisions on his behalf because he is too young to give informed consent. However, permitting a doctor to amputate a perfectly healthy body part, without a compelling medical reason to do so, was not a choice that I felt comfortable making.

Now that my son knew about circumcision, I wanted to assure him that no one would ever cut off his foreskin. After all, I didn't want him to think that I was just waiting around for some later date to have his pediatrician snip it off. (He is already traumatized enough by the routine finger-stick blood tests that check for lead poisoning. The last time I brought him to the doctor, for a mild case of pinkeye, Jason made me tell every nurse and doctor who came into the room that there were to be "no blue needle stick things today!")

I told Jason that while he was growing inside my body, I made a promise to him that I would not tell a doctor to cut off his foreskin. I told him that making this decision was just one of the ways I took care of him while I waited for him to be born. I said that I also ate lots of good foods to help him grow and to keep myself healthy and strong; I took regular long walks around a lake ringed with willow trees for exercise; I read all kinds of books and magazines about babies; I went to classes to learn about giving birth; and I got mad about all of the smog and traffic in Washington, D.C., where we used to live, as I breathed in all kinds of nasty, polluted air. I told him, "I wanted to stomp my foot and yell at the big, stinky trucks, 'I'm trying to grow a person in here, darn it!'"

Jason smiled and filled in the end of the familiar story of his birth, saying, "Then I grew, and I grew, and I grew, and I came out of you, and you said, 'Oh, my baby Jason!'"

This time I added, "And then I snuggled you close, and when the doctor asked me if I wanted him to cut off your foreskin, I said, 'No!' And so he didn't, and you have your foreskin, and you always will."

That week things went smoothly. Jason didn't seem troubled by his new knowledge that some boys' parents decide to have doctors cut off their foreskins. He liked to tell people about his "special private teelee thing," which is how he began to refer to his new ability to retract his foreskin. Although I tried to avoid shaming him, I did attempt to stress the *private* part of that statement. After all, he couldn't march up to just anybody in our apartment complex and expect them to listen as rapturously as I would to his latest description of what his foreskin could do.

One evening, I decided to check in again with Jason to make sure that he was still feeling comfortable and safe. I incorporated the topic into a casual good touch/bad touch conversation. I began by telling him that no one should ever touch his private body parts—his teelee, his foreskin, his scrotum or the hole in his bottom where poop comes out—unless the person was his parent, his preschool teacher or a doctor or a nurse keeping him healthy and clean. I told him that he could always tell me if someone touched him in a way that he didn't like. (And then, I thought to my usually pacifist self, somebody will have to hold me back from trying to kill that sick person with my own two hands.) Finally, I asked Jason if he knew that no one would ever cut off his foreskin.

"Yes," he said, nodding his head. "When I was a little tiny baby," he began, "Mom-mom brought me to the doctor and she said, 'Don't cut off Jason's foreskin.' And the doctor said, 'Okay, I won't.'"

I know that we will have more teelee talks as time goes on and he comes up with further questions. In the meantime, he is a happy little boy with a healthy three-year-old pride and curiosity about his special private teelee thing and the rest of his miraculous body.

The Perfect Name

Peri Escarda

"What's dat?" says my eighteen-month-old daughter, trying out her newest phrase.

"That's your eye," I answer carefully.

"What's dat?" she continues with a grin.

"That's your nose," I answer obligingly. We are sitting on the patchwork quilt that covers our bed, and I am enjoying the game as much as she is.

She considers my answer for a moment, finger smooshed up against her nose, and then plunges her finger downward.

"What's dat?" she demands, and my eyes follow her gaze. She has pointed between her legs, and I realize that I am at a loss for words—at a loss even for a single word.

I have thought about this moment, of course. And I have promised myself that I will offer my daughter better answers than the ones that were given to me as a child. But the moment has snuck up on me—as parenting moments will do—and I find myself ill-prepared. I silently ask her to forgive me, to give me just a little more time, and then I cheerfully change the subject.

"Let's blow some bubbles!" I suggest, and she scampers up into my arms.

In the backyard, I send out volley after delicate volley of bubbles from a yellow, plastic wand. They are just standard bubbles, pulled forth from the standard, cheap, plastic bottle. But each shimmering bubble is a miracle to my daughter—a bit of mysterious mama magic—and she toddles eagerly after each one. She is delighted, and her consuming delight gives me time to think . . . precious time to remember all the experiences that have led me to this moment.

Language can be as powerful and swift as the surgeon's knife. What is not named, does not exist. —Harriet Lerner, *New Woman*

When I was about five years old, I became curious about the differences between me and the five-year-old boy down the street. So one day, my buddy and I paused in our play, lowered our pants and took a peek.

Unfortunately, my grandmother appeared, looming over us with the look of an avenging angel, and swooped down upon the offending scene.

"What are you doing?" she gasped. She grabbed my friend by the arm and marched him toward the door. "You go home now!"

Then she knelt down to me and grabbed me by both shoulders.

"Don't you ever do that again!" she said in a terrible voice as if I had been found strangling kittens. My gentle, sweet grandmother had never spoken to me before in that tone, and I was badly shaken. I got the message all right: What was "down there" was bad, dirty and incomprehensibly dangerous.

Little did my grandmother know that I was already being stalked by a budding pedophile: a thirteen-year-old boy who was unusually interested in the very young girls in our neighborhood. A smiling thirteen-year-old boy who lured me into his bedroom with promises of candy. A deceptively violent boy who bullied me into taking off my pants. Then this boy, who is now living freely somewhere as a man, pressed my tiny face into the carpet while he tried repeatedly to rape me. Repeatedly, until my panic carried me crying from his room. And when my mother asked me what was wrong, I could only remember the incident with my grandmother. I could only believe that I had disobeyed her by agreeing to take off my pants. I could only believe that I was in the wrong. And so I said nothing. I said nothing because I had no words to describe the abuse. No words that did not fill me with shame.

A majority of women believe to this day that their genitals, in one way or another, are not quite "normal." —Joani Blank, *Femalia*

When I was nine years old, I slipped while walking on top of a fence. I landed right on my crotch and could not believe that such pain existed.

Even though I was worried that I had seriously injured myself, I did not tell my mother about it. Instead, I snuck into the bathroom and took a look with a hand mirror. But since I did not know what it looked like normally, I did not know if it had been damaged or not. I didn't even know what to call it down there, and the thought of drawing attention to "it" filled me with embarrassment. So I hid my tear-stained face and suffered in silence.

Menarche [had become] a matter of consumer decision making, and . . . coming-of-age was a process to be worked out in the marketplace rather than at home. —Joan Jacobs Brumberg, *The Body Project*

When I was eleven, my mother nervously handed me a pink packet. Inside was a series of pamphlets that described the basics of menstruation. The packet stressed the importance of hygiene over and over again. The answer to this hygienic problem was always given in large letters: "Kotex" with a little "TM" next to it. Kotex assured me that it offered the best protection available. Protection from what? Protection from smell, protection from staining, protection from the horrible possibility of anybody knowing that I was menstruating. The pamphlet then went on to assure me that this was a perfectly natural thing that they were protecting me from. Perfectly natural. Not a thing to worry about—as long as you could pay for their protection.

I guess a lot of women can't imagine a place where there's so much freedom involved with finding out what they want and then getting it. Getting what you want sexually is a huge achievement, and it seems to frighten a lot of women. —Claire Cavanah, co-owner of Toys in Babeland

When I was fifteen, I noticed an interesting fact. None of the boys in my school ever wanted to admit they were virgins, and none of the girls ever wanted to admit that they were *not* virgins. One of the worst names you could call a girl was "slut." But of course, nobody wanted to be known as "straight" either. It was assumed that every guy craved sexual pleasure, but not so for the girls. To behave as though you were a girl who craved sexual pleasure was to lose the respect not only of the boys in school, but also the respect of the girls. To take pleasure only as far as you (and you alone) felt comfortable meant risking being labeled a "tease." And if you had the misfortune of being labeled "straight," well, the world just always seemed to pass you by. It was a difficult tightrope to walk: One seemed always on the verge of falling into the label of "straight," "slut" or "tease."

Technologically oriented medical practitioners who are sure that childbirth is something to be wrestled into submission feel that the sound of a mother wailing in pain is a sign that she is "losing it" and ought to be medicated.

—Joanne Dozer and Shannon Baruth, "Epidural Epidemic," *Mothering* magazine

When I was thirty, I lost a pregnancy at five months gestation. I went in to the hospital and listened to the tiny heartbeat fade into silence. The doctor came in to my room. He was wearing cowboy boots. He ordered drugs.

He reached his hand inside me and applied painful, opening pressure to my cervix. His fingers reached far up and found the fetus. He twisted and pulled. Eventually he gave up, saying, "I'm going to have to stop pulling now or I'm afraid I will sever the fetus's head from its body." Then he left. I felt as if I had been raped. You see, the problem was that the doctor did not trust my body to deliver the pregnancy on its own. Yet in the end, that is exactly what it did. When finally left alone, that quiet little life slipped out into the world—without the help of the doctor's invasive fingers.

But that pregnancy had been followed by the birth of my daughter, and now that daughter was pulling insistently at the unused bubble wand hanging limply in my hand. I reached down and pulled her fiercely into the circle of my arms. I would give her a word that was free of shame. I would find her a worthy name for what nestled between her legs. I owed her this much, for she had come to me, had come through me and had brought with her a powerful healing.

I remembered the day my daughter was born. On that day, I labored in my living room. Sunlight streamed in through the lace curtains and fell upon my back as I lay, encircled in my husband's arms, completely consumed with the work at hand. On that day, I found out what it meant to be a woman. I reached deep down inside of myself for that last bit of strength.

I found it and offered it. I added that strength to the contraction that bore down with a will of its own. Then I realized that what I had offered—the sum of all I had offered in blood, sweat and tears—was not enough. So I reached deeper, into a place of myself that I had never been before: a reservoir so deep and still, a subterranean lake of strength.

This reservoir had remained hidden and untapped, but on that day, its waters moved through me. I was a vessel, and from me poured life.

The lips of my vessel are perfectly formed to protect; they unfurl like delicate petals around a pink bloom. The muscles surrounding the opening are thick and springy. During birth, they flatten and spread, fanning out around the baby's head, but afterward, they return immediately to their thick and muscular form. The clitoris at the top is a bundle of nerves that is deliciously sensitive to the slightest touch. Somehow, despite the sordid collection of offenses perpetrated against me, I had learned to stroke from that clitoris storms of orgasms that moved across the landscape of my body—storms of orgasms that made me discover the pleasures of every one of my curves and hollows. Even so, I had struggled with a name for what brought me such pleasure. I had grown up surrounded by the daughters of the sexual revolution, and yet we all seemed to be struggling for a name. What name, I wondered, would make the perfect offering for my daughter?

Well, the word "pussy" is common, but this term always sounds a bit submissive. The word "cunt" actually has a very powerful history: It is related to words that were once titles of respect for women, priestesses and goddesses. Inga Muscio, in her book titled *Cunt*, makes an impassioned argument for reclaiming that ancient term. But "cunt" is too powerful a word for a toddler to wield. Perhaps it would be best to wait until she understood the consequences of shouting out "cunt" in a crowd. Harriet Lerner, the writer/educator, asks that we differentiate between "vulva" and "clitoris," in the hopes that we don't forget that we have these separate parts. And many women fall back on the word "vagina." But that term just always sounds so damn clinical: fine for when you're discussing yeast infections, but not very endearing in general.

Which brings me to the term "yoni." I first heard this word on the day my daughter was born. My midwives had made hot compresses soaked in boiled ginger water. The midwife placed the compress against me, smiled and said, "Push into the warmth. Feel your yoni beginning to give and stretch."

"My what?" I gasped, as the sweet, pungent smell of ginger filled the air.

"You haven't heard the word 'yoni'? It means 'the gateway to nirvana' or 'sacred place.' The word 'vagina' is of Roman descent and means 'sheath for your sword.'"

This was all very interesting, but labor tends to put linguistic lessons on hold. Still, I would always remember the word "yoni" as one more pretty thing that the midwives had offered me. Even during the work of labor, my mind was fascinated by the concept of "yoni." My sacred place. My gateway to the other world. Having been present at other births, I know that it is an incredible experience to watch that door open in a laboring woman, bringing a new life from that holiest of places. But it is something else to *be* that door, to feel that gateway steadily opening in the most intimate part of yourself. There is no word to describe it. But "yoni" comes pretty close.

And I needed a word that bestowed honor on that particular part of womanhood. But why limit my daughter to just one word? Why not give her the word "pussy" when she wants to whisper, "cunt" when she wants to growl? Why not give her the word "clitoris" when she looks for it, and the word "vulva" so that she's sure not to miss it? But certainly, we need at least one word that addresses the power of childbirth. For, as any laboring mother can attest, the moment of the baby's crowning is a moment unlike any other in life.

I recall that feeling as I gather my daughter up and carry her inside. As always, I revel in the fact that she was once contained inside me. Now that we are seated back on our patchwork quilt, it is not long before my daughter and I are playing the name game again. This time when she points between her legs and asks, "What's dat?" I tell her very solemnly, "This is no passive piece of equipment. This is your sacred place: your yoni. There is no greater source of strength in the world."

She stares back with minimal comprehension, but still, decides to take a closer look. As we bow our heads together to better see what lies

between her legs, I am sure that no artist could ever create a more perfect balance of delicate fragility and astounding strength. No other sym-
bol could better express the resilience of woman-spirit. The life-giving
force that each one of us contains.

FEEDING

Marianne Apostolides

She lies along my chest, her feet dangling at my side. Her hands perform in a slow-motion dance, opening and closing at a mesmerizingly languid pace. Her soft ear wiggles just slightly as she feeds, taking the milk from my breast.

Feeding is the foundation of the intimate relationship developing between me and my three-month-old daughter. As she eats, my daughter can sense the warmth of my body, smell the mingled scents of me and my milk, feel my chest rise against hers with each breath. Feeding was her primary pleasure in her first weeks of life, before she could play or explore; it will always be her first experience of comfort, safety and caring.

Looking down at my daughter during these quiet moments of breast-feeding, I often feel an urgent need to protect her from my own problems with food—my decade-long struggle with anorexia and bulimia, and the hints of those eating disorders that remain. I haven't been bulimic for several years, but I still sometimes make disparaging comments about my weight, mope about when I eat a self-proclaimed "bad" food like a piece of cake, or get anxious if a meal seems bigger or more fatty than I anticipated. I feel myself pulled into that familiar hole, slowly at first, resisting, then faster as my mind spins, faster as I rush through calorie calculations and compensation strategies, still faster as numbers and judgments and remorse and anger gather in my mind, chasing each other in a circle that doesn't stop for my husband or myself or my baby. Not even for my baby. If I don't let go of the last remnants of my eating disorder, my daughter will sense a problem. She will not be able to identify that problem consciously, but she will understand at a young age that food is dangerous, that the body is threatening, that desire is frighteningly untamable. As we sit for dinner, she will feel my energy charge the room, a current of panic pulsing from my skin. If she is exposed to that current long enough, she may assume my behavior as her own, because all children primarily learn how to relate to food, their body and their emotions by observing the behavior of their parents.

I learned by observing my father. I learned on weekends when the family would schedule our "one big meal of the day." I learned on vacations when I would lie awake in the darkness of morning hearing my father exercise in the pitch-black hotel room. He gave me his unhealthy obsession in the nervousness and sadness that filled the house, never discussed, openly denied. As a child, I felt those emotions in my skinny body without knowing how to handle them. Years before I became an anorexic teenager, I learned to "handle" them by growing angry, closed off and obsessed with controlling my body—training it to achieve in sports, teaching it to reject food. Although my father was not clinically anorexic or bulimic, he used food- and weight-obsession to avoid emotions he could not handle in a healthy way. Those emotions are rooted in a childhood in Greece during World War II and the Greek Civil War when he hid in a homemade bomb shelter and felt hunger gnaw at his tiny belly. His father disappeared early one morning during the Nazi occupation; he was killed by Greek Communists, the family was told a year later. The body was never found.

My father's childhood was so dangerously out of control that he tried to find safety in controlling his food. For decades, he has focused on his body, making his muscles stronger and stronger so their walls keep the memories of his childhood locked away. The fear is still inside him, along with the anguish, loss and anger. But he refuses to acknowledge those emotions, to feel them fully in order to free himself of them. Instead he hides from them in food.

Even now, at every lunch and dinner we share, my father begins the meal by commenting that his portion is too big. His words slap me in the face. I feel the anger rise from my chest, well in my throat like blood. I am a teenager again, feeling judged by my father as I eat my food, feeling guilty as I plan my binge for that night. Only later do I wonder why he can't refrain from making those comments when he is around me, his only daughter, his child whom he has seen diet to a sickly eighty pounds, whom he has heard vomiting in the bathroom. Only later still do I forgive.

As I think about my father's failings as a parent, I can't help but contemplate my own future failings: I wonder how I will hurt my child and whether I will be so caught in the spinning of my own obsessions that I will be unable to focus on her needs.

When I was floating in that shimmery moment of pregnancy—the time when I had no confirmation that I was pregnant but knew in my body that I was carrying a child—I shared my suspicion with my therapist, who immediately gave me a book. In *The Drama of the Gifted Child: The Search for the True Self,* Alice Miller presents the theory that mothers are largely responsible for the emotional problems of their children. A mother may use her child to fulfill her own emotional needs instead of making herself available to recognize and meet the needs of her child. That child will then repress her feelings and act as her mother wants her to act. Since she is unable to experience her own emotions, the child feels insecure, empty and alienated from her true self. This "exploitation" of the child is most likely to occur when the mother herself was not respected and protected when she was young. Therefore, she constantly seeks to find a sense of security and affirmation from the one person who cannot leave her: her child.

Miller wrote this book for therapists and for adults trying to understand the childhood foundations of their adult emotional problems; I read the book both as an adult looking back on my childhood and as a woman about to become a mother. Reading the book from these two perspectives gave me a sensation of vertigo. My emotions rapidly switched from security to panic, from understanding the past to fearing the future. I would read one sentence and feel embraced by the book because it confirmed that my problems had a true basis, that I was not simply an ungrateful, hateful, angry child; but the very next phrase would make my foot twitch from anxiety and fear that I would be unable to deal with my problems before my child was born, before I began to hurt her as my parents had hurt me. In my less panicked moments, I realized that unless I changed, my baby would learn from me what I learned from my father: to hide from her emotions because there is already too much anxiety, hunger and fear in the family; to numb herself because no one is able to hold her safely while she ventures into the complexity of her own feelings.

After reading Miller's book, I once again began to focus on letting go of my anger and self-alienation. More than ever, I have found my center: I have found peace and security within me. If I keep working to release myself from the destructive patterns of the past, I will be able to express and fulfill my own needs rather than use my daughter to do those things for me. I will be able to observe my child in a situation, respect her feelings and empathize with her, responding based on what she needs rather than what I need. For example, we will inevitably have to deal with the death of our pets. If I am unable to feel, understand and contain my own emotions surrounding death, I will need my daughter to be stoic and "strong"; she will most likely comply with my unspoken request, even if she needs me to comfort and sustain her as she experiences sadness, confusion, grief and fear. We will either hide our grief together, depending on each other to suppress it, or we will both let ourselves feel the range of our emotions, with me helping her through the crisis because I am a mother and she is just a child.

This psychological self-examination is the new element that our generation brings to parenthood. Unlike my father, we come from a culture and a generation that values understanding emotional processes. My father doesn't have the language or the need to explore his obsessive-compulsive behavior and the traumas underlying it. He, like many of his generation, gave the effects of his traumas to his child. Because of the "exploitative" way my parents related to me, I spent ten years of my life locked in the desperate, roiling anger of an eating disorder. As an adult I was able to use the tools available to my generation—tools that include psychotherapy, yoga, shiatsu and acupuncture—to begin to let go of the anger and fear my father carried since World War II and, subsequently, gave to me.

I have made a promise to myself and my daughter that I will continue that work. I will not unconsciously give her the burden of my past. Instead, I will work to lay down the past so she can experience every moment of her present.

As I breast-feed my daughter, holding her small body in my arms, I can't help but imagine who this child will become; I can't help but wonder what nourishment will sustain her as she moves through this world.

MORENA

Caledonia Kearns

The neighborhood women in our barrio who play dominos in front of our loading dock on hot nights think that my husband's mother is my mother because she is white. When she comes to visit, they see Miguel, a Puerto Rican man, and this Irish-looking older white woman. And then they see me, a younger woman, blond and fair, and assume she belongs to me.

Miguel's father is black and Puerto Rican. He once said to me, "It's the mix—my children are beautiful because of the mix." And they are.

When Miguel's niece Isabella was born, she looked exactly as I had pictured my own child with Miguel would look, except she was longer because her parents are tall. She was light brown with dark black hair and a sweet African nose like her father's. She was black, white. Ethnically she is Puerto Rican, German, Scottish, Irish, English and Italian. Isabella is lovely. She is a Martínez like her father, her uncle and her aunt. When her sister, Hana, was born, we were all a bit surprised. She wasn't brown like Isabella. She was white. It occurred to me that my baby might resemble an Irish princess more than a Latina one.

When Selena was born, everyone at the birthing center said she looked exactly like Miguel. She had dark brown hair, and her skin was not white. The midwife said she had jaundice, but I thought it was the African in her. And while her African heritage remains, as she approaches her first birthday, our daughter is now fair like her mama. Miguel says she's a white black person. When she was born, my relatives asked my mother who she looked like. They wanted to know what color she was. Genetically, it was like rolling dice: She could have been black or white, red- or chestnut-haired.

My father, an old beatnik, calls on the phone to tell me that what's wonderful about Selena's heritage is that she can choose what she wants to be. I repeat this to Miguel and he says, "No, Selena can be everything all at the same time." Her ethnicities are not separate; they are part of the mix. Miguel calls himself a Scottorican. He wore a kilt to our wedding and walked down the aisle with his parents to the strains of a Puerto Rican cuatro player. His maternal grandfather emigrated from Aberdeen, Scotland. Plaid is the motif of choice among his mother and her sisters. A bagpiper led me down the aisle with the traditional Irish song "Maire's Wedding."

I grew up in Boston in the mid-seventies knowing I was a white girl. With busing and desegregation the norm, you could not ignore race. My mother and I spent my childhood living in mostly black neighborhoods all around Dorchester. My school culture was urban. We listened to early rap in music class and I learned the "rock" and the "freak" from my classmates. In the school talent show, I danced with my friend Christa to Michael Jackson's "Working Day and Night." My mom and I went to Houghton's Pond on hot summer days, and I remember her saying to me, "I never have to worry about not being able to spot you, you are so white you stick out like a flashlight."

I am just about as white as you can get. I don't tan. I am happy in my freckled skin, but as a child I had wished for long eyelashes, dark curly hair and, most definitely, skin that did not crisp immediately upon contact with the sun. Though I know that white skin is privileged skin and that young girls of all colors in America feel the tyranny of the blond and blue-eyed ideal, I did not grow up thinking my hair and skin color made me beautiful. The grass is always greener, I know. But I grew up thinking brown was beautiful.

There are many words in Spanish for skin color. *Morena, trigueña, blanca, negra.* They roll off the tongue sweeter than sugar cane. They are terms of endearment; in English, the words: "white," "black" and "mixed" don't convey affection the way Spanish *cariño* does. "Little white girl" or "little brown girl" does not sound loving the way *blanquita* or *morenita* does.

Selena and I go to the playground with her cousins. My sister-in-law says that Isabella knows what color people are, unusual for a three-year-old. As my sister-in-law names the members of our family, Bella correctly identifies who is brown and who is white. She knows Hana and Selena are white. She knows she is brown. Miguel and his brother and sister were not raised to think about race, even with a black father and a white mother. It wasn't until he reached high school that he began to think about difference.

Selena and I go to the bookstore to buy Spanish books for Isabella's birthday. The woman at the register looks at me and says, "Isn't it a bit early for Spanish?" I tell her my daughter is Puerto Rican, and she says, "Oh, she's my race." She then looks at me and says, "You're not Puerto Rican?" "I'm not," I say, and I think about that word: "race." How she immediately connected herself with Selena. I think about how Selena looks white but has mixed heritage. We share blue eyes and a widow's peak, but she is also her father's child. In a few years we will take her to the St. Patrick's Day and Puerto Rican Day Parades. She can take step dancing and salsa.

Selena's middle name is Burke, for my great-grandmother, whose birthday she shares. I wanted my daughter to have both Irish and Spanish names. We had planned to name her Lola-Maude—Lola after Lolita Lebron, the Puerto Rican *independentista,* and Maude for Yeats's love, Maud Gonne. But she was born on the new moon, with a big round face, so we named her Selena-Alicia. It means moon Goddess.

Isabella comes over to play, and I say, "You know, Selena's first name is not Selena, it's Selena-Alicia. And Titi's name is not Rita, it's Rita-Alicia. Your name is Isabella Clay." "No, no," she says, "my name is Isabella-Alicia." We are now living with her *titi* in Miguel's parents' house. Titi teaches me Spanish songs, and she speaks only Spanish with Selena. My mother-in-law had a pediatrician pierce her daughter Rita's ears when she was a month old because Miguel's *abuela* wouldn't stop pressuring her. It's tradition. When Selena is almost seven months old, we take her to a Russian beauty salon, where women look at us like we're crazy to put a needle through this small child's ears. We can tell that the ear piercer does not want to do this to Selena, but we have paid our twenty dollars, and we are ready to hold Selena still. "It's tribal," Miguel tells our audience in the salon. "She is Puerto Rican," I explain. They look at us and sort of laugh. Having to restrain Selena so she doesn't move is awful, but by the time we leave the salon, she has almost stopped crying. My mother didn't want me to pierce Selena's ears. She could hear her grandmother's voice saying that only gypsies have holes in their ears. I had to beg and plead to get my ears pierced at age eleven. Piercing Selena's ears, for me, was a way of honoring her Latina heritage, as is making sure she is bilingual.

Selena's baby sitter, Evelyn, only speaks Spanish. Though my Spanish accent is decent, I understand more than I can speak. I know some basic vocabulary but am ignorant when it comes to verb conjugations. Evelyn understands more English than she speaks, so we meet halfway. One afternoon on my way home from work, there is a fire in the subway and I use the pay phone on the platform. Evelyn answers. I am scared to speak Spanish over the phone. Will she understand me? "Evelyn, esta Caledonia. Una emergencia en el tren. El numero dos. Soy tarde. En la casa a la cinco." I forget the word for fire. I speak gringa Spanglish, but a Spanish-speaking man who overheard my conversation tells me I did okay. Embarrassed, I ask "Fire?" He responds, *"Fuego."*

When Selena and I visit my mother in Boston, she plays the bodhran, an Irish drum, for her granddaughter, and performs endless jigs and reels. What connects Miguel and me is that our heritage matters to us. We are urban. We are Irish and Yankee and Scottish and German and Afro–Puerto Rican. We are brown and black and white. Miguel grew up knowing that family is not about skin color, and this is what Selena will learn. She and her cousins are blessed. They are Martínez girls; they belong to each other.

MOTHERING CHAOS

Sarah Talbot

I've been reading a magazine article for a good two and a half minutes when I smell something funny. Like any mother of a four-year-old, I respond now, not when I finish the sentence. Caleb is dancing barefoot in a puddle of whitish liquid. When I walk into the kitchen, he smiles up at me.

"Well," I say aloud, "you'll smell tasty." It's vanilla extract. I pick up the empty bottle, grab a dish towel and kneel down so I'm in his face.

"Naughty," I sign. Actually the sign means bad. I don't know the sign for naughty, but that's the word I'm thinking and I hope that my facial expression somehow shows the difference.

"That's messy," I sign. His blue eyes catch mine long enough to show he understands. Less than a second really. I clean off his feet and turn his face toward mine.

"Jammy time," I tell him. He glances at me, then turns away. I can't hold his face and sign at the same time. I hope he understands.

I pick up my thirty-pound love child and carry him to the bedroom. On the way he grabs door frames to steer me into my room. I grab a clean pair of jammies off the floor and squeeze us through the door before he shuts it. Caleb is compulsive about open doors. They bother him the way car alarms bother most people. I hold up his bottoms and he points his legs in. He smiles when they are around his waist, then he giggles like an angel and runs off. He doesn't like the top part. I think it scares him when it goes over his head. I hold the shirt above him. He holds his feet up as if to put them into the sleeves.

"No," I sign to him, "shirt now. Stand up. Come on." He smiles sweetly and giggles. I smile and kiss him. I don't know how a child so sweet could come from my body.

After the shirt and hugs, it's time for medicine. I mix soy protein with vitamin C, vitamin B_6, a B complex, GABA and Oscap. These are the natural things my husband and I give him twice a day to keep him from starving since he won't eat much, and to help his brain act like a regular brain. Caleb is dancing an homage to his higher power, a magnetic smiling clock face on our refrigerator. He steps up and down quickly and flaps his arms around his head. His face is tense, his lower jaw jutting out. He must be bitching at the face. I pull him down to the ground, sit on him with my knees pinning his arms down and feed him the disgusting goop with an oral syringe. He takes it well, since we do this every night. Next is Tegratol, a medicine for people with epilepsy and schizophrenia. It seems to help Caleb sleep at night and focus during the day, but it's a liver toxin and requires regular blood tests. I hate giving it to him, but he doesn't mind because it tastes good.

Caleb is a beautiful child. It's not just my parental bias, it's part of his diagnosis. The head of deaf services for Seattle Children's Hospital put it in a report substantiating the severity of Caleb's autism: "Caleb is an attractive, three-and-a-half-year-old, ethnically mixed (Caucasian and

Native-American) male with a diagnosed bilateral profound hearing loss. He was referred to this clinician for a second opinion regarding diagnoses of Landau-Kleffner syndrome or autism . . ." That psychologist used the same diagnostic techniques as every doctor we've seen (more than a few); they all ignore Caleb and ask me a bunch of questions I try to answer as honestly as possible, given that Caleb is about as enigmatic as a child can be. I sometimes wonder if maybe it's me who is autistic.

People stared at me when my daughter Maia was born because I was young and hairy, and I breast-fed everywhere. I cut my hair, got a real job, and my children outgrew the titty bar, but people still stare. I think they look at first because my children are so beautiful. They continue to stare because I sign ASL to Caleb. Then they stare more, because I'm usually signing to the back of his head. I try to sign to his face, but autism gets in our way a lot.

People also stare because Caleb's behavior is bizarre and my reactions are anything but normal. He runs. Away. Fast. I sprint to catch him, don't say, "Come back now, please," like a normal mother would, and often hold him kicking and screaming under my arm in such places as grocery stores and libraries. I don't take him many other places. I took him once to see an author speak, and I ended up swinging him by his ankles through most of the conversation. It's fatiguing, but he loves it so much he stays quiet. I found myself explaining Caleb's entire medical history to the audience because I thought they might think I was abusing him.

I hate having to explain Caleb to random strangers. Last week Caleb and I rode in an elevator with another four-year-old and his mother. The other child chattered happily. Caleb kept trying to pull out the emergency stop button. I danced around trying to restrain him, and signed "No," repeatedly. Both the mother and the boy stared. I might have explained, and they might have understood, but I didn't feel like going through all that just to ride an elevator.

Then there are those less polite, more interested strangers like the volunteer at Caleb's swimming lessons. "What's he got?" she asked me. No chitchat or introduction, just, "What's he got?" like some alien probe. She was young, maybe twenty.

"Pardon me?" The first time she said it I thought my son might have grabbed some forbidden toy or tool from the pool's narrow side. Just like when I thought that first neurologist said, "Your son is clearly artistic." Though I knew what each of them really meant, I hoped both times that people weren't really that insensitive.

I made her repeat it about six times, and she didn't prove me wrong. She really did want to know what he had. I couldn't answer her question though; I have a description of his behavior that they dare call a diagnosis, but Caleb hasn't "got" anything at all.

So I rephrased her question for her: "Do you mean why does he act so weird?"

She had the nerve, and just enough time, to be indignant before Caleb pulled me away, "He's not weird! I work with kids like him."

As she spoke Caleb was laughing maniacally and struggling to put his head under water; the other children were shyly blowing bubbles. Never has there been a kid like him. Even the autism experts struggle with him. Caleb's teacher, who has worked successfully with autistic children for fifteen years, has never worked with a "kid like him." And this prat believes she knows whether he's weird, though she's seen him from a distance maybe three times? She believes, perhaps, that if she has a label for him it will allow her to help him?

The neurologist doesn't help him, the speech pathologist doesn't help him, the drugs don't help him, the naturopath doesn't help him, the physical therapy doesn't help him, the carefully developed educational program doesn't help him, the exercise therapy doesn't help him, the Reiki doesn't help him, the vitamins don't help him, the acupuncture doesn't help him, the astrology doesn't help him, the sign language doesn't help him, the social worker doesn't help him, the testing doesn't help him, the love from his mother doesn't help him. A well-meaning stranger in a pool, even knowing what he's "got," will not help him be anything other than weird. That question pissed me off, and I didn't do anything to help but scare her silly. She still avoids me.

Luckily, that kind of idiocy is rare. Most often we just get stared at. And if the people staring in public, where we're on our best behavior, saw what we're like in private, they'd wonder even more.

Right now my husband is trying to get Caleb to sleep. Caleb is screaming, and I imagine Bob is restraining his flailing limbs, trying to rock him in the dark room. We do this every night. He sometimes goes to sleep like a champ, but on nights like tonight he stays awake for hours crying and kicking and fighting. I am learning to deal with my temper during these nights. Sometimes he and I cry together over our mutual frustration and exhaustion. For a while, he would go to bed with no trouble at eight o'clock every night, when I would commence praying. Then I would go to bed, and at one in the morning my prayers would be soundly rejected; he would wake, happy, and I would learn to be angry without hurting anyone. For three weeks I taught high-school English full-time on between three and five hours of sleep a night. It's been like having an infant for four years straight.

The learning curve has been steep. I haven't ever hurt him, but I have left him alone in the house while I sat in the car, I have strapped him into a car seat in his bedroom and left him there, and I have signed mean, horrid things in the darkness. I hope he didn't see or understand any of them. I hope that none of those experiences were as scarring for him as they were for me. I hope it gets easier someday.

Becoming a mama has totally heightened my sense of interconnectedness with the world. I have always had the idea that there is one basic element common to all living things (and the living earth, too). Now it is much more than an idea to me; it is a physical truth. It's not like I looked at my newborn and magically discovered the meaning of life; rather, it's a realization that I came to slowly while contemplating the cycles of our lives and preparing to become a parent. —Mamalama

What I love: the quiet of the woods. My pond with the pink lily pads and cattails and dragonflies. My many dogs. The way my sweaters smell after being stored with cedar blocks all summer. My neighbors. A quiet glass of wine with the baby asleep and a candle burning while sitting at my grandmother's table and hearing an owl. The sound of crickets. The first fire of fall. Lying on the imitation Persian rug in the living room, feeling the cool night air blowing in, and looking up at the exposed beams on the ceiling and thinking about what could be . . . —Cecile

THE JOURNEY HOME

Allison Abner

You have to understand. When my brother and I were growing up, we didn't have a choice. We lived where we did because of my parents, went to the neighborhood public school because of where we lived, and had the friends we did because of the school we attended. So, through no fault of our own, we became the only kids of color who lived in the school district in this all-white area of Los Angeles. (The neighborhood was half Jewish, but in L.A. Jews are simply white, and Anglos, Italians, Poles, etc. are indistinguishable from each other.) When we were growing up people were categorized as white, black or "Mexican" (regardless of where the Latino person in question was actually from, including the United States).

So, now you know the context. My brother and I went to school, sometimes driven by our father's driver but usually on the bus, in our afros and "black power" sneakers (black, with red and green stripes, my dad had picked them up at a Jesse Jackson PUSH rally). We had blond love interests with long, straight hair, and teachers who treated us, for the most part, fairly because we were in many ways indistinguishable from the white kids in the district, and we performed better academically. We played on white fear at the time, terrorizing the kids who took advantage of the weak by trying to raise their status through sleazy power moves, like making fun of a destitute or outcast classmate. In a Robin Hood reverse-racism stunt, we'd tell the kids their "ass was grass after class." And it usually was, but they deserved it—truly.

And so, in this way, we'd go to school, day after day, year after year. Not learning terribly much, knowing we were different but not shrinking into the background because of it. Unlike the other kids who were bussed in, starting in third grade. These kids did their best to stay out of trouble, not be seen, maintain a neat appearance. If I heard anyone make fun of them, his ass was mine, and he deserved it—truly. Others came in buttoned-to-the-neck dress shirts, hair greased down, in an attempt to fit in with the "rich kids." Their parents didn't know that we lived in ripped Levis, rumpled plaid shirts and long, feathered hair. (I made an unsuccessful attempt in sixth grade to blow-dry my afro, so my wings would go with the lip-gloss I shoplifted from the drugstore.) Kids talked about the "smell" of the bussed kids, particularly Joseph, who was white and in love with all the girls in our class. At the end of the day, they would load into the yellow bus and get on a series of freeways to another part of L.A. where they lived—I still don't know where. All this trouble was still preferable to attending their neighborhood schools.

As it did for the bussed kids, school life contrasted with our life at home, at least life inside our house. Our Hollywood Hills neighborhood was all-white, too, studded with stoner celebrities, children who were survivors of famous parental suicides, Jewish transplants from Brooklyn, and Europeans who sought refuge after World War II. In the house, my mother talked for hours to her family and friends back in

Chicago. All her closest relationships, apart from those with us, were conducted over the phone. Off the phone, she spent her time caring for us, overseeing house renovations and the building of our pool and going to industry parties with my father. My father held a glamorous position as a high-level music executive, and parties, concerts and socializing with superstars were part of his job. But he was also a soldier of justice, always involved in uplifting poor blacks or getting independent record companies to form alliances so they could take a stand against the majors. He had marched with King in Selma, financed the Black Panthers in Chicago, supported Jesse Jackson and black politicians in D.C. in various campaigns, including the effort to honor King's birthday as a national holiday. (It really becomes clear how divided our nation actually is when someone tries to pass a national holiday in honor of anyone who wasn't a white slave-owner.) Our house was lively with music, phones ringing off the hook. We had four phone lines and an answering service to handle the volume of calls for my father's business and my blossoming social life. The smell of gumbo or chicken fricassee and my father's booming voice pervaded the house as he cut deals and put out fires. Some of our friends' parents would invite us over just to grill us about the celebrities he worked with. But we were under strict orders not to discuss any matters—personal or business—with these nosy white people.

Instead of trading on our proximity to stars, my brother and I stayed in the vortex of the cool pack by smoking pot, drinking and remaining ahead of the sexual curve. It was the seventies, things were loose. Parents supplied their kids with pot, or the kids stole the stash from the fridge. My friend Heidi's mom was into coke, so there were little brown glass vials scattered throughout the house. Sex was something still a ways away, but halter-tops and deep-purple hickies were at the height of fashion. Still, my parents hated drugs and frowned on men with wandering hands, especially when young girls were around. So most of our nefarious activities took place at the houses of our friends with absent parents or parents who just didn't give a shit because they were high or caught up in the sexual revolution, or both.

This fantasy life all but evaporated when we sold our house in the hills and moved to the beach. My brother and I started private school. Gone were the days of cozying up to a teacher for an A, or spending most evenings on the phone. Homework took over an hour each night, but I didn't figure that out until after my first two report cards—really until after my first two years of private school. But by then homework time had worked its way up to two hours a day, even on weekends.

Privilege was a distant goal for the families in the old neighborhood compared to these private-school kids. The progeny of owners of famous hotel chains, Vegas casinos, movie studios, cereal companies and automobile manufacturers, they knew how to live idle lives. Some had two, maybe three, cars (a racing BMW, an SUV, and a kick-around classic or Model T Ford). They snorted pharmaceutical coke and had entire houses to themselves (guest "cottages" off the pool). But in my six years at that school, I witnessed a change: As the public schools declined and bussing increased, our school became increasingly selective. The only billionaire jack-offs allowed to stay were those whose parents donated a new science building or film library.

And forget diversity. The admissions people didn't know enough brown-skinned families in all of L.A. to invite even twenty to apply. To this day, I believe I am the first black girl to have graduated from my school, and I was in the ninth or tenth graduating class. Though I had outgrown using intimidation (I grew to a mere five-two, and the school had a zero-tolerance policy about fighting), I remained in the cool crowd. But in private school, cool is very relative. So it wasn't hard. And ultimately being cool was tired compared to becoming rich and successful in our own right, at least for those of us who didn't have trust funds. (Trust fund kids lacked ambition simply because they could afford to. Why go to college? Why work? Ever? So grades and studying for tests and taking the SATs were laughable to them. They didn't need a work ethic, they were rich, dude.) I was there to learn, get into an Ivy and never ask my parents for another dime.

And that's basically what I did. After graduating from Vassar, I was on my own. Free to create my own life. And I imagined it to be as far away from the abovementioned experience as I could get. I saw myself moving to New York, working in some creative field, having serially monogamous relationships with artsy, successful men in my downtown loft. And I did live out my dream. I met my husband, moved into his Tribeca loft with him. He was a successful, artsy type, and I did earn a living as a TV producer and freelance writer. Then I got pregnant, married. And had my baby, Miles.

Here was our plan with Miles: We would live the *Metropolitan Home*–meets–*Mother Jones* lifestyle. In the world's most diverse city, we'd send Miles to the local public school, which was really good, and surround ourselves with an array of friends of varying hues, economic backgrounds, religions. Manhattan would be the setting in which we would raise this new generation. My husband had an almost identical childhood, except his took place eleven years before mine in Westport, Connecticut, and he was surrounded by brilliant medical researchers and Nobel laureates instead of Hollywood powerhouses. His father also marched with King in Selma, and my husband raised money for the Panthers. Tangentially, his cousin was a leading member of the Panther group that my father was financing in Chicago.

And here in this fantasy we remained, until at 105 miles per hour we crashed into the unyielding cement wall of reality. It started when we counted up the inconveniences. Life would be so much better if we had a car to drive the mile home from the weekly shopping, instead of balancing grocery bags in two arms and on the stroller in twenty-eight-degree, hellishly windy weather. Or nicer if we could slide open the screen door to feel the grass crunch beneath our soles, instead of walking the humid half-mile to the park, that one spot on the back of our necks sizzling like an ant under a magnifying glass. Or more comfortable having the bikes in the garage along with the camping equipment, the old tax files and the overly colorful eyesore toys Miles played with, instead of stacking them in the hallways and laundry room. So we moved to the suburbs of Westchester, where we paid thirteen thousand dollars in taxes so one day Miles could attend a great neighborhood public school. Sure the neighborhood lacked the diversity of Manhattan, but Tribeca hadn't been exactly diverse anyway since it became the area of convenience for migrating Wall-Streeters.

Life in Larchmont was every bit as isolating as suburban life is cracked up to be. I missed so much: the spontaneous intercom buzzes from my friends who happened to be lunching down the street; the walks up and down Wooster, Greene, Prince, to relieve my writing blocks; meeting my husband at the Angelika for the latest indie. But we had space, greenery, ease and fresh air.

My pursuit of convenience derailed the real question temporarily, until Miles approached school age. The question wasn't "What will I do when Miles starts school?" It was "What will I do with Miles once I find a job?" My job would be in the city, and it would take me twenty-six miles away every day. For everything I gained being out of the city, I would pay dearly when Miles began school and I returned to work. I wanted to write for movies or TV, but a weekly commute to L.A. was out of the question. My best options were editing for a national glossy or writing another book (sadly, the era of gravy book deals had just ended).

I began slowly to panic over the issue of caring for my child while working in the city, most likely at a job I didn't really want. The more I realized how time-consuming my job would be, the more I agonized over having to hire someone to take over my role in cooking, cleaning and caring for Miles before and after school. I'd essentially be handing over my personal life (sans my spot in the bed) to a stranger. After talking to other working mothers in the neighborhood about hiring "nannies," the picture was clear: I had to get the fuck outta there.

So after a two-year run in suburbia, we moved to L.A. Miles started preschool, and I started a B.S. job doing post-production editing on a B.S. TV show to support us. Miles and I moved into my mom's place while my husband put the house on the market and quit his job. Four months later, he joined us. We left everything behind. Couches, lamps, towels—sold in the yard sale or given to the Salvation Army. Volvo—sold to the first buyer. We stored our bed and a smattering of furniture and shipped out the SUV. Like middle-class immigrants—"only the shirts on our backs" and the money from the sale of our house in the savings account—we were pursuing the new American Dream so popular on network TV dramas this fall: returning home.

Of course, my husband wasn't returning home. I was. He was leaving home for uncharted waters, based on my faith and hope. "It will all work out" is the worst reason for doing anything, and the best. But coming to L.A., as drastic and scary as it was, as far away from our original dream for raising Miles, was still far better than the course we had been on. We were kidding ourselves to think that living near New York City was the same as living in it, especially if you're not white. Once you cross through the tunnels or over the bridges, you might as well be anywhere else in America, because you're no longer living the city experience. You visit it on weekends. What's the point?

My father had recently died, and I wanted to be near my family. My mother didn't work and wanted to help us care for Miles, so we wouldn't have to rely on a baby sitter. She would get him from school, fix his dinner, supervise his homework, music practice and TV viewing—all the things that would be impossible to ask of a hired hand. She was an incredible mother and her offer to assist was impossible to refuse.

Once home, I had the time and energy to muster a script to land an agent and another script to land a job as a writer on the show *The West Wing*. Meanwhile, I also obsessed about Miles's education. He was in his last year of preschool. There are only three good public schools in all of L.A., and we didn't have the 2.3 million dollars necessary to buy a house in these districts. So private school was inevitable.

I filled out the applications, went to the open houses and interviews, and took Miles to the tests. It was a gauntlet more strenuous than any I had gone through for college. Except one school. There the only requirement was that your child test 145 or above on an IQ test, no preparation necessary. Many parents were fearful of the test, anticipating the disappointment that their children wouldn't be as "smart" as they believed them to be. I had the same fear, which was relieved when Miles tested into the school. (The entire issue of taking an IQ test at age four is highly debatable, and deserves an entire book.) Lucky for us, the school was also not even a mile from the house we had recently purchased, which was not even a mile from my mother's.

Conveniences aside, the school required uniforms, was 70 percent white, had a traditional academic approach and no kindergarten. This was not the educational utopia that we had envisioned five years earlier, with diversity as the cornerstone of Miles's socialization. But when we got the acceptance letter, we took them up on the invitation.

So, here I am. The next generation. As my parents did, I've moved my family to L.A. to work in the "biz." I'm raising a multiracial child in a mostly white environment and living in a house in the hills with the same view of the Valley I had as a child.

We've done a little better, in that Miles's school won't have the drugs and sexual abandon (at least not until junior high). His classmates aren't nearly as hip as ours were, but then again he won't be their only living example of a "real-life" person of color. He's one of four racially mixed kids in his class of twenty, not the freak that my brother and I were. And we're not the only family in the neighborhood with a darker hue. L.A.'s population now has a non-white majority, and immigrants with serious cash continue to arrive. Where we were once the neighborhood oddity, now Middle-Eastern, Asian and European families pepper the landscape.

When I told myself twenty years ago that I would never raise my child in the same environment that I was raised in, having him struggle with issues of racial identity and belonging, I certainly didn't picture ending up right where I started. But I guess to get a little perspective, you have to leave home and see for yourself that your parents made some damn good choices. Given the same circumstances, I couldn't have done better myself.

On the Road (with baby)

China

Looking at her face in the morning, it was hard to believe I didn't feel the newness of my month-old baby—not in the way I had expected. When I stared into her eyes, she just did not seem brand new to me.

My day began with the grogginess of waking up with not enough sleep again, with my suckling sweaty under my sleeping bag. But once up, I felt refreshed. After I pissed behind a tree that didn't hide me, I brushed my teeth in the trailer park water hose, and changed my milk-stained shirt.

She sleeps a lot, not quite in this world yet. I've heard that humans dream more as newborns than at any other age.

I tie her into her makeshift car seat, and Stacy turns on Metallica. The baby sleeps through this as she has slept through all of our music. (I did turn down the Butthole Surfers when I thought the screams might be too emotional for her.) We are back on the road.

Driving through Texas late last night, we set up our tent, in the trailer park in front of the Sheraton Hotel, without paying. It was right off the highway. We were so tired, but our conversation dripped with profound thoughts. Stacy told me that the *National Enquirer* ran a picture of a World War II plane found on the moon. She thought it was funny. She didn't believe the stuff she read in the normal newspapers, either. "What if everything they print in the *National Enquirer* is true?" I said. "No one believes it. You know, just like how most people won't see reality staring them in the face because it's too much for them."

We had driven for twelve hours or more in our truck. Stacy was leaving behind a broken heart; she and Helga wanted to escape. But me, with my baby—I kept wondering, *What am I doing?*

We drove. We drove by great white mountains and mesas, longing to climb up and sit Buddha-like on top. We had driven through New Mexico. We drove by volcanoes and great expanses of land.

We stopped in a roadside town, and I filled my daughter's prescription with Medicaid in a drugstore. All the towns were like other worlds. I watched the beautiful young children in these towns. I supposed they were descended from the indigenous tribes of North and South America. I watched sad cowboys walk across big parking lots.

Texas was full of tacky steak houses. Metal oil pumps that looked like they were sucking up every juice left in the earth. Nonstop surrealism. We watched dreams cut the earth as we drove, and we watched the earth rise and fall. We passed neon signs for headstones, the Home of the Ding Dong Daddy, a giant cow statue fronting an Old West amusement park, and a dead cow by a fence. Scenes and places and people's faces flashed by me in patterns.

The night before we left Boulder, Stacy's roommate's little black cat had her kittens. They had been talking about it for weeks: "Sassafras is about to pop." That night, I arrived at their house for the first time, and a few minutes later, Sassafras went into labor. I felt like my presence triggered it.

Laura had been petting Sassy when, right in the middle of the carpeted floor, a white bubble came out from her, and she started licking it. Laura screamed, "Oh Sassy, the babies are coming! Oh!" Stacy ran in from the other room and yelled, "Laura, don't touch her! Oh God, Oh God!"

And me, I just watched. I wanted to know what birth looked like—this thing I felt not too long before. I knew what it felt like to be the one delivering, but now I was going to see what it looked like, being on the outside of the experience.

I don't think Laura and Stacy had ever seen a birth before. Sassafras seemed to trust Laura so much, and she climbed into the box we laid out for her. Scared, Stacy had fled the room. We called to her, "Come on back, you have to see this." We settled down to watch. The kittens looked dead at first. Little wet creatures, they didn't even look like kittens until they were licked and licked and then finally opened their tiny mouths to cry and we were all just amazed.

I slept over that night, and a funny thing happened. When my baby woke and cried to be nursed, Sassafras ran over to her—with her eyes so round—trying to respond to that cry. She didn't know what to do. But the small young cat was now a mother, and as a mother, she had that strong tug in her gut to respond to a baby's cry.

It felt right to witness birth the night before we left. That night was also the biggest, fullest, brightest orange moon that I have ever seen.

Right near the horizon. At first I did not even recognize it as the moon. It marked one complete lunar cycle since the full moon when my baby had been born.

It was early in the morning when we stopped at Denny's for coffee. Texan accents and square-dancing outfits were everywhere. Our waitress zeroed in on my new baby—she had two children of her own. It was strange to connect with people who would have stayed distant before. It was like we all belonged to a secret club of motherhood.

Of course, everyone stared at us. Stacy in her Doc Martens, tattoos and spikes. She had shaved off her mohawk and was now bald. She was a GBH punk getting into speed metal, a good person who roared with laughter when she laughed. Helga had a nose-ring and long, bleached dreadlocks, like a lamb. And I looked like most new mothers who barely get the chance to piss or change their shirt. I'd turned into a mess and didn't care. I wore tennis shoes and let the green dye wash out of my hair without touching it up.

We were different folk for this town. It was fun to see how different people lived.

Speculation and talk was an all-day affair as we rode in the truck, Helga driving. My conversation revolved almost entirely around my as-yet-unnamed baby. The people I knew and the people I met didn't know much about birth, so I felt it was up to me to tell everyone about my labor and eating the placenta, and her. And her! That I loved her like I had never loved—like a mother.

And all my life, I will love her. Physically, like the gush in my breasts. I love her in the way that shapes what is bent awry back to its true form.

She taught me that my breasts were mine and I could show them if I wanted. She taught me that my body worked and was not inadequate or dysfunctional, as I had felt most of my life. I carried her to fruition, and I birthed this perfect child at home with the light assistance of my midwife. I did this. I trusted myself more than I ever had before. I trusted my child and I trusted this life. I came through the fear and mystery of pregnancy to the clear light of day of motherhood.

I have leapt chasms, spat like mountains, gushed like rivers and screamed better than the demonically possessed. I learned I was life, and life and I merged and growled with each contraction. I have raised the red toast of placenta to my lips. I am the earth who drinks the same old rain again, but it is cleansed. It keeps getting polluted. I know it's harder than ever to get clean, to rise lighter than trash into the sky, and fall to do it again, and again, like a tired slut walking home in the morning hour, to do it again. But birth raises brand-new flowers and little blades of green grass. It has a will so strong some can't understand it, so they call it instinct, as if it had no choice. It's always going to do it—to raise the dead. This is sex. This is love.

My daughter had the most beautiful face I have ever seen. I watched her, and I thought then that there could be no death: If this child could come from me, could grow to be a woman, then why couldn't a corpse change into something new—it was no larger a feat than birth! I felt different about life itself, because of my child.

And it wasn't just me. Others were surprised by her flexibility, strength and composure. A man in New Orleans held her gently like she was an egg, and stared at her in wonder. She was the first infant he had ever held, ever truly seen.

I was initiated into an underground sisterhood. I took the child and showed her—like a key, like a message to the world—to the people who would ignore her if they could, to the people who were startled and to the people who smiled. I was her food, balance and escort. I was her good and loving mother, and she was my child. It was love that was born. It was something that I could not have foreseen.

In the town we had left, I could look into the eyes of other mothers who knew and who loved, and they would embrace us fully in their conversation. Waiting in the welfare office, I felt the warmth of motherkind in small-town greetings. It was my special place. These women would look at the young one in my arms and remember when their child was a newborn. Sturdy women who would come down from the Colorado mountains, to wait in line on food-stamp day.

We arrived in Florida at our destination—Helga's parents' house. My suitcase explodes, like a jack-in-the-box, in their spare bedroom.

"Is she really supposed to nurse that much?" someone asks me. I don't know. My baby's like a young alcoholic with the milk, but who's going to say no to her? Not me. Could nature be that crazy? "I suppose she is supposed to do what she does," I answer. My life drips milk and stains everything we touch.

Helga's mom says "It's not right," when I tote the baby to the grocery store. "Babies that young shouldn't leave the house," she says. "And they should sleep bundled in a cradle, not by their mother's side."

Stacy says, "It's such a fuckin' drag to know there's nothing left anymore. Just . . . hell. You can't even get on a bus. A bus out of hell going back to hell." She cracks me up, but she is right. I write a poem called "The Humor of our Lives":

It's hard to get around with a baby hangin' on your tit. It's hard
to settle down when you got no town, just other people's places.
We shuffle from here to there. We dry our eyes so we can cry

them out again. We run in the mud and are free for a while. We shuffle and flee from you to me. Life is a thick pea soup we must swallow whole to be free. We sit in a suburban house in Florida and are confused. Someday you will look back and laugh, they say. We laugh so hard today, how can we laugh any harder tomorrow?

The South is the terrain of the subconscious. Trees grow Seuss-like, snaky and parallel to the ground with spikes and scales. It's a primeval world here, full of alligators, dragons, wild boars and palmettos. The plants and trees grow thick here, reaching out for each other, making one impenetrable clump. The sun is a hot fireball. There are mugwumps in the Everglades and prehistoric pelicans in the coastal sky. People go crazy, trying to hack out a bald spot to plant themselves some grass to water.

We go to a barbecue, and I hear the sounds of monkeys in the backyard. They escaped from the set of a Tarzan movie in the 1950s and have been living feral around these parts ever since.

There is a beautiful biker-mom chick at the party who mesmerizes me. She is so perfect, in a classic blond Malibu Barbie kind of way, wearing very short cutoffs. She sits on the sofa, flawless except for the absence of one entire leg. She lost it in a recent motorcycle accident and is going in for surgery again soon. With a cool, proud demeanor, she tells me how her husband has been so wonderful through the whole thing, watching their two young children and supporting her.

Stacy got on a bus going back home to Boulder, Colorado. I grew up an army brat—I wasn't from anywhere to speak of. I only stopped in Boulder to have my baby (I had been on the road for the first half of my pregnancy, too) and left when my best friends wanted to. There was no reason to stay without them. And now they were growing distant from me.

It was time to leave Florida, so I headed north to my parents' house in suburban Maryland. I stayed there for a bit, sheltered from the world and isolated, until I was invited to go on a road trip to an anarchist convention in Canada. So go I did. I waited for my young, punk friends to get ready, finish packing the van. It was after midnight when we left. I was tired and worried about being in the company of those who like to stay up half the night. Sleep was so important to maintaining my sanity while being responsible for the care of my child.

I lost ten pounds in Toronto, breast-feeding and living only on toast. My daughter's colic really kicked in, and I walked with her, patting her back, holding her as she wailed and screamed. People came out of their houses to look at me and see if I was killing her.

When we got to the anarchist gathering, I went straight to the daycare room and stayed there. What joy to meet other parents like me. Our conversations made me feel sane: "Do you feel left behind, too? Do you feel you can't keep up? So it's not just me!" "Parenthood is just as big of a subculture as being a punk. I felt relieved to find others like myself."

I'd seen enough of the road. So I went west with high hopes of finding the ideal place to raise a child and settle down. I can't say I ever found that place. But this story ends here, by the Pacific Ocean, where my child grows strong playing in tidal pools and under cafe tables, in Santa Cruz, California.

My daughter was eight months old by the time we moved into our very own apartment.

Roots Deep in the Soil

LaSara W. FireFox

It is sometime in the late 1970s. I am a small child. I run free in the wilderness. We live in the hills, barely ever go to town. Occasionally we see our neighbors, who live a mile away. My family is large.

I am taught at home, don't go to school. We survive off the land. Sometimes we go hungry. We eat fresh veggies from our huge garden, slaughter animals for food. Often we augment our diet with government cheese and commodities.

It is 1985. The front-page headline of *The Grapevine,* the independent newspaper in Ukiah, reads "The End of an Era." The topic of the article is the demise of my parents' relationship. The last of the homesteader hippies have finally folded under the pressure.

The dream of self-reliance is waning. The drugs of choice in the bohemia of Northern California have switched from those with expansive properties to those with contractile: from hallucinogens to booze and coke. My folks have been ostracized because they don't use. Well, my mom doesn't. My dad is an alcoholic. Thus, the demise of their marriage.

Somewhere in the beautiful, earth-friendly, righteous move to low-impact living, my parents gave up their independence, their dreams. Four kids later (plus two from my mom's first marriage), there is nothing left but resentment, prize crops going to bloom and then to seed in fertile soil, dead cows and now-feral goats. The ducks fly away.

It is 1986. Home is a tent in Tent City. Mom has taken us out of Mendocino County, in part to escape the ugliness of the divorce and in part to gain her own independence. We are marching from California to Washington, D.C., on the Great Peace March for Global Nuclear Disarmament. I turn fifteen on the peak of the Continental Divide. Loveland Pass.

We do not achieve world peace, but we arrive in D.C. after nine months on the road, living on the charity of our supporters, and learning new ways of being in community, being at home, being together. Leaving the ground we tread on cleaner than we found it, we are a traveling village, idealistic, committed, successful.

It is 1989. I have my own place. A room in a house off campus. The house has electricity, hot running water. My first time living full-time with modern amenities, I get used to it all very quickly. Except for the fact that I can feel the electricity humming in the walls.

◯

I am nineteen. I spend the summer traveling in Europe with friends. We find home in an anarchist squat in Berlin. The political unification of Germany is upon us. There are riots every day. The squatters' unity is strong, in response to the daily fear of the destruction of our home.

I am happy to be angry, and not alone in it. For the first time I feel at home with people of my own age. *Down with governments! Let the black flag fly!*

It is 1991. Back in the States, I'm couch surfing. My friends are generous, and I find my home in many houses. I throw parties, create change, protest the Gulf War and finally finish the semester at university, never to return.

Home has been transitory, elusive. I have seen home flitting about the periphery of our discussion and action groups. We talk about getting land together, creating a community dedicated to anarchist ideals. We are in love with one another, in love with the struggle, in love with our ideas. We are young and don't know it. I'm more jaded than others. I know love doesn't always last like we think it should.

I move to L.A. for love and martial arts. I am living with a lover for the first time. We work and study martial arts. I never find a home in L.A., the city with no heart. I cannot put roots down here, with no soil to nourish my growth. After thirteen months I move north again, telling my lover he can follow me when he will.

At the age of twenty-one I finally have a home to myself, a tiny cottage in Oakland worth less than I pay for it. Still, it is a great feeling to have my own space. I am strong in my independence, although still in love with my lover in L.A. I spend a lot of time alone. My cottage is surrounded by a garden, and I am happy to smell the earth again.

The lover moves up to the Bay Area. He convinces me I shouldn't be paying so much rent. He's moving into a martial arts school that a friend is starting. They are converting a warehouse space into a dojo and living quarters. Even though I am no longer the avid martial artist that I was in L.A., I move in. It is a mistake. My lover and I fight about everything. We fight loudly and fuck loudly, and everyone simply loves living with us.

We finally break up, and go on a road trip to Mexico together to celebrate. I get pregnant on the way home. I tell him about the baby, and he says "You aren't thinking of having it, are you?" I don't say all the things I could, like, "I would if it weren't yours," and say, "Not now."

I have an abortion. It nearly kills me. It is a menstrual extraction, performed by women whose names I'm not allowed to know. I take this route for two reasons: money and political idealism. I am willing to let my body be a pawn in the fight against the patriarchy. With women like these around, we will never lose our ability to have abortions. I do it to support their existence.

I say I don't want injections. I want to feel it all. It hurts like hell, almost enough to separate body and spirit. I do feel it all. I feel our baby, or the promise of it, being torn from my womb. It is horrible.

I will never forgive him. Finally, the relationship is over, and I can move on.

I live where I am. I park wherever, sleep wherever. I have wheels under me and a camper shell over me. I fear nothing.

I sleep in Oakland, Lower Haight, outside whichever bar I close. I drink a lot, have sex with strangers, let people I don't know sleep in my truck with me.

I spend some time in Mendocino County, then head up to Seattle. My truck, Turtle, and I are a nation unto ourselves. I feel like a cowgirl. The Lone Ranger.

Home is fluid and solid at the same time.

I ponder the idea of moving to Seattle, but settle back into Mendocino County at my mother's urging. I spend some time living in my truck on the land where I grew up. It is nice to be home, but also confining.

After nearly a year in motion, I decide I want a house. I find a place to live in Ukiah, the town nearest the family land.

I am used to my living room being a bar, and need to phase my way out of habitual binges. My new room feels like a cave—dark, a little dank, but I throw great parties.

All my old friends are doing the same old things: speed, booze. Everyone has slept with everyone, and everyone's best friend. I'm not interested in being part of it.

I start hanging out with younger friends. I don't know these people yet. They have come into their own in the years I have been away from here. I find home in this circle of youth.

The minds of my peers are already atrophying with overindulgence in bad drugs. Longing for fresh awareness, I get down with the next generation. I'm a bad influence. I corrupt many pure souls, sully many mothers' young ones. I love being the bad girl.

I next live as a caregiver for an old woman who is dying. I sit with her, talk with her, listen to her stories. I get high with her. We smoke pot.

She passes through the veil. Her final stroke pushes her over the edge. She doesn't eat for days. She slips into a coma. She dies, and I am the last one to see her breathing. She is taken out wrapped in a sheet after her daughter cleans her body and dresses her in a fresh nightgown.

It is beautiful. I am honored to witness her death.

I stay on in the apartment, renting out the room that had been hers to a friend. It takes a while for the distinctive scent of death to fade.

My roommate leaves town, and I feel it is time to move on. I throw a moving-out party with a cross-dressing theme. All the young men I know show up as girls. The girls they think they want to meet. It is so great to see the boys flirt with one another. We're in rural Mendocino County. Some of these guys wear cowboy hats in real life. They are grabbing each other's asses, commenting on one another's legs and breasts. Even kissing.

I move back to Greenfield Ranch, the land where I grew up. Not to the parcel my family lived on, but to a friend's place. It's a tiny and isolated yurt. My friend is leaving the area.

I spend an autumn and winter drinking and praying. I work a graveyard shift and spend my time searching for enlightenment à la Kerouac. My home is my cloister, and I am seeking the hand of God to intervene and pull me out of my depressive hell. I seek divine love. I go celibate, devote myself to love, talk on the phone with my mother, drop out of sight.

Divine love comes in the form of a beautiful young man with flowing blond hair. We hook up and rapidly become inseparable. I find home in his arms. He feels familiar.

On Sadie Hawkins Day I ask him to marry me. We've been together for twenty-five days. I call him from work on my break, from a pay phone outside. I say, "You don't have to answer me now. Just think about it." He says, "I want to answer you." I'm scared. He says, "Yes." And I'm even more scared. But I'm in love.

Home is our car. We are car camping and couch surfing together in Sonoma County when I get pregnant. It's a condom baby. One of the .01 percent, or whatever. A miracle. This little spirit bonds our fates together as no words can. We decide to marry before the baby is born, to the relief of his mother.

I have met his parents twice when he tells them he's having a baby. They say, "With who?" Mercifully, I am not present for this discussion. We have been together for three months. His father says, "There are options, you know . . . " He says yeah, he knows. Dad says, "Well, do you love her?" He says, "Yes."

We are living on the land where I grew up. It is a trip. We camp on the platform where I spent my summers as a child. The dirt smells good. My husband-to-be is going insane with the quiet of country life. I tell him, "Stay with it. Notice what's happening. You're going through detox." Detoxing from years of urban distraction, noise pollution, visual overload. And he is. He does. We are home on the land, grounded. Life is solid.

I am sick as hell with pregnancy, but I feel safe on my motherland.

It is September, 1996. We are to be married on Greenfield at the Ranch House Community Center.

We spend the night before the wedding apart. I stay with my women friends, my sisters and my mom at the yurt where I lived when he and I got together. It is a sweet place, a sweet way to spend my last night before the big day. He stays at the Ranch House. It serves to build the tension of our impending union.

In the morning, I walk the mile to the Ranch House from the yurt barefoot, stop to throw flowers in the common land pond, sing songs with my bridesmaid, best friend, buddy. I take my sweet time. I am late for my own wedding.

By the time I arrive, he is getting antsy. But it is the best day of our lives. We are high on the intensity. We're so in love. We share amazing vows. We have prepared ourselves for this ceremony with days of ritual.

About two hundred of our friends and family witness our union. Many of my past lovers are present. People are in shock. LaSara, the wild one, is getting married.

We feast on a sheep we helped my father slaughter two nights prior, feast on our potluck wedding supper. My brother makes a toast. We all laugh at how fast it's all gone.

My husband and I stay in a room in the Ranch House. We don't leave the party, but retire, still enveloped in the sounds of revelry. We fall into bed early, exhausted. In time with the heartbeat, drumbeat, of our day of honor, we make sweet and satisfying love as married folks expecting a baby.

We arrive home after the wedding weekend and move into the house my parents built. It has been more or less empty of human life since my folks separated. We have spent the summer cleaning it out and patching the apparent holes. It is strange to be living in the shell of my parents' dreams. But the house is lovely, and the land is manna from the gods. All the same, it is a hard life. We don't have hot water or a phone or electricity. We are walking in my parents' footsteps. We are living lightly on the land. We are on welfare to cover the lack. We are on Medi-Cal to cover the pregnancy.

We have a Thanksgiving party with twenty-three guests. The house is festive. We feel full of home. I am seven months pregnant. I am the matriarch in the family house. This causes some tension with my mother.

My family is present: Mom, my two brothers, one of my sisters and her newborn boy. So are many friends, old and new. The house is glowing, and it reminds me and my family of years earlier.

Valentine's Day, 1997, two weeks after my due date, I go into labor. We are having a home birth. After three days of pain and exhaustion, we decide to head out to the hospital. I am passing out between contractions.

The baby, a sweet glowing little girl, is born halfway to the car, on the path, under an oak tree. It is 1:03 A.M., a waxing moon, an almost balmy February night. She is born, whole and perfect, and I am relieved. She is sweet and lovely. She looks at her dad first. I am seeing spirits. It's amazing. I'm on drugs, the natural kind, produced by my own body. She nurses and nurses. I have dirt, blood and amniotic fluid all over my ass. There are leaves and dirt sticking to me.

My daughter is a daughter born at home of a daughter born at home of a daughter born at home, an unbroken line back to the beginning of daughters being born. And never a one in a hospital.

We struggle with the demons of low-impact living. We make many improvements on the land. We have hot running water, a limited photovoltaic power system. We have lights and a cell phone.

It is beautiful land, God's country. There are spirits in the hills, fairies in the trees. We see mountain lions, bobcats, bears. We slaughter and consume a deer wounded by a predator.

We live close to the earth, feel the strong storms, cold nights, hot days, long summers, longer winters. We heat ourselves with the power of fire, drink pristine water from a spring on the hill above us.

Our daughter's first food is blackberries from the front yard. She smiles through the red smear on her face. It looks like she's just devoured some small red-blooded creature raw.

She crawls on hard, wood floors, learns to walk on soft dirt. We kill five rattlesnakes one summer to keep her safe. We eat them as well. We keep the skins, destroy the heads in our fire pit.

I get pregnant again. My husband and I are both working. On my days at home I sit with my older daughter outside. We lounge naked in the sunlight. It feels good to be exposed to the elements. Soft breezes caressing my body, gentle sunlight warming my skin. We read together.

I cannot work on my days at home. Our daughter gets to see one video a day. The electricity is rationed. She knows that if it's cloudy, she doesn't get to see a movie at all.

After three years on the family land, I am pregnant with my second child, trying to launch my career and tired of the amount of work it takes to survive in the outback. I cannot face the austerity of the low-impact life we have led any longer. My husband's parents support the idea of us re-entering the civilized world, and we begin looking for our next home.

We find a place, still in the middle of nowhere but with indoor plumbing. A paved road. A watertight roof. A phone. I can get my email from my house! It is a home, a house, with electricity and amenities.

My husband and I feel like we are wimping out. We are leaving the Garden. We are sorry that our children will not live on this ancestral land. Our hearts break in making the choice.

Our new home is two acres on the Eel River, outside a tiny town called Potter Valley. It is much more manageable. I work a lot. Do a lot of writing. Let my daughter of nearly three years watch television while I sit at my computer and type for hours at a shot. I feel guilty that she is not playing outside.

I am somewhat at home in my identity as a self-employed writer, a work-at-home mom.

Our next daughter is born in the Seventh-day Adventist hospital in Ukiah. A C-section. We move closer to the center, become less judgmental. I am happy to be alive, happy my daughter made it. Our lives have been saved by the intervention of the Patriarchy.

I am at home in the love of my children. The possibility of death has brought me into living. I am so alive. But I swear I will never have another child. I was not built for this.

Try as we may, home will not stabilize, and we spend more and more time in the San Francisco Bay Area. Work calls me there. My husband becomes less and less satisfied with life as a service-sector grunt worker. Our art calls us more and more strongly. And our art is not at home where our bodies live. We are still too rural. We feel very alone.

We decide to move to the city. We follow our dreams to the

metropolitan center of Northern California. We are taken care of. Home is a basement apartment in a friend's place in Bernal Heights. We are supported in our move.

San Francisco is a different home. My roots are still strong in the soil of Mendocino County. We struggle in the noise, speed, paranoia and claustrophobia of city life. Cities have always reminded me of rat cages. I don't believe people were meant to live this way.

We are loved here, supported, and my husband needs to go back to school so we can get somewhere in our lives. We are both at the end of our twenties. I am rubbing more roughly against thirty than he is, but we both feel it.

Here in the city, home is a hearth of friend-light, the fire a virtual one, formed by a community of minds. Ideas that encourage and encompass our own. We are surrounded by the light of a new eon, a generation of new thought. We are not alone here.

Raised money-poor and dirt-rich, I pass on the legacy of land to my daughters. Even from the city, pitch-black nights with only star glitter for light and shockingly quiet mornings are a day's drive away. The scent of clean dirt, sweet, clear water, the comfort of a fire-warmed house and air that feels like love in my lungs, achingly pure and sensually satisfying, call to me.

Home is where I am standing. I stand in different places day to day. Home appears, a composite view. Home is everywhere I have ever loved. My heart is shattered into millions of pieces, scattered across the planet.

Home is the people and places I have known, everywhere I have ever belonged.

Home, elusive and transitory, solid in the earthy history of my blood, strong in the currents and eddies of lover and beloved. Home is where the heart is, and my heart is held strong in the sweetness of my children, family, tribe. Home is a verb, stated in present tense.

Confessions of a Heathen

Ana June

They must have thought I was a Satanist. I was cleaning out my car on a warm morning in May. Junk that had accumulated in the nether regions of my vehicle over a ten-month period of time was strewn hither and yon on the driveway. Dirty clothes, toys, stinky coffee mugs, sippy cups and even a bag of soiled cloth diapers. Lord knows how long that had been stewing in the trunk. The children danced around in mud-stained clothes, rat's-nest hair. Soren, age five, had chosen a mid-thigh-length dinosaur T-shirt and soccer shoes to wear that day— and nothing else. Mirabai, nearly three, sat in the dust playing with old Power Rangers.

The kids saw the two men in suits before I did, and Soren ran to greet them. I looked up and smiled stiffly, then remembered that I was still wearing my nightshirt—the one on which a skeleton in a Mickey Mouse hat smiles and waves cheerfully (inscription on the back: "At least I'm enjoying the ride"). My hair, hastily bound in a ponytail, was as yet unwashed. My jeans, ripped and stained. Shoes—was I wearing shoes?

"Morning!" I said. "May I help you?" I stopped short of offering a grubby handshake.

"Hello," said Suit-Man One, "we're from Santa Maria de la Paz Catholic Community. We're in the neighborhood today to invite anyone who doesn't already have a spiritual home to join us. Do you have a spiritual home?"

"Well, no," I said blithely, then winced as he started to offer me a piece of paper. "But we're definitely not Catholic!" I added, pasting a most genuine smile on my face.

"Ah, okay. Thank you anyway." They turned to go accost my neighbor.

"Nice to meet you!" I called. I think they grumbled a response.

I returned to my car, my mind rolling over thoughts of God and sin and holiness and virtue and, well, religion, plain and simple. When I was a child, a couple of girls down the street invited me to their Baptist church one night. I went. I went a few more times after that, too. My parents knew about it and were dubious, which didn't surprise me. They were always dubious about religion. So much so, in fact, that I learned little about it from them. In order to reconcile the stories of hell and damnation that I heard from my mostly Catholic classmates, I had to believe in God at least a little. This translated into fearing Hell, a lot, wanting to die before I became an adult so that I would be "an angel" (old people apparently became ghosts, which was far less desirable) and even making up my own God. His name was Karu, and I pictured him somewhat like the alien I drew for a creative arts project in third grade: small and furry, not unlike a gremlin. My gremlin God didn't get me very far, however. Neither did going to church with my friends. My naiveté drove me to raise my hand when the preacher polled the congregation one day, asking who was ready to commit themselves to God. Through baptism.

I didn't know what baptism was all about. All I knew was that everyone was excited that I had chosen to "commit." I was led to a back room by the mother of my friends and given a corduroy robe that looked like a dress. I was supposed to take off all my clothes and put on the robe so that the preacher could baptize me. But my friends' mother stood there, talking to me, watching me, and I was frozen in nodding politeness, wanting nothing more than for her to turn her back so I could undress. When she finally got the hint, she sighed and turned around, then remarked that in her family everyone just walks around naked. "It's only the three of us girls, you know."

When I was ready, the preacher walked me to a small room. He wore an identical corduroy robe, and I knew—without even blushing—that he was naked beneath it. Just as I was. In the room was a pool of water, and for some reason I was sure it would be cold. It felt strange to step into warm water instead. One side of the wall was covered by a curtain, and as I stepped into the pool the curtain began to open.

I was shocked when I realized what lay beyond. The entire congregation stood and started singing when they saw me. I froze. I didn't know what would happen next, what to do, even who I was. Behind me the preacher was saying something, but I didn't pay any attention until suddenly he grabbed me by the shoulders, leaned me backward and dunked my entire head beneath the water.

To his disgust, I came up coughing and spluttering. He must have known then that I would make a lousy Baptist.

After I changed back into my clothes, I was escorted to the altar, where people were lined up to shake my hand. I stood there, bewildered, as my hair dripped down my back. By the time I was delivered home, I was cold, nearly shivering, and my parents greeted me with wide eyes.

They joke about it now.

"Hey, remember that you're a Baptist?" they say, and we all laugh. Invariably my mom adds how upset she was that they not only baptized me without parental consent but brought me home in the dead of winter with a wet head. All I can recall is the confusion of being in that warm water with a preacher in a dress and a church full of people watching and singing.

Since my run-in with the Baptists, I have had a few other religious experiences. When I was still young enough to attend Sunday school, I once went to church with my grandparents. I remember little from the experience, except this: The Sunday-school room smelled like barf. Strongly, deeply like barf. And everyone, kids included, tried to pretend that all was normal. There we were, singing and playing churchy games in a barfy room, and there was absolutely no missing that odor. No mistaking it.

I survived the ordeal without barfing in response and even felt strong enough to begin attending church many years later with the man I would marry. Memories from those churchgoing days include playing the "in bed" game with the hymnal (in which we'd take the title of a hymn and add "in bed" to the end: "How Great Thou Art . . . in bed," for instance), trying not to giggle too loudly and making fun of the man who led the singing on certain occasions. He sounded exactly like Kermit the Frog.

Malcolm's church factored strongly into our wedding plans. We attended premarital counseling with his minister and then asked him to officiate. Though we chose the vows (I threw in a couple of poems by Kahlil Gibran), we were also encouraged to let the minister add a Christian touch. We tried desperately not to giggle as he read, "Look there, my lover, see him bounding across the meadows, he grazes among the lilies," or something to that effect.

After the wedding, we settled into a life that did not include weekly church attendance. Malcolm even discovered Wicca, which I decided was not to my taste after attending Yule festivities during which everyone harmonized along to "God Rest Ye Merry Pagan Folk." We did, however, go to a Sunday service during a family visit to Texas. I believe the church we attended that hot morning was Malcolm's grandfather's church. Indeed, every single member was elderly.

To this service we brought two-month-old Soren, and we all—Malcolm's mother and cousins included—tried ever so hard to be polite as Soren began nursing, smacking his lips, belching and farting. You could hear him from across the room. I would have taken him out, but we were crammed in the pews, and I kept hoping that he'd just be done with it. This scene was nicely topped off with an incomprehensible sermon that had something to do with making sure you get "certified seed."

Since that episode, we've attended a few more services and some church functions—barbecues and baby welcomings—but nothing "took." No light appeared for me, nor did I fully expect one. *Poor Catholics*, I thought, as I cleaned unidentifiable food particles from the floorboards of my car. *If ever there were a lost cause.* But as the children raced around the car, kicking up dust and wailing like banshees, I was reminded of that new Christian catch phrase: What Would Jesus Do? *Hmmm* . . . The Suit-Men must have sent their thoughts to me via some celestial radio frequency.

But hey, what *would* Jesus do? I've seen the foreshortening of that saying—WWJD—on everything from bumper stickers to keychains but haven't paid it much attention. I mean, Jesus was a great person and all; he had a cool message and was gentle and loving—an enlightened guy. But he doesn't cross my mind on a daily basis. It isn't Jesus, or even the Bible, that fills me with doubt or suspicion. Instead, I find the distortion of his message by mere mortals to be entirely off-putting. Would Jesus baptize a child without parental knowledge or consent? And wouldn't he at least warn her before shoving her under water? Would Jesus send her home with a wet head?

I am pretty sure Jesus wouldn't plead for money on cable TV. He wouldn't wear a toupee and sit on a tacky, golden settee. He certainly wouldn't paint a grand piano gold and hang with Tammy Faye's alter ego. He wouldn't molest altar boys. He wouldn't kill in the name of God.

But I could believe that maybe, in his enlightened benevolence, he would help me clean my car, play with the children, conjure dinner out of the measly scraps of leftovers lurking in the back of my fridge. I'm sure he would know some soothing bedtime stories. And after he got the kids peacefully to sleep, I'm sure he wouldn't mind shooting the breeze with me for a while. I'd be curious to know what he thinks about such current controversies as evolution, prayer in schools, evangelists. And did he know about the dinosaurs?

But really, I'm hardly worthy. That's why I have a limping car with an oil leak and stained upholstery, after all. So I question myself. And, since religion plays a large role in many people's lives, I worry about my kids.

Growing up in the predominately Spanish town of Santa Fe, New Mexico, I learned the importance of religion in family life. I watched my classmates prepare for First Holy Communion and heard their stories of grand get-togethers with extended family. Many of these families were eligible for land grants or could trace their ancestry back to the conquistadors. All of them could lay claim to New Mexico by virtue of being there for countless generations—they were rooted in the deep clay earth. I can barely summon a tomato plant out of a piece of my homeland, a term I use loosely since I was not actually born there. In New Mexico, place is vital. Place is linked to heritage and heritage is tied directly to God. By not raising my children with a formal belief in God, I am often concerned that they will grow up with no mooring in tradition. I worry that they will feel adrift, as I sometimes do, and unsure about their heritage.

Thus, given my suspicion of Christianity, I sought to reconcile my search for identity by looking into Buddhism. What I learned made perfect sense to me, which I attributed to my East Indian blood. Never mind that it's only a few drops. Never mind that most of that side of the family is actually Christian. Never mind that the Indian heritage was strongly denied by that side of the family, so much so that one of my dark-complected aunts was actually hidden away after her arrival in the United States, lest she somehow challenge the British and French lineage my family held so dear. Though this woman, Mabel, was alive and well when my mother was young, the two never met. In fact, my mother knew nothing of Mabel's existence until a couple of years ago.

Discovering this skeleton in the ancestral closet (and a few others) served to deepen my own sense of pride in my Indian roots. And since I have found less to be proud of in my British and German lineage, I have mixed what I know of being partly East Indian with a bit of what I have learned, and have arrived at something approximating a religion. I prefer to think of it as an identity. A heritage. A "spiritual home," if you will.

For truly, I have seen too much beauty in this world not to believe in a God of sorts. Yet, so have I pondered the "mystery" for too long to find any meaning in established religion. When I am still, when I pay attention, I see God in everything. In the face of my first-born, a split second after birth, I saw God—innocent, pure, gazing back at me. Likewise with my daughter, who burst into life to the welcoming chorus of early morning bird song. After both births I saw God flit away, laughing. Joyous. Yes, my God is joyous.

But I have not completely re-created the idea of God. Every Christmas I am moved by the spirit of old songs around my mother's Steinway.

"Joy to the World," "Cantique de Noel." We always set up a tree, a live one, and decorate it with ornaments that have been in the family for years. Some of the ornaments are handmade, obviously by children. Every Christmas I pause to recall who made them. I stitched the puppy ornament, with help, when I was three. My husband drew this Santa Claus glued to a Styrofoam cup when he was six. My children are adding to this collection now.

And as tradition dictates, we spend Christmas Eve walking the bitter cold streets of downtown Santa Fe, singing carols and marveling at the paths of farolitos stretching out along the roadsides, on walls, rooftops, in tree limbs. The amber light glowing from within those small bags means Christmas to me. Likewise, warming icy fingers by the blazing luminarias. Among strangers.

I teach my children of their roots, from India and Europe to the dusty wagon ruts of northern Arizona traveled by their great-great grandfather over a hundred years ago. And I speak with pride of their place. Of Soren's native town of Española, of Mirabai's native Santa Fe. I remind her that she drew her first breath in the house that saw my own life's growth. Malcolm and I share our stories with them, and they are privy to the wisdom and memories of all their grandparents and two of their great-grandparents.

So when those Catholics visited and left me pondering my beliefs, I could truly find nothing lacking in the end. In their eyes I am undoubtedly headed to hell in a handbasket (or a bucket, if you believe my shirt). But I am certain that if God created me to be who I am, then he or she must also know that I have no place in a Catholic church—or any other.

As for my kids, maybe they will grow up to renounce the family belief system. Maybe they'll laugh at the idea of seeing God in everything. Maybe they'll dabble in Christianity and get baptized, lead cheerful

Sunday-school activities in stinky church rooms, take the hymnals and the sermons seriously. Perhaps they'll frown on people like me who make fun of preachers and sacred songs. They might even have stand-up/sit-down weddings in grand cathedrals. Or perhaps they'll celebrate Yule instead of Christmas, Beltane in lieu of Easter. These things I cannot know. I can only trust that they, too, will find their paths. Along the way I hope they will be thankful that they know their family history, that they are loved.

I say this with conviction, but I'm sure I will have many more moments of doubt and insecurity. Wanting to do right by the children I brought into this world is the strongest drive I feel, but the answers about certain things are not clear-cut. For most of this parenting gig, I've been winging it. In moments of lucidity, I know that's okay. I know my children are strong, have good heads on their shoulders.

And I know that no matter how hard I try or how much effort I expend as I help them walk the path from childhood to maturity, I'll always worry about them. I'll always wonder if I made the right choices, protected them adequately, helped them grow to their fullest potential.

But I swear, if they stick one more piece of half-eaten fruit in the space beneath their car seats so that I am forced to turn the car practically inside out in search of whatever-in-*hell*-that-foul-stench-is, well then, I may just have to sacrifice them both. Ahem. To the gods.

LEARNING TO SURF

Jennifer Savage

I stumble into my daughter's preschool, escaping the glare of the sun against the sand and sidewalk outside. I cocktail nights at Bogart's, a punk—or is it grunge?—club, and this morning I am hung over: one too many shots during after-hours cleanup. I hold the door open for my daughter, who trails in after me, all mismatched clothes and crazy hair. What can I say? Chelsea likes to dress herself. Fine by me. I'm dressed quite fashionably myself—jeans with the knees ripped out and a flannel shirt. I am twenty-two years old. My daughter is two. Her dad, Bobby, and I are getting married next month.

I pull my sunglasses off my head, tuck my keys into my jeans and scrawl my name in the sign-in book. I smile good morning at the three moms congregated in the lobby; I can't help myself. They stretch their lips in a thin upward motion and look away. Fuck 'em. I walk Chelsea to her classroom, say hi to her teacher, Ms. Joan—a sweetheart of a woman who raves about how clever my daughter is—and murmur bye to Chelsea, managing to get a kiss and a hug.

Back outside, my beat-up 1973 Super Beetle with the Red Hot Chili Peppers sticker on the window is bookended by minivans. As I drive away, I try to imagine what those other moms think of me. But I can't. I don't know how thirty-year-old, minivan-owning brains work. They probably think I'm on welfare. I wonder what would be worse to them: being on welfare or slinging drinks to a heavily pierced crowd as a band called "Lubricated Goat" screams onstage.

In addition to serving drinks at night, I work two days a week at Bogart's, answering the phone, selling tickets, coordinating sound checks and playing gin rummy with my co-workers who drop by. Sometimes Bobby brings Chelsea in to say hi and, if the timing's right, she'll get to watch the sound check. She loves the shininess and noise of the drums; I love watching her bounce in time to the beat.

When Chelsea's happy, I think maybe I'm doing okay as a mom, maybe she'll remember the good times: watching the bands, playing at Mother's Beach, riding around the city on the Blue Line train. But I worry. I don't know if the good mom stuff outweighs the bad. I yell. I throw things. I bounce checks.

I want to be a good mom. But how? The very idea of having kids had always sparked a strong "no way!" reaction in me. No kids for me, no marriage, just well-paying jobs; I was going to be "free." Then I found myself pregnant. Worse, I'd fallen in love. Several people advised me to get an abortion, but I couldn't. This little blip inside me had actually been conceived in love. Well, okay, maybe conceived in an empty banquet room at a friend's wedding reception, but still, I did love her dad. Bobby and I had been together a long time by then, a whole year and a half.

When I decided—no, "decided" sounds like too rational a word— when suddenly a long-buried bit of hope surfaced from underneath the layers of cynicism I'd cultivated since adolescence, when I found myself in the grip of an unnamable, unstoppable emotion that had me saying, "I want to have this baby," the feeling signified a monumental shift in attitude. Before getting pregnant, I'd viewed the world as a collage of betrayal: Politicians lied, schools failed to educate, parents divorced, men broke trusting young girls' hearts. Only by focusing on money and staying emotionally aloof could a woman survive intact, I thought. But the decision to bring a child into this rotten world planted a bit of optimism inside me that took hold and grew along with my baby.

I set about reading every parenting book and magazine I could to figure out how to be a mom. The theme of everything I read was, "Never do anything except what is best for the baby." However, "what is best" varied from book to book, magazine issue to magazine issue. At no time did I ever read anything like, "You can do this. Trust yourself." I could have used a little reassurance because the world, with scarce exception, was less than thrilled about my joining the ranks of motherhood. Pregnant nineteen-year-old high-school dropouts, even if they did go to interior design school, are not a highly sought-after marketing demographic. Nevertheless, determined to be a responsible mother, I quit drinking, moved into my dad's house and started scouting for employment.

I found a job relating to the interior design courses I'd been studying: I became a "wallcovering consultant." Only, this nice little corporate job I had found, the one that provided health benefits and steady raises, also offered a forty-five-minute commute each way and a pair of sexually harassing bosses. For six months after my daughter's birth, I endured leaving her in daycare for twelve hours a day so I could go to a place where round, bald men leered at my postpartum C-cup breasts. One day, as I was driving to work, a truck driver ran a red light and totaled my car. I wasn't hurt, but I couldn't commute anymore. The town I lived in didn't have bus service or trains, and at twenty-two I was too young to rent a car. "I can't get to work," I told my boss. He replied that they'd have to let me go. I didn't want to be a cog in the corporate machine, anyway. I didn't want to drive ninety miles a day; I wanted to take care of my kid. I wanted to smell the ocean again, to discover what a life that wasn't money-driven could be like. Chelsea and I moved to Long Beach to be with Bobby, and we began the next stage of our lives together.

Marriage turns out to be even more difficult than motherhood. Looking for ways to avoid fighting with Bobby, I stay later and later at the club, partying with my co-workers. This does not help my marital problems. Bobby and I split up two months before our first wedding anniversary. Chelsea and I move into our own place, closer to the preschool. I let her pick out a cat at the animal shelter and try to make the separation as painless as possible, but the right words are hard to find. I'm mad at myself because I'd sworn I would never put my own kid through a divorce, but I don't know what else to do. I'm not ready for divorce; I just can't stand the way my marriage is going and need to leave to make my unhappiness clear. Bobby agrees to marital counseling if it means we can get back together, even though he thinks counseling is mostly a crock. But the counseling helps. A weekend in Santa Barbara, just the two of us, helps more. A fist unclenches from around my heart, and I feel a rush of love return. We get back together and move into a new apartment with wood floors, big windows that let in the afternoon sun, and a built-in cat door. A month later, I discover that I'm pregnant again. My immediate response is to freak out, but I come to terms with the idea when I have my tarot cards read. The woman reading my cards has no idea I'm pregnant, but she assures me that I have enough love inside me to turn whatever burdens I'm experiencing into joy. Corny, but just what I needed to hear. I leave the reading cradling my belly, thinking, *I can do this.*

Unfortunately, Bogart's closes down five weeks later. Bobby gets laid off from the graphic design firm. By Christmas, we are living at my mother-in-law's in Quartz Hill, a desert suburb sixty miles north of Los Angeles. I read a story in the paper about the trend of young adults living with their parents. I am six months along and wondering how to make a life.

Kathleen—"Kaylee"—is born fourteen days early, on the vernal equinox. I manage to labor drug-free, which pays off when the natural adrenaline high hits postpartum. What a rush. I bounce around my birthing room, ready to zoom off with my new baby. Bobby, Chelsea, Kaylee and I leave twelve hours after delivery, visit my mom, then return home in time to go out to a Thai restaurant for dinner. At dinner I feel like Super Mom, but by dessert the high has burned off. We return to my mother-in-law's and I collapse into bed with Kaylee snuggled next to me.

In June, the temperature outside reaches 115 degrees. My mother-in-law doesn't believe in running the air conditioner. Kaylee is sweating so much her weight drops from fourteen to ten pounds in twenty-four hours. I take her to the doctor; they draw blood. We rush to Children's Hospital in Los Angeles when the results come in—severe dehydration. Thankfully, the hospital does believe in air conditioning. With five days of cool air and an IV, Kaylee recovers. We return to my mother-in-law's, having nowhere else to go.

I need somewhere else to go.

<hr />

Bobby, the girls and I go on a road trip, from our desert city near Los Angeles to a family reunion in Seattle. This is the first time I have traveled north of San Francisco. I am amazed by how much California there is between San Francisco and Oregon. We are also checking out places to move: Arcata, a little hippie town in Humboldt County (got a rave in *Vegetarian Times* and the *Utne Reader*), Portland (the new Seattle by all accounts) and Seattle (because it's Seattle). But when we get to Arcata, I know. This is it. Redwood trees tower over us. The Pacific, whose tides mimic the moon-rhythm of my body, crashes violently, beautifully along rocky coastline. Coastline without condos. This is where I want my kids to grow up. At the end of the trip my conviction stands: Portland and Seattle impressed me, but Arcata connected.

When we return from our three weeks on the road, I finally share something I'd been keeping to myself: another pregnancy. I hadn't told anyone other than Bobby because I was afraid of judgmental looks and words: *You're poor, uneducated, living with your mother-in-law. Your husband wants to be an artist. What are you thinking?* And the worst: *Again?* But I'm surprised. Even without my expounding on the failure rates of birth control, most of our friends and family offer congratulations that seem sincere.

Nicolas is born on November 5, 1995. Eight days later, I turn twenty-five. I have three kids. I have three kids! An obvious fact, but one I have to repeat daily to believe. Like dyeing my hair orange and then tripping out for a week on how strange-yet-familiar I look. I see these kids of mine every day, wipe their noses, read them stories . . . but still. I. Have. Three. Kids. When asked how many kids I have, I answer "three," and surprise colors my voice every time. Having one child changed me; having three solidified those changes. There's no subtlety with three. I can't glide into restaurants, dash into grocery stores, cruise into other people's houses. No, my children and I descend upon places. Like locusts.

We are our own crowd. My days of passing unnoticed, slipping through the masses, are long gone. So is my VW Beetle. We needed a five–seat-belt vehicle, so we "upgraded" to a 1969 red-and-white VW bus. Between the bus and my husband's waist-length hair, we're looking awfully hippie. S'okay though; it's beginning to suit me. As I brought children into the world, something else came, too: a renewal of caring, of hope. The future suddenly matters. As I figure out how I want to raise my kids, I have to decide what kind of example I am going to set. For instance, I've always rejected sexism: I led the argument for the ERA in sixth grade, rebelled against gender stereotyping in my junior high's reenactment of a pioneer wagon train. But I still bought fashion magazines and dreamed of being anorexic. Now that I have girls of my own, I no longer obsess out loud about being fat; I don't want to screw up my daughters by passing on warped body ideals. So I grit my teeth, silently wishing my jeans hung a little lower on my waist. Yes, I still have issues, but I try to have them out of my daughters' earshot.

Another year goes by, and we are still in Quartz Hill, surviving, missing the ocean. I have to escape this cultureless, Republican, fundamentalist, chain-store-saturated, mall-centered, skinhead-harboring, speedfreak-breeding, child-abuse-capital-of-California town. If one more person remarks about "the good old days when Reagan was president," I am going to rip his or her head off and fling it into the goddamn wind that blows sand into my eyes at fifty miles per hour 362 goddamn days a year. I grew up aching to leave this town so badly the pain forced me to self-medicate with alcohol and a variety of drugs. I've outgrown the substance abuse—and besides, I'm a mom now—but I can't cope sober. I cannot raise my kids here. I am tired of people trying to feed my vegetarian kids Happy Meals, as if the three of them are somehow deprived. Friends and family I love live here, but still I dream of Arcata. My own house. At least I have some friends, I tell myself. I have no money, no real home, but I still have friends and children and laughter. At least I have my job at Hang-n-Java, the one cool, noncorporate coffee house in this place. It's more than a job, really—it's a life line. The coffee house, my friends and my kids are all that keeps me sane.

In June, unable to make enough of a profit to survive, Hang-n-Java closes.

In September, Bobby gets laid off. After seven years of surviving just above the poverty line, we plunge below it and into the Department of Social Services. In December, in a desperate leap of faith, we pack up our belongings and prepare to move to Humboldt County.

In January we move into a tiny three-bedroom house on a third of an acre. The house is in Eureka, just south of Arcata, and closer to my new school, College of the Redwoods. The first sixteen days, rain falls without ceasing. El Niño rips through an old-growth redwood in which a woman named Julia Butterfly has been living for a month. I have fallen into a Tom Robbins novel! The rain continues. I plant flowers, tomatoes, lettuce. Play with my kids. Start college. Discover the woods and explore the beaches. Breathe deeply. Humboldt County smells like a freshly showered lover wrapped in last night's love-stained sheets. Like a salty ocean breeze mixed with sweet forest rain. Vanilla. Musk. Nag Champa incense. Like organic Sumatra coffee. Cinnamon, clove, cardamom, ginger, allspice and skunky bud. Like life. The rain continues. The clouds break. Sun shines through. Rainbows surround us.

Within a year, I am doing a parenting show on KMUD, our local community radio station. Bobby scores a couple of art openings. The kids know the forest, the river, the beach. A bear—a real, live, wild bear—makes an appearance in the woods near our house. We still don't have much money, but life is sweet. For the first time, I feel grounded. I imagine being eighty, still living in Humboldt County, still planting dahlias and romaine in the backyard.

Can it be that only eight years have passed since Long Beach? It feels like a lifetime. Chelsea is ten—half as old as I was when I had her. Kaylee is six; Nick, four. And I'm thirty. Thirty! Why did I ever think thirty was old? I'm not sure I know how to be thirty. I don't despise minivans anymore; several of my favorite people drive them. Some of my friends were determined to get married or to have reached a certain tax bracket by age thirty. Me? I bought a surfboard. Music remains a big deal in our house, as Bobby and I (together twelve years now!) try to influence the children's musical tastes, something that is getting harder to do as the girls come home from school singing Britney Spears songs. My own CD collection, culled from BMG catalogs and the "used" bins at music stores, only partly reflects my actual tastes. I wonder if this lack of diversity makes me a bad mom. Will whoever judges such things check a box by my name: "Failed to provide an appropriate and well-rounded music selection"? Chelsea, a longtime Nirvana and Smashing Pumpkins fan, found my old Madonna tape and has been singing "Like a Prayer" and (to Bobby's chagrin) "Papa Don't Preach." She takes violin lessons during the day at school and falls asleep at night to Love and Rockets. Kaylee leans more toward chicks with guitars, from Michelle Shocked to PJ Harvey. She also performs Louis Armstrong's "What a Wonderful World." Beautifully. Nick loves "wild guitars—loud!" Can't be too cranked for him. He almost blew out a stereo speaker blasting the new Foo Fighters CD. Plus he knows the words to "Born to Be Wild." All the kids do.

The Future? Life: change and chaos. And learning to surf, which, so far, is a lot like learning to mother: I bought the gear, I understand the theory, and I have occasional success. But the ocean won't stay still and neither will my kids; they keep getting older. Stable ground exists but only under powerful, ever-changing currents. Paddling out takes strength, persistence and the ability to roll under the waves as they crash down. Make it out past the break . . . and wait. And, when the right wave comes, it must be recognized, caught, stood upon, stayed upon and ridden in. So far, I've done a lot more falling down than anything else. But I keep going out, keep watching the surfers who have found their groove, their sweet spot. I can always tell the people who are good at something by the easy habit with which they do it. I want, long for, that kind of grace. I'm learning. Last week, I caught the first wave that rolled under me. Then I spent the next hour paddling like an idiot, catching nothing. But that first small taste, those few seconds of reward, hooked me. Even as I'm battered by waves, exhausted from fighting the current and feeling like my body weighs five hundred pounds, I think, *One more time, just one more time* and then I'm up, knees bent, standing, riding, grinning. I've had days with the kids when I've thought, *I'm not going to make it*, only to forget my worries as the sun shines in the window, lighting up Chelsea's eyes, Kaylee's smile, Nick's grin. Or I remember the quick healing power of getting out of the house; we take a walk in the woods and all is well again. Or, after they don't eat the tasty, healthy meal I've made, refuse to put on pajamas, don't want to brush their teeth—just when I am about to go over the edge—they decide to get into bed and wait patiently for bedtime stories. And we lose ourselves with Harry Potter or Frog and Toad for a while. I figure I have about ninety-two more times to go before I'm any good at surfing.

Meanwhile, the sun bounces off the water, the redwoods rise on the hills, and I inhale the beauty that surrounds me.

I figure I have about the rest of my life to go before I get this parenting thing down. Meanwhile, the kids make me laugh, amaze me with their brilliance, and I soak in the love that surrounds me.

GOD THE MOTHER

Julia Mossbridge

I told the whole fourth grade that I was taking sex ed in Sunday school at the liberal church our family attended. It made me popular every Monday. Even the cheerleaders listened with rapt attention to my lunchroom lectures. I like to think I wouldn't have talked to the cheerleader girlies at all unless I was shocking them with terms like "fisting," but I probably would have talked to them about muffin-baking contests, or whatever Republican suburbanite kids talk about, if they would have befriended greasy-haired, six-foot-tall, comb-in-wrong-pants-pocket me.

One Sunday, driving home from church in a rusty, red Datsun sedan, my father made the Announcement. He told my sister and me that our mother didn't like men anymore, and that they were getting a divorce. When we picked Mom up at the train, she seconded the story—except the part about not liking men. Instead, she said she didn't like my dad in particular. But it was true that they were going to divorce, and that she had fallen in love with a woman. Curled up crying in the back seat, my mind swirled with images of my mom performing cunnilingus on some large-booted lesbian lover.

Why did our dad have to tell us in this way—driving home, with us in the back, unable to see his face? Why couldn't both of them tell us together, in one of our weekly encounter-group-style "family meetings"? Even though my church was at the forefront of the gender-neutral-God movement, from the time of the Announcement on, I saw God as a dad. He made harsh announcements from afar. He was very much like my father—a red-bearded giant with an Amish farmer's hat and no tact.

My mom's lover turned out to favor smallish flats, not large boots. She was one of my mom's therapist colleagues; in fact, she was the kindly butch therapist who a month before had cured my anxiety disorder in one session. The session went something like this:

Me: "I feel like I'm left out of the family circle."

Kindly Butch Therapist: "Ah! So you feel like you're left out of the family circle."

Me: "Exactly. I'm better now."

Kindly Butch Therapist: "You know, your mom's kinda cute."

After a while, I found myself living with two moms. Though I promised never to speak to either of them, I did. Karen understood me, she helped me understand myself, and she would unpack the groceries by tossing them to me from across the room—even the eggs. She was cool—cooler than my other two parents. Certainly cooler than I was.

But as great as my stepmom was, I was in shock. It seemed my mother had changed from a rhubarb-picking, pie-making, warm-lap-to-cry-in, apron-wearing mom to a please-don't-bother-me, I-don't-care-that-you're-dating-a-drug-addict, it's-my-time-now mercenary mom without leaving me so much as a note of explanation on the kitchen table. Just when I was moving into my Reviving Ophelia years, my mom entered her Reinventing Sappho decade and left her old self, and me, in the dust. So you could say my two models of motherhood were set right there—it's either all about the kid or all about you. And nothing in between.

My mother and Karen were both present for my son Joseph's birth last November. Karen held my feet and calmly encouraged each push; Mom whirled around and made sure everyone was doing something productive. I was on all fours so I didn't get to see this baby until he was on my belly, but when I saw him, I wanted to eat him. I wasn't thinking *Oh! He's so beautiful I want to just eat him up!* It was more animalistic—he seemed like a wounded bird, all slippery and fragile and moving in random spasmodic bursts. In my postlabor confusion, my primitive brain thought maybe the best thing for everyone would be if I ate him.

The birth was shockingly final: Here is a child; now everything changes. But eating him wouldn't solve the problem. Even if he were safely tucked away, tiny toes in my belly, I'd still know I was a mom. That was the real issue. Shocking to have a child, yes, but for me it was bone-gnawingly shocking to be a mom. If I were a mom, which kind should I be? The existence of each kind of mom obliterated the other. Apron mom had no self. Mercenary mom had herself, but no child. As soon as I felt Joseph slip onto my belly, I heard the voice of that tactless Amish farmer: "Apron mom or mercenary mom. Choose now. And, for Chrissakes, don't change your mind."

At first I headed for apron-mom heaven, where babies are perfect and days are perfect and husbands are perfect. At the end of each day, I'd massage my jaws to relax my aching smile muscles. I'd look at Joseph and beam, saying "hi!" repeatedly, insanely, trying to get him to acknowledge me. I'd call my friends with kids to chat about how amazing it is to be a mom. Just momhood—so satisfying! I somehow never got around to talking to my friends without kids, until I noticed mercenary mom's fast approach.

The first time it happened, I was walking by the scissors I had left out on the table to cut pictures for Joseph's baby book. Joseph was probably puking over my left shoulder, as was usual in those days. I thought, *I could take that scissors and ram it into Joseph's soft spot.* I had a mental image of me doing it, and I couldn't erase that picture. The next day I saw a knife and the same image flashed in my head. Then I saw a sharp piece of glass. Why stop there? I saw a piece of concrete by the el stop that looked like I could sharpen it into some sort of soft-spot piercing implement with just a little effort and some sanding tools. I quickly became the Martha Stewart of Anne Lamott–style infanticide fantasies.

For a few weeks I kept this to myself. Who could I tell? My mom friends who were fifteen seconds away from offing their own kids? So I confessed to my childless friends. As I told them, I realized what a monster I'd become. At least in her mercenary moments, my mother admitted her selfishness and broadcasted it well: "Stay away! I'm going through a mercenary phase!" And here I was, hiding an ice pick behind my "Kiss the Cook" apron.

Here's the part of the story where I should tell you that I integrated my apron strings with my ice pick. That I started going back to school to finish my Ph.D. while still spending most of my time with Joseph. That I love Joseph more than honey *and* mangos and can walk through an entire cutlery store without thinking ill thoughts. That I realize now that my mother has always been not just apron mom or mercenary mom, but both. All that is true.

Although I think I should, I can't write a new mom story where everything turns out fine and I remark that momhood is so satisfying, in a much deeper way than I originally guessed. Because I can't point to any moment with my child when I am having that thought. The thing is, when I'm with him, I can't think. I act like a cat or musk ox—I become infinite, timeless, animal mom. Mom is flailing around, still struggling to choose between herself and the baby. Mom is sometimes wanting to eat her young and in the same moment fending off intruding predators. Mom is the apron mercenary, not in a high-minded, whole-person, well-integrated sense but in an everyday, can't-get-sick, must-sleep-*now*-or-I'll-kill-you sense.

No part of me finds this kind of work satisfying. It's disorienting, exhausting, confusing. It drains me of everything I have to give, then asks for more. And it sucks me dry while leaving others—like my husband—completely ready for puking, flailing, playing baby action. So he can't even sympathize. In fact, he is jealous of me—how fun it must be to spend the whole day with our baby!

I am jealous, too. No, I don't want to work all day and be away from my kid. No, I don't want to stay home all day and be with my kid. What I want is to be my kid, all day. He gets to sleep wherever he wants. Like a prince, he's carried on his mother the donkey. Thirsty? Miriam's sippy-cup well eases his throat in the parched desert. Hungry? Endless manna from heaven is delivered via his mama's boobs. Want to break down and cry for a day? It's okay, Mom will rock and hold him patiently and lovingly.

At four-thirty one morning I realized I want a mom. A mom who both meets her own needs and finds time to meet all of mine just as perfectly. An apron/mercenary mom who tends her garden out back while keeping snarling leopards from my path. Like a gift, I suddenly saw her: thick-armed, all-powerful Mom wielding lightning bolts. I saw her. Where before I could only see sideburns beneath the hat, that morning I saw God tossing her wiry black hair and parting the menstrual waters of the Red Sea as she gives birth to tribes and nations.

That day, at the bookstore, I checked out the 40 percent–off rack. I saw *Charlton Heston Presents the Bible* with a cover sporting Charlton offering a large book up to me, the reader. I opened it up to see if Charlton could shed light on my new God-Mama image. I opened right to a section where Moses is reminding God that he wasn't the one who made all these people in the first place, God was. There was some oblique mention of Moses holding his people to his bosom—very suspicious, I thought. I found a real Bible and read about Moses' whining in detail:

Have I conceived all [these] people? Have I brought them forth, that Thou shouldest say unto me: Carry them in thy bosom, as a nursing father [*sic*] carrieth the sucking child, unto the land which Thou didst swear unto their fathers? Whence should I have flesh to give unto these people? For they trouble me with their weeping, saying "Give us flesh, that we may eat." I am not able to bear all [these] people myself alone, because it is too heavy for me.

All those "nursing fathers" out there might disagree, but I think Moses is saying, "Hey God, I'm not a resourceful mom like you. Help me deal with these cranky kids you made." And what is God's response? Like a good mom, she takes his complaining for immaturity and offers some food to him and the rest of the gang, while at the same time scolding him for lack of respect. At that moment in the bookstore, I saw God wink at me with her everlasting flood-proof mascara in place. For the first time, I was in the popular crowd. God and me—we were two mamas on a walk.

By being moms, we can do God's work—God's actual daily work of loving and bringing forth souls—and we can get credit for it. Is this the secret? Have mothers always privately seen themselves in God in order to save their own lives and their children's? Maybe. For me, this is the secret. This is how it all turns out fine. God is my mother, and with her I am well pleased. And it's true what they say—her company is more deeply satisfying than I originally expected.

CONTRIBUTORS

Alex McCall is a thirtysomething freelance writer of edgy features and fiction who lives in Denver, Colorado. She is an alumna of the University of Denver, ex-employee of *Westword*, former editor of *Entertainment Scene* and contributor to the late, lamented *Hooligan*.

Alisa Gordaneer is a thirty-one-year-old mama of one, plus one on the way. She lives in Detroit with her husband, kid(s), dog and cats, and works as an editor at an alternative weekly newspaper. Her poetry has been published in the anthology *Threshold: Six Women, Six Poets,* and her fiction in the anthology *Love and Pomegranates,* both from Sono Nis Press.

Allison Abner lives in Los Angeles with her son, Miles, and her mother down the street. She writes for the television series *The West Wing.* She co-authored *Finding Our Way: The Teen Girls' Survival Guide* (HarperPerennial, 1996) and *The Black Parenting Book* (Broadway Books, 1998); her work has appeared in many anthologies, including *Child of Mine: Original Essays on Becoming a Mother* (Bantam, 1998).

Allison Crews is the editor of girlmom.com, a point-of-view journalist for Oxygen Media, the founder of the Coalition for the Empowerment of Teen Parents and the proprietor of StarBottoms Baby Supplies (www.starbottoms.homestead.com). She plans to major in journalism and women's studies when she starts college next year.

Ana June now lives in Oregon with her three children, one husband and a very dumb snake named Ghost. Alhough her current car doesn't limp, it does leak oil and is chronically messy—especially with the recent addition of a third car seat.

Andrea Buchanan is a senior program editor for *Stagebill* magazine. Trained as a classical pianist, she is also a freelance writer whose work has been featured in the online magazines hipmama.com and oxygen.com, where she is a regular contributor. Andrea works from home in Philadelphia, where she lives with her husband and daughter. Andrea's most recent solo piano recital took place at Carnegie Hall's Weill Recital Hall.

Angela Morrill is a Native-American, second-generation welfare mama of a bald baby named Leroy. Her parents were activists. She hopes to attend the revolution.

Australia Sims is a mom, painter, writer and occasional corporate executive. She lives with her husband and son on a tiny urban ranch in Texas. Her recent work includes a series of essays on pregnancy and a group of images toying with scenes from family life.

Ayun Halliday is the creator of the *East Village Inky*, a quarterly zine chronicling her adventures in New York City with her daughter, India. *East Village Inky* was recently improved with all new baby brother power, following the birth of Milo. Contrary to the title of the zine, Halliday and her children live in Brooklyn.

Beth Kohl Feinerman is a thirty-two-year-old MFA student in writing at the School of the Art Institute of Chicago. She is the mother of eight-month-old Sophia.

Beth Lucht is a mother, freelance writer, popular DJ, social worker and associate editor of hipmama.com. She lives in Madison, Wisconsin.

Caledonia Kearns is the editor of two anthologies of Irish American women's writing: *Cabbage and Bones: An Anthology of Irish Women's Fiction* (Henry Holt, 1997), and *Motherland: Writings by Irish American Women About Mothers and Daughters* (William Morrow & Co, 1999). She also contributed to *The Encyclopedia of the Irish in America* (University of Notre Dame Press, 1999). A writer and book reviewer, her work has appeared in the *Boston Globe*, the *Chicago Tribune* and *Newsday*. She is currently working on a collection of essays about her daughter's first year. She lives in Brooklyn with her family.

China has been writing every day since she was twelve; most of her writings are in boxes under her bed, a file cabinet at her grandmother's and a trunk at her mother's—but she has self-published four small (Xeroxed) books and put out a zine called *The Future Generation* for the last ten years. She currently writes for *Slug and Lettuce,* and lives with her twelve-year-old daughter outside Baltimore, Maryland—in the same house for the last three years.

Coleen Murphy is a mother, a feminist, an advocate for young people, a social justice ninja and a punk rocker. She lives in Mississippi with her two young sons and their dad. She works in her local community and also in the world community via the Internet and frequent road trips. Her writing is a response to the world as it is, but with an underlying motion toward the way it should and could be.

Dan Savage is the author of "Savage Love," a widely syndicated sex-advice column, as well as the memoir *The Kid: What Happened After My Boyfriend and I Decided to Go Get Pregnant . . . An Adoption Story.* Savage's writing has appeared in the *New York Times* magazine, *Rolling Stone, Salon, nest, Travel & Leisure, Travelocity* and other publications. Savage is the associate editor of the *Stranger* in Seattle, where he lives with his boyfriend and their three-year-old son.

Gayle Brandeis is a writer and dancer living in Riverside, California, with her husband, Matt, and their two kids, Arin and Hannah. Her guide for women writers, *Fruitflesh*, will be published by HarperSanFrancisco in 2001.

Jennifer Savage grew up in the Southern California desert but much prefers the Northern California coast. When not desperately trying to maintain the illusion of order, she can be found reading Shel Silverstein to her kids, wandering the Humboldt State University campus or grinning on her surfboard in the Pacific. She is constantly grateful to her friends and family but forgets to tell them so.

Jessica Rigney is mother to one son, Imagine. A published writer and photographer who occasionally takes on graphic design as well, she recently became part of a female cooperative zine called *Rag*. She is also training herself to say no to taking on new projects.

Joy Castro lives with her son and husband in Crawfordsville, Indiana, where she teaches twentieth-century literature, women's literature, ethnic literature and creative writing at Wabash College. Her work has appeared in *Quarterly West, Puerto del Sol, Chelsea, Mid-American Review, A Ghost at Heart's Edge: Stories and Poems of Adoption* (North Atlantic Books, 1999) and other journals and anthologies.

Julie Jamison is a careless wife and sarcastic mother of two. Her weekly column "Ranting Chick" (www.rantingchick.com) contains social commentary from a pissy Midwestern type. Julie has performed commentary for NPR's "All Things Considered" and is a regular columnist for *NetWits Magazine*.

Julia Mossbridge is a writer and psychoacoustics graduate student at Northwestern University in Evanston, Illinois. Her current writing project is "The Unfolding Experiment," a self-taught course in working with your nature and purpose to repair the world. Her long-term goal in science is to continue her work on dolphin and whale communication.

June Day was born and raised near Yakima, Washington. She spent endless days of her youth sitting in trees and running through fields and looking at cows. Her parents were wonderfully ordinary and kind. She lives in New York City now, where she is writing historical fiction, go-go dancing and performing online (rosetta.myifriends.net).

Kara Gall lives in the San Francisco Bay Area with her three-year-old daughter. Her written documentary, *Fresh Voices*, chronicled the Gallery 60 Summer Program at Chicago's Boulevard Arts Center. She currently writes short stories, poetry and essays.

Kai Ro is a reformed social recluse who enjoys full-time mothering, name-dropping, hanging out with other cool moms and feeling intimidated in record stores. Kai's incredibly foxy partner, Bean, moonlights as a punk rocker while kicking butt during his day job as an ultra-square college professor. Her future radical activist daughter, Ember, likes nursing, standing on mama's tummy and flirting with rockabilly boys in coffee shops. Motherhood has taught Kai not to hate people as much, not to give a damn what other people think and to function on five or six intermittent hours of sleep.

Kimberly Bright was born in Indiana in 1971 and raised by golfing Republican Protestants. She attended a Jesuit prep school and Butler University, where she did extensive independent study in self-destructive antisocial behavior before graduating with honors in communications. She began writing professionally at eighteen, after playing guitar in various unsuccessful New Wave and punk bands. A contributing writer for the *Bloomington Independent* newsweekly, her work has also appeared in magazines, newspapers and zines, in addition to four poetry chapbooks. She lives with her husband, Peter, and their two children, Tommy and Maggie. Mrs. Bright has no unusual piercings or tattoos and has never been to a rave.

LaSara W. FireFox is a wyld red-haired country grrl who left her heart in Mendocino County, California, but is forced to live in The City from time to time. She is mother to two wonderful daughters, a writer and a neofeminist sex radical. She is happily married to a lovely man, yet identifies as queer. She is an anarchist, existentialist and a clergy member ordained by the Church of All Worlds.

Liesl Schwabe is a graduate of Antioch College and is now balancing her life as a stay-at-home mother and aspiring writer. She is currently preparing to return to India with her partner and their one-year-old son. She lives in Brooklyn, New York.

Marianne Apostolides is the author of *Inner Hunger: A Young Woman's Struggle Through Anorexia and Bulimia* (W.W. Norton & Co, 1998). The book referred to in *"Feeding"* is *The Drama of the Gifted Child: The Search for the True Self,* by Alice Miller (Basic Books, 1987).

Megan Lambert is a twenty-four-year-old writer and manager of an independent bookstore in Northampton, Massachusetts. At twenty, she graduated from Smith College with a dual degree in government and African American studies, scrapped her plans for law school, had a baby and is now pursuing a master's in children's literature at Simmons College. She lives with her son, her partner Dana and their cat, Fiona T. Feline.

Min Jin Lee was born in 1968 in Seoul, South Korea. She immigrated to the United States in 1976. At Yale College, she received the Wright and Veech prizes for non-fiction and fiction, respectively. Her essays have been published in the *Korea Times* and in the anthology *To Be Real: Telling the Truth and Changing the Face of Feminism* (Anchor Books, 1995). Her short fiction has been published in *The Asian Pacific American Journal* and *bananafish*. In 1999, she was a finalist for *Glimmer Train*'s Fiction Open. In 2000, she was awarded second place in the *bananafish* Fiction Contest. She received a fiction fellowship from the New York Foundation for the Arts in 2000.

Peri Escarda spent many years as a bookseller and professional student before embarking on the mission of motherhood. With more than a little help from her adoring husband, and in spite of a couple of miscarriages, she has managed to bring two miraculous children into our midst. She is one of the founders of The Body Objective (bodyobjective.com), a Web site dedicated to celebrating the female body in all its wondrous forms. Writing has always been her tool of choice for distilling life experiences, and the printed word will always be her great joy and salvation. Her extended family surrounds her like some crazy, messed-up tribe, and she lives among them in the wilds of Northern California.

Phaedra Hise is an author and pilot. She passed her instrument tests while pregnant and takes her three-year-old daughter flying regularly.

Hise's husband caught the flying passion and has earned a pilot's license and instrument rating as well.

Sara Manns lives and works in a small town in the Midwest, where her queer, trans-cultural, mixed-race adoptive family gets stared at a lot.

Sarah Talbot lives and breeds in Olympia, Washington—the hippest town on earth. She enjoys being run ragged by small, strange children, and teaches high school English for food. She co-publishes *Rag* magazine and her work can be found there and, on occasion, in *Hip Mama*. She is the single mother of Maia and Caleb, who continue to teach her to laugh and love.

Sherry Thompson is a poet and mama living in Waterloo, Ontario. She has performed at many readings and festivals and is currently working on a manuscript-length series of poems. If she attains her every wish and heart's desire, she might consider dealing with the shameful state of her kitchen.

Yantra Bertelli is a queer single mother of two children, Aiden and Miles. They live in Northern California with their treasured computer, fuzzy green couch and painting easel. Yantra can be found nightly banging at the keys searching for a story, throwing rich texture onto a makeshift canvas or dancing with a sink full of bubbles and dirty dishes.

THANKS AND WE LOVE YOU

Bee would like to thank her family—Byron, Mina, Aubrey; her mother, Laina Lavender; and Moe Bowstern.

Ariel would like to thank the usual suspects, including her daughter Maia and the writingmamas.

Together they'd like to thank all of the excellent breeder chicks who submitted their work/shared their stories; the hipmama.com and girlmom.com communities; the moderators; Leslie Miller, Jennie Goode and the Seal Press ladies for their patience, wisdom and ever-coolness; Jonny Thief for the art; Cheyenne at Tiger Lily for the tattoos; The Amalgamated Everlasting Union Chorus Local 824 for the songs; Marisa Anderson and the Dolly Ranchers for watching the home front and providing a soundtrack; Reading Frenzy, Radical Women, Misty Fitzgerald, Stella Marrs, Teresa Dulce, the Portland hip mamas; Sonja Smith, Gina Covarrubias, Ethan Cruze, Julie Talbutt, Susanna Rankin-Bohme, Eileen Alden, Eva and Joe Zirker, Lynn Marsh, Tamar and Chris Kern, James Luckett, John and Sue Ann Cook, Ana Helena, Beth Schulman, Lli Wilburn, Sallyann Kluz, Kim Haines and everyone who put us up and put up with us when we were on the road. Plus, Utah Phillips, Woody Guthrie, Inga Muscio, Mary Kay Blakely, Michael Moore, Nina Hagen, Sandra Bernhard, Susan Sarandon, Victoria Woodhull; Emma Goldman and Loretta Lynn for the inspiration; the hippies for making breast-feeding and home birthing cool; the feminists for making reproductive freedom and childcare priorities; the labor movement for the weekend; the anarchists and anybody who doesn't need a cop to tell them what to do; and Marlo Thomas and Carol Hall and the other folks who made the album *Free To Be . . . You and Me,* for teaching us that "mommies can be almost anything they want to be."

Ariel Gore is the founder and creator of *Hip Mama,* the award-winning zine covering the culture and politics of motherhood. The author of *The Hip Mama Survival Guide* (Hyperion, 1998) and *The Mother Trip* (Seal, 2000), she lives with her daughter in Portland, Oregon.

Bee Lavender is a thirty-year-old mother of two children. The editor of hipmama.com and the founding editor of girlmom.com and mamaphonic.com, she is also a much-married, working-class cancer survivor and renegade public administrator.

SELECTED TITLES

The Mother Trip: Hip Mama's Guide to Staying Sane in the Chaos of Motherhood by Ariel Gore. $14.95, 1-58005-029-8. In a book that is part self-help, part critique of the mommy myth and part hip-mama handbook, Ariel Gore offers support to mothers who break the mold.

The Single Mother's Companion: Essays and Stories by Women edited by Marsha Leslie. $12.95, 1-878067-56-7. In their own words, the single mothers in this landmark collection explore both the joys and the difficult realities of raising children alone.

The Lesbian Parenting Book: A Guide to Creating Families and Raising Children by D. Merilee Clunis and G. Dorsey Green. $16.95, 1-878067-68-0. This practical and readable book covers a wide range of parenting topics as well as issues specifically relevant to lesbian families.

The Adoption Reader: Birthmothers, Adoptive Mothers and Adopted Daughters Tell Their Stories edited by Susan Wadia-Ells. $16.95, 1-878067-65-6. With eloquence and conviction, more than thirty birthmothers, adoptive mothers and adopted daughters explore the many faces of adoption.

Sex and Single Girls: Straight and Queer Women on Sexuality edited by Lee Damsky. $16.95, 1-58005-038-7. In this potent and entertaining collection of personal essays, women lay bare pleasure, fear, desire, risk—all that comes with exploring their sexuality. Contributors write their own rules and tell their own stories with empowering and often humorous results.

Cunt: A Declaration of Independence by Inga Muscio. $14.95, 1-58005-015-8. An ancient title of respect for women, "cunt" long ago veered off the path of honor and now careens toward the heart of every woman as an expletive. Muscio traces this winding road, giving women both the motivation and the tools to claim "cunt" as a positive and powerful force in the lives of all women.

FROM SEAL PRESS

Young Wives' Tales: New Adventures in Love and Partnership edited by Jill Corral and Lisa Miya-Jervis, foreword by bell hooks. $16.95, 1-58005-050-6. *Wife.* The term inspires ambivalence in young women the world over, for a multitude of good reasons. So what's a young, independent girl in love to do? In a bold and provocative anthology, women in their twenties and thirties attempt to answer that question, whether they are trying on the title "wife," deciding who will wear the gown in a lesbian wedding or demanding the space for solitude in a committed relationship.

Wild Child: Girlhoods in the Counterculture edited by Chelsea Cain, foreword by Moon Zappa. $16.00, 1-58005-031-X. Daughters of the hippie generation reflect on the experience of a counterculture childhood, presenting a fresh perspective on our current world as seen through the legacy of sixties ideals.

Body Outlaws: Young Women Write About Body Image and Identity edited by Ophira Edut, foreword by Rebecca Walker. $14.95, 1-58005-043-3. Filled with honesty and humor, this groundbreaking anthology offers stories by women who have chosen to ignore, subvert or redefine the dominant beauty standard in order to feel at home in their bodies.

Listen Up: Voices from the Next Feminist Generation edited by Barbara Findlen. $16.95, 1-58005-054-9. In a new, expanded edition of the classic collection of young feminist writing, *Listen Up* gathers the women of feminism's "third wave" and allows them to explore and reveal their lives. Contributors address topics such as racism, sexuality, identity, AIDS, revolution, religion, abortion and much more.

$\sim$

Seal Press publishes many books of fiction and nonfiction by women writers. If you are unable to obtain a Seal Press title from a bookstore, please order from us directly by calling 800-754-0271. Visit our Web site and online catalog at **www.sealpress.com**.